Also by Ronald Goldfarb:

THE CONTEMPT POWER

RANSOM

A Critique of the American Bail System

by

Ronald Goldfarb

Foreword by Justice Arthur J. Goldberg

HARPER & ROW, PUBLISHERS, NEW YORK

FIRST EDITION

LIBRARY OF CONGRESS CATALOG CARD NUMBER: 65–14684

I–P

For Joanne and Jody
With love and thanks

CONTENTS

Foreword

by ARTHUR J. GOLDBERG
Associate Justice
Supreme Court of the United States

If it is true that "the quality of a nation's civilization can be largely measured by the methods it uses in the enforcement of its criminal law," then the American bail system as it now operates can no longer be tolerated. At best, it is a system of checkbook justice; at worst, a highly commercialized racket. These are strong words, but that they are accurate is confirmed by the overwhelming evidence detailed in Ronald Goldfarb's timely and valuable study. His book demonstrates the inadequacies and unfairness of the American bail system and also makes valuable suggestions for overdue and much needed reform.

A basic defect of the present bail system is that it operates to the prejudice of the poor. Yet it is the central aim of our entire judicial system that, "all people charged with crime must, so far as the law is concerned, 'stand on an equality before the bar of justice in every American court.'" The simple truth is that, despite this most basic concept that equal justice be afforded to the poor and to the rich alike, the bail system operates to discriminate on account of poverty. After arrest, the accused who is poor must often await the disposition of his case in jail because of his inability to raise bail, while the accused who can afford bail is free to return to his family and job. Equally important, he is free during the critical period between arrest and trial to help his attorney with the investigation and preparation of his defense. In a recent case a defendant was imprisoned well over two years between the time he was arrested and the time he was ultimately acquitted on appeal, solely because he could not raise the small amount of money necessary for bail. This is an example, too often repeated, of justice denied or a man imprisoned for no other reason than his poverty.

Recent studies in the area of bail which are reviewed in this book establish that if carefully screened defendants are released pending trial on their own recognizance and treated with dignity they will appear at trial. Mr. Goldfarb properly reminds us of the appalling and needless waste—to the government, the family, and the community—every time a responsible person presumed by law to be innocent is kept in jail awaiting trial solely because he is unable to raise bail money. It is becoming more and more apparent that careful screening and release without bail should be made the rule rather than the exception throughout the country. This does not mean that release without bail should be allowed in every case. It does mean that it is feasible in a great many cases.

It is said, in defense of the present American bail system, that the government cannot be expected to equalize all economic disparities. Of course it cannot, but this does not mean that it should not try to minimize inequities in this critical area of administration of criminal justice. The real question, as put by the Attorney General's Committee on Poverty and the Administration of Federal Criminal Justice is: "Has government done all that can be reasonably required of it . . . to render the poverty of the litigant an irrelevancy?" Mr. Goldfarb's book demonstrates that government in this country, both state and federal, has not done all that can reasonably be required of it to render the poverty of the litigant an irrelevancy in the operation of the bail system.

Another valuable contribution of this book is its discussion of the programs underway to eliminate these inequities. The Manhattan Bail Project, under the auspices of the Vera Foundation, has served to awaken the country to the archaic and unjust nature of the bail system. The first National Bail Conference in May, 1964, cosponsored by the United States Department of Justice and the Vera Foundation, was a milestone in stimulating interest and study, the first steps in reform. The Report of the Attorney General's Committee on Poverty and the Administration of Federal Criminal Justice deservedly promises to have a constructive influence in this and related areas. The proposals by Senator Ervin for federal legislation, and the program under consideration or adopted in the various states, represent welcome recognition that we need not and cannot continue under the present system.

✹ Mr. Goldfarb's book contributes to this re-evaluation of the bail system by offering important suggestions for fundamental reform. I am sure that the author would agree with me that it is not important whether his specific suggestions be followed; what is important is that the abuses of the present bail system be corrected, here and now. ✹

In reading this scholarly book, with its appeal to our conscience on behalf of those charged with crime, we are again reminded of the words uttered by Sir Winston Churchill more than a half-century ago, speaking in the House of Commons as Home Secretary:

The mood and temper of the public in regard to the treatment of crime and criminals is one of the most unfailing tests of any country. A calm, dispassionate recognition of the rights of the accused, and even of the convicted criminal, against the State—a constant heart-searching by all charged with the duty of punishment—a desire and eagerness to rehabilitate in the world of industry those who have paid their due in the hard coinage of punishment: tireless efforts towards the discovery of curative and regenerative processes: unfailing faith that there is a treasure, if you can only find it, in the heart of every man. These are the symbols, which, in the treatment of crime and criminal, mark and measure the stored up strength of a nation, and are sign and proof of the living virtue within it.

Preface

A recent report by a committee of The Association of the Bar of the City of New York included this pathetic, pessimistic, and entirely accurate conclusion:

. . . it would appear that the form of bail has triumphed over the substance of what is sought to be achieved. This has occurred because the administration of bail is beyond the knowledge or interest of the citizenry generally and their legislative representatives particularly. But one class is personally involved in the problem, the criminal defendants, a class to which few aspire and whose problems are not only not thought about, but avoided by most people. The only others concerned are the technicians—the lawyers, prosecutors, judges and bondsmen who are responsible for the administration of bail. To the great majority of them the problems have become commonplace, the capacity for the indignation and reform has become attenuated, and the familiar has become endurable. Perhaps it is only after the community as a whole has become acquainted with this problem and reviewed it that any fresh or new approach to what is admittedly an antique problem in our jurisprudence can be developed.

My main reason for writing this book—my obvious interest in the subject aside—was to present the story of our bail system to the broadest public community. My hope is that general knowledge of our system's faults will bring indignation; and that this indignation will bring the necessary change.

The impact of the American bail system upon our modern social and judicial values demands this consideration now.

There is relatively little literature on this subject. I had one critical decision to make in developing this book: whether it should be a formal, fully documented legal treatise, or instead a book of more general interest in thrust and style. I chose the latter. While my hope is that the book will be serious and complete enough to be useful to lawyers, judges, legislators, and other professionals interested in improving the bail system, my motivation is to reach the public, without whose support these former groups cannot be fully successful. Most of the bench and bar know about the faults of the present bail system. When the public does, too, the impetus for reform may arise.

There are complete bibliographies on the subject of bail. I see no need to repeat them and add another. This book is not intended to be a legal brief; only possibly to support others' briefs. Anyone interested in a bibliography can get one from the Criminal Justice Section, Department of Justice, Washington, D.C., or from the Institute of Governmental Studies, University of California, Berkeley, California.

Acknowledgments

I wish to formally thank the directors of the Walter E. Meyer Research Institute of Law for their generous grant which enabled me to detach myself temporarily from other pursuits to work on this book. I am also grateful to the Institute for Policy Studies in Washington, D.C., which administered this grant. In arranging this award, Professor Ralph S. Brown, Jr., of the Yale Law School and the Meyer Institute, and Richard Barnet, codirector of the Institute for Policy Studies, were especially kind and helpful.

Though on the one hand our bail system is archaic, unjust, and in need of reform, on the other hand the first steps toward that much needed reform have been taken. During the past few years there has been some significant research and experiment and discussion, the proving ground for the far-reaching change that must come. A handful of men are chiefly responsible for this beginning, and in tribute to their accomplishments and for their generous advice and counsel to me while I wrote this book, they have my great respect and gratitude.

Professor Caleb Foote of the University of Pennsylvania Law School and Herbert Sturz, the director of the Vera Foundation, are both at the front of the small, dynamic group which has led the way toward bail reform. Both graciously shared their ideas with me, and commented wisely on my manuscript. They have my fullest gratitude and admiration.

Others, including Professor Charles H. Bowman, Ollie Gresham, David Hall, and Harry Subin, gave me advice about specific parts of the book, and for this they have my thanks. Several individuals read all or parts of the finished manuscript and offered valuable criticism at stages where it may have helped. For this I wish to thank Judge Skelly Wright, Professor Paul Oberst, Louis Claiborne, Steve Kurzman, Daniel Steiner, Milton Viorst, and Robert and Wendy Weinberg. I am especially in debt to Louis Claiborne, a brilliant attorney in the Office of the United States Solicitor General. He patiently, almost torturously, consorted with me during the time I wrote this book. His criticisms and suggestions were invaluable; and while he is not to blame for my errors, he does deserve credit for any parts of the book which the reader may consider worthwhile. He is a fine friend and a great critic.

Others who generously provided me with specific pieces of valuable information, and who checked my report for accuracy were: Louis Kauder, John Rosenberg and Burke Marshall of the Justice Department's Civil Rights Division, Jack Greenberg, Mike Meltsner, Leroy Clark, Charles Jones and Norman Amaker of the NAACP Legal Defense and Educational Fund, John Pratt of the National Council of Churches, Commission on Religion and Race. Louis Lusky of the Columbia Law School, and Carl Rachlin of CORE were consulted and provided me with helpful information.

Nanine Meiklejohn typed the early drafts of the first few chapters, and Liz Riemer deftly handled all that followed. Both were kind, thoughtful, and a big help. They have my appreciation.

Writing is hard and lonely work. Fortunately for me, after most of my research was done and about the time I started to write this book, my daughter was born. She was beside me almost constantly while I wrote; she grew with the manuscript.

And in merely being there she made the hardest days delightful, the sunny ones beautiful.

My wife, besides designing the book's jacket, acted as my constant critic and sounding board. With little thanks and much abuse, she read all drafts and constantly found the soft spots. I hope she found them all.

For these reasons and others, I have dedicated this book to my wife and my daughter with my thanks, as well as my love.

Alexandria, Virginia   R.G.
June, 1965

RANSOM

Prologue: Ransom

Although ideally the American system of law is based on equal justice for all men, in reality this is not always so. There are times when the scales of justice are weighted or tipped in favor of the rich and the "connected," and even at times in favor of the guilty, while the poor, the friendless, and sometimes the innocent are punished.

Millions of men and women are, through the American bail system, held each year in "ransom" in American jails, committed to prison cells often for prolonged periods before trial. Because they are poor or friendless, they may spend days, weeks, or months in confinement, often to be acquitted of wrongdoing in the end. A man is accused of stealing a few dollars from a subway change-booth, spends six months in jail before trial, and is finally acquitted. Though innocent, he has been punished by the American system of "justice." His only crime is poverty—he could not afford the $105 fee for a bondsman to put up the $2,500 bond set by the judge. A bootblack spends 121 days in jail charged with taking clothing from an automobile. But he is found not guilty. Yet a man with means, accused of far more serious crimes and eventually to be found guilty, may have to spend no time in jail before trial; his only virtue the fact that he could pay his way out of jail and wait comfortably at home for his trial to begin. As a result, his chances at the time of trial, and even at sentencing, are better.

The system of bail is used also by society as a social and political weapon to punish in advance of trial and sentence those it does not like. The power of law, for example, is used in the South today to express the anger and hostility of law enforcement officers toward those Negroes and whites who demonstrate for civil rights. A judge may deny bail altogether, as one did in an Alabama town when about two hundred demonstrators were arrested for violating an injunction against civil rights protests and held in jail. Only a habeas corpus petition freed them. A prosecutor in one Georgia town announced that refusal of bail to several civil rights demonstrators was done as a public lesson, to teach them their place.

So, too, bail may be set so high that even civil rights demonstrators who have come armed with funds may find themselves held "in ransom." One seventy-year-old minister languished in jail in Georgia for seven months with bail of $20,000 pending his appeal of a conviction—bail far in excess of that which would normally have been required, even for a dangerous criminal whose freedom before trial might endanger society. The same judge set bail at $20,000 for each of two women, one pregnant, arrested for protesting segregation at a restaurant.

Sometimes those arrested are charged with a number of crimes, with separate bail set for each alleged crime, multiplying the funds needed to a sum the defendants cannot raise. Mass arrests of hundreds of persons protesting racial injustice place a tremendous burden also upon civil rights organizations, forcing them to limit the number and occasions of demonstrations, a consequence the setting of excessive bail seems designed to achieve. When freedom riders were arrested in Mississippi in 1961, hundreds were sentenced. To appeal their convictions would have cost the individuals or the civil rights organizations $372,000. Money had to be raised by special collections. The cases, long delayed, are still pending, and the money raised is still tied up in the hands of Mississippi courts. In Birmingham, a quarter of a million dollars had to be raised overnight for bail for 840 prisoners, most of them youngsters. Even when such money is eventually returned, the delay serves to frustrate the activities of civil rights organizations. Again, the system of bail is used to hold for "ransom" persons either convicted of no crime or, even when convicted, whose sentence months or years later has been overturned by higher courts as unconstitutional. In one Virginia town a requirement of $400,000 worth of bail for release of civil rights demonstrators forced the end of antisegregation protests in that city. Such a use of bail as a political weapon is a corruption of the principle of equal justice.

Such practices are not confined to the South. When civil rights pickets were arrested at the 1964 New York World's Fair, charged with breach of the peace, sitting on the grass, and similar "crimes," each person had to raise $500 bail. A total of more than $10,000 was demanded in one night.

Yet the system of bail was never intended as a denial of justice, as a sentence before trial. It was intended as a device to make sure that a person charged with a crime would be available for trial. Yet the persons arrested and held without bail or under exorbitant bail today are often, as in the case of civil rights demonstrators, responsible and even noted personalities, neither dangerous nor intent on evading the law; many are children. Most have never been arrested before, yet they are subject to penalties which hardened criminals usually escape.

Bail does not even protect society. The major racketeer, on the other hand, who might present a menace can easily afford bail and be on the streets before his trial, threatening witnesses, destroying evidence, and generally endangering the community. He often works in cohorts with the bail bondsman. Recidivists who can afford bail are often released before trial and may commit multiple crimes while out on bail, unable or unwilling to resist. In 1963, a convicted criminal who had recently completed a term for burglary and armed robbery was caught again in the act of burglary and released on bail of $7,500. While free on bail he was caught committing a second burglary, released again, this time on $4,500 bail; then he was rearrested twice, once in possession of arms and burglary tools, once in the act of yet another burglary, released again in somewhat higher bail, $15,000, rearrested the same afternoon in the midst of still another burglary. Bail was set once more, at $5,000. He was rearrested three more times, released each time. When he went to trial, he had been arrested nine times and freed each time. He pleaded guilty to the ten indictments that had accumulated and was sentenced. In his case, as in so many others, bail had proved no deterrent to crime. In his case, as in the case of so many hardened criminals, bail was easily available. It is the amateur, often the innocent amateur, who waits in jail—often to be finally proved innocent. In the Appalachia case, bail was set in some instances as high as $100,000, but presented no problem to the defendants, who were quickly freed. This is the other side of the coin; the poor who can't afford bail are kept in jail while the wealthy but dangerous criminal against whom some controls are needed is not deterred by the requirements of bail.

 The American bail system is a scandal. It typifies what is worst and most cynical about our system of justice. It discriminates against the poor, against those who advocate or represent unpopular courses of action. It compromises and prostitutes the administration of justice by the courts. It is not only unfair; it is illogical; it does not even work well. The bail system is to a great degree a socially countenanced ransom of people and of justice for no good reason. It is an unworkable and unreasonable abortive outgrowth of historical Anglo-American legal devices which worked once in a far different time and place and in a far different way. Bail doesn't work. In one recent program, in Manhattan, which tested the utility of bail, more people on bail jumped than those in a group released on their own trust.

Every American should be shocked and moved by this ungainly legal process. It affects millions directly each year; and its mere existence should outrage and offend those who have been fortunate enough to avoid it. It is paradoxical that while the American public is moved by aspects of the legal process such as capital punishment which, whatever its horror, affects only a dozen or so persons each year, it is ignorant of or complacent about the workings of the bail system, which affects more than ten million Americans each year. How the bail system works, who operates it and with what weird and unworkable effects, should interest every person of sensitivity and arouse the American public to action.

CHAPTER I

The Nature and Origin of the
American Bail System

The word "bail" has a variety of legal connotations. All have
something to do with a situation in which one holds something or someone for another. Some say that etymologically,
the word derives from the old French word *baille*, meaning
to deliver, or a bucket or scoop used to dip water out of a
boat. Sir Edward Coke, former Lord Chief Justice of the
King's Bench, in his *Treatise of Bail and Mainprize*, said
that "baily is an old Saxon word, and signifieth a safekeeper
or protector . . . and therefore when a man upon surety is
delivered out of prison . . . he is delivered into bayle—that
is, into their safekeeping or protection from prison." There
are similar words in other languages. The Greek word *Bārrevz*
means "to deliver into hands."

In practical usage the word "bail" has come to connote the
process of *getting out*. One bails out a boat; one may bail out of
a plane; one bails out a person who has been arrested when he
is released on one's promise to return him to lawful authority
and on fulfilment of certain conditions in support of that
promise. Though there are other meanings, in the most common form of legal jargon bail describes the system for determining the official status of someone charged with a crime

pending his trial. This book will deal only with that system.
When is the bail system set into motion?

The police investigate a minor neighborhood complaint.
Clues indicate who the culprit is. A criminal charge is made
against a certain man. What should be done with him until he
is tried a week or a month or many months later?

A policeman on duty catches a burglar red-handed. He
arrests him and brings him to jail. Charges are preferred. What
should be done with him until his trial?

A man goes berserk and fires a gun into a crowded store.
He has seriously wounded many people in front of many
witnesses. What should be done with him after his arrest
until he is tried?

Public enemy number one is caught after an informant
decides to testify or reveal evidence to the police. In the past
when other charges against him have been brought, essential
evidence and witnesses have disappeared before trial. Should
this dangerous person be freed during the period before his
trial?

A questionable, purely circumstantial case is developed
against a person of impeccable background. He is very poor.
He has a job which he cannot leave without great sacrifice to
his family. He professes innocence and says he can prove it.
What should be done with him before he comes to trial?

The pillar of the community is indicted for a technical financial maneuver. Experts disagree about its illegality. He has
family, fortune, and deep ties in his community, and no plans
to leave. He announces that he will fight the case through the
courts. What should happen to him before his trial?

In all these hypothetical but typical cases, the status of
the defendants before trial is governed by the American bail
system. The period before trial may be long. It is always a
crucial time. It is a time of parallel and competing interests,

a period when the defendant must prepare his defense, and arrange his affairs; when the prosecution must prepare the government's case; when, perhaps even more than usual, the police must maintain peace and order. It is a vitally crucial period for all concerned and for society in general. Society needs to know it is safe and that the laws are enforced. It also wants to know that community affairs are conducted fairly and competently and that its fellow citizens are treated justly.

An individual's conduct has been questioned by his government. The wheels of the accusatorial system have begun to turn. Both sides begin the preparation of their case. If the case is a serious or generally interesting one, the press media will cover it and the public will be informed. A judge will have to decide what will be done with the defendant until some indefinite future time when he will be discharged as innocent or convicted as guilty and perhaps imprisoned. The judge's decision is a perplexing one.

Some conclude that fairness demands that all defendants ought to be free until they are convicted and sentenced to jail; others, that for the general welfare all suspects should be imprisoned until the charges are dismissed or until any danger is abated. There are serious questions about both these absolute approaches. Society must protect itself from clear and present dangers. Yet if the totalitarian results of guilt by accusation and the fearful consequences of the inquisitorial system, which punishes first and returns freedom only after ordeal, are to be avoided, imprisonments without due process of law cannot be countenanced. If the crime is ended upon apprehension, the chief nonpunitive reasons for incarceration before trial are the prevention of flight and new crimes.

The bail system is a compromise between these two extreme alternatives. Instead of simple release or imprisonment before trial, defendants usually are allowed conditional release. The condition of release is the pledging to the court of a sum of money to assure the defendant's presence for trial. This pledge may be made by the person involved, or by another, or most frequently by one who is in the business of bailing out defendants and insuring their presence for trial. As a general rule, all the defendants in the hypothetical cases cited earlier would be given the opportunity to buy a bailbond and go free. If they could not afford it, they would be jailed.

⟨The manner in which organized society treats people who are accused or suspected of having committed a crime is a telling gauge of that society's maturity and sophistication. The bail system is a measure of the political, even philosophical, quality of American society, and civilization, the relationship between government and the individual, our attitudes toward individual freedom, public welfare, equal justice, law, and order.⟩

John Seldon, the eminent Elizabethan antiquarian and historical scholar, once described bail as "the highest remedy." That was, no doubt, because bail was, as it still is, the door between confinement and freedom. The United States Supreme Court made a similar value judgment when in a 1932 case[1] it stated that the interim of time between the institution of formal charges and the trial was ". . . perhaps the most critical period of the proceeding . . . when consultation, thoroughgoing investigation and preparation (are) vitally important. . . ." For these reasons bail plays a crucial part in the pretrial system of criminal justice, and its implementation is worth careful consideration.

One considerable debate ranges about the question: What is the purpose of bail? Every reasonable student of the bail situation recognizes that a purpose of bail is to assure the

[1] Powell v. Alabama, 287 U.S. 45, 57 (1932).

presence of an accused at his trial if he is released before trial. However, there have been serious arguments over the question whether this is a purpose of bail, the primary purpose, or indeed the only purpose. In 1835, the Supreme Court held that: "A recognizance of bail, in a criminal case, is taken to secure the due attendance of the party accused, to answer the indictment, and to submit to a trial, and the judgment of the court thereon. It is not designed as a satisfaction for the offense . . . but as a means of compelling the party to submit to the trial and punishment which the law ordains for his offense."[And so, in modern articles and comments one is made quickly aware of the prevalent attitude that any aim of bail other than assuring the presence of an accused at trial would be a prostitution of the bail power.]

Others have expressed the view that judges have duties to others than an accused, and that at times the bail-setting power can and should be manipulated for the public good. The concept of preventive detention, that is, denying bail in order to restrain certain people or to protect society, will be given considerable attention in Chapter IV.

Preventive detention raises the most difficult practical and philosophical questions. Along with the obvious relief of his immediate discomfort, release before trial has long-range practical importance for an accused. It is during this time that a trial defense is prepared, and pretrial freedom may be conducive to ultimate success and freedom. And it is during this time that a defendant can arrange his affairs in case he is later convicted.

Preventive detention also raises more ponderous questions about the proper balance of values: Is unreachably high bail or the denial of bail a proper instrument for preventing potential misconduct; is it a fair way to assure a defendant's appearance;

2 Ex parte Milburn, 34 U.S. 704.

and is it a proper way to teach a lesson or punish one who is thought undesirable? Is preventive detention practiced through the manipulation of the bail system, and, if it is, *ought* it to be?

Preventive detention involves predictability. Can the likelihood of flight or the future criminality of a man be accurately predicted? If so, with what divine powers, upon what clairvoyant criteria? Are lower court judges the best ones to decide this impossibly difficult question, clear only in a few extreme cases? Should not some more scientific basis for taking this severe action or for avoiding injustices be sought before institutionalizing this practice? Is this an area of legal proceedings for which computers could be suitably developed? Or are human estimations alone appropriate?

Aside from the use of pretrial detention to prohibit future crime, is it a proper way to deter flight? One might well ask whether worrying about flight before a trial is not really premature. The police can catch up with those who do not submit voluntarily to the judicial process. If so, and if most people do not flee, is there a need for bail procedures at all? As one writer has said: "Of course no precaution will prevent an accused on bail from absconding if he is really determined to do so; that is an inherent risk and the chief deterrent must be the efficiency of the police in capturing those who abscond."[3] Is flight a police problem to be brought into play after the fact, or is it a judicial problem of insurance before the fact?

If pretrial detention is proper sometimes, when are those times? Should judges have absolute discretion to decide when? While judges are trustworthy, they are sometimes wrong, even corrupt. Americans prefer a government of laws and not of men. What law then should govern the judge? Presently, the law generally allows judges discretion to set or deny bail in

[3] Devlin, *The Criminal Prosecution in England*, pp. 89–91.

capital cases, but requires them to set reasonable bail in other
cases. This rule is subject to numerous questions. Capital
offenses are often one-time crimes, while petty offenses are
likely to be repeated and to present a continuing danger to the
community. The criterion of capital versus noncapital offenses
for determining pretrial incarceration may therefore not be
wise. Moreover, if a person *should* be jailed before trial, he
should not be allowed out on bail at all. His ability to put
up some money does not allay society's fears. The criterion of
bail for pretrial release may not be wise. Is there some other
way to classify offenses to keep the dangerous defendants in jail
and allow the others to go free? Is classification of the crime (for
example, release unless a crime of violence is involved) rather
than the gravity of the sentence a better formula? If so, then
what function has bail? Should we simply lock up some defendants and release others, regardless of their ability to afford
bail? If the decision is limited to whether the defendant ought
to be in or out of jail before trial, does the need for the present
bail system vanish as an irrelevancy?

The bail system is currently used indirectly to detain certain
defendants before trial. Judges manipulate the bail system,
which on its face does not so provide, to meet the needs for
preventive detention. Where incarceration is deemed appropriate, judges deny bail or set it unattainably high and accomplish the same result. Is this a proper subterranean function of
bail?

District of Columbia Court of Appeals Judge Bazelon recently argued that even if a defendant's dangerousness to the
community is a proper consideration in granting or denying
bail in certain cases, it is *not* a proper consideration in setting
the *amount* of bail. "Setting high bail to deny release discriminates between the dangerous rich and the dangerous poor and
masks the difficult problem of predicting future behavior

which is, in itself, fraught with excesses and injustice."[4] His inquiry could well have gone farther. If there is no specific legal procedure for preventive detention, is it not also wrong to deny bail to accomplish this end?

Is the bail system really geared only to one relatively small aspect of this problem of pretrial control of defendants, assuring the presence of the few defendants who can afford bail and who would be inhibited from flight by fear of losing the bail money? Is it related in any real and direct sense to the problem of deterring danger to the community during the time before trial? Is there a way to draw some new classification to guide judges which would sift both the defendant's dangerousness and his likelihood to flee, allowing only those who present neither of these two dangers to go free? Are these criteria related, or consistent or possible?

At the 1964 National Bail Conference, Professor Caleb Foote gave an interesting example, and made these clear and damning comments concerning the competing concepts governing the decision to release or incarcerate defendants prior to trial:

Neither our decisional law nor our present or proposed Federal rules of criminal procedure have gotten to first base in dealing with this riddle.

In 1835, a man named Lawrence fired two loaded pistols at President Jackson. He missed, and when he was brought up for preliminary examination, Chief Judge Krantz of the District of Columbia Circuit questioned the prisoner and supposed that in view of his very limited economic circumstances, $1,000 bail would be enough, because, "To require larger bail than the prisoner could give would be to require excessive bail."

When the Government objected because of the danger to the President's life, Judge Krantz in effect threw up his hands, increased

[4] Hairston v. U.S., District of Columbia Court of Appeals (Feb. 25, 1965).

the amount to $1,500 and remarked that *if the ability of the prisoner alone were to be considered, $1,500 was too much, but if the atrocity of the offense alone were to be considered, it was too small.* [Italics added.]

That there is not, then, a single intellectually respectable judicial decision on this problem in the ensuing 129 years is probably a testimonial to the fact that *the riddle is insoluble in the context of the bond system.* [Italics added.]

Another significant problem is reconciling any pretrial incarceration of any accused for any purpose with the traditional American jurisprudential rule that everyone accused of committing a crime has the benefit of a presumption of innocence. How can this be so if he is jailed, or forced to buy his provisional release before he is tried? The answer to this question depends upon definition. What does the presumption of innocence mean; and upon a value judgment, how is that presumption to be balanced with the other compelling demands upon the bail system? One commentator has said: "The presumption of innocence, in Britain at all events, is a rule of evidence to secure fair trial, and implies that the guilt of an accused must be proved at his trial beyond all reasonable doubt. It does not mean that those who discharge executive or administrative functions prior to trial should be bound to act as though the suspect had behaved, and would pending trial behave, as a law-abiding citizen. This would be to contradict the experience of mankind over the ages."[5]

On the other hand, Caleb Foote has said that the presumption of innocence is not a reference to any statistical probability of the defendant's actual innocence, but is merely the iteration of a value judgment. Individuals are not treated like criminals until the processes of the law have determined that

[5] T. B. Smith, *Bail Before Trial: Reflections of a Scottish Lawyer,* 108 *University of Pennsylvania Law Review* 109 (1960).

they are criminals. The presumption of innocence is not conclusive nor does it dispose of any conflict, but is indicative only of the proper weight to be given to this judgment in the judicial balance of competing interests. Senator Sam Ervin, Jr., the chairman of the Senate Subcommittee on Constitutional Rights, recently told the Senate: "Under our judicial system a man is innocent until proven guilty. Pretrial detention is equivalent to pretrial punishment."

Can the question of the presumption of innocence be raised at the bail stage when it is a rule of evidence applicable only at trial? The rule is uniformly followed in the United States that no inference of guilt is to be drawn by the jury from intermediate steps in the criminal trial process before conviction, and that the burden of proving guilt at trial rests on the prosecution. One can ask, then, what this has to do with bail proceedings that take place before trial. Or is any pretrial incarceration in conflict with the spirit or the philosophy of the presumption of innocence?

Aside from the possible inconsistency of pretrial detention with the presumption of innocence, is it inherently prejudicial for a defendant to be treated as a prisoner before trial? Is he not prejudiced when he is treated this way in front of the court and jury? If pretrial imprisonment itself does not imply a presumption of guilt, does it add to the likelihood of a finding of guilt? Aside from the practical problems of physical restraint by jailing before trial, is an insistence upon bail at the arraignment stage a form of economic punishment? Is jail instead of bail an unconstitutional form of trial and imprisonment without a jury?

Some of these questions can be answered only after deciding whether bail itself is primarily a power of the government or a right of the individual.

Numerous legal questions arise about the nature of the

right to bail. Is there some enforceable guarantee that one must be entitled to bail? Or rather is the right only to non-excessive bail when bail is allowed? What is excessive? How is this determined? A bail of $500,000 might not be excessive to a wealthy man, whereas $25 would be excessive to a poor man. How do we deal with these extremes?

The financial emphasis of the American bail system raises provoking and perplexing problems about the equality of the administration of justice. What if a man has no money? Should he be denied a chance for freedom before trial simply because he is poor? What if a man has a little money, but cannot afford to use it for bail? Suppose he has a family, a limited bank account, and a job that brings a meager living. The recent studies about the conditions of poverty in America pointed out how common this status is. One-fifth of our population, approximately thirty-five million people, fall into the poverty class. One out of four families earns less than $3,000 a year. If a man has a wife and two children, and he earns about $60 a week, can he afford to spend a week's salary for bail? The answer is obvious. Yet, not being able to afford it, he must go to jail. There he loses his earning capacity for periods averaging about a month, and possibly loses his job. We help least those who need us most. Justice Brennan has said: "A just man must feel uneasy when an accused, pending trial, must languish in jail because, although he is eligible for bail, he cannot raise the necessary funds."

Is the ability to afford bail or the gravity of the crime charged a rational basis for determining pretrial status? What does either have to do with the likelihood of flight or the commission of later crimes? Our federal courts historically have ruled that in fixing bail a judge should consider both the ability of a prisoner to give bail as well as the atrocity of the offense with which he is charged. How much consideration ought to be given to each factor has never been defined. The facts and experiences which will be described in this book will show that the poor are special victims of the workings of the bail system. Only recently Justice Douglas, long an outspoken critic of laws that discriminate in their terms or in fact against the poor, offered an opinion about the present situation with regard to bail and the poor:

The fundamental tradition in the country is that one charged with a crime is not, in ordinary circumstances, imprisoned until after a judgment of guilty. . . . This traditional right to freedom during trial . . . has to be squared with the possibility that the defendant may flee or hide himself. Bail is the device which we have borrowed to reconcile these conflicting interests. . . . It is assumed that the threat of forfeiture of one's goods will be an effective deterrent to the temptation to break the conditions of one's release. But *this theory is based on the assumption that a defendant has property. To continue to demand a substantial bond which the defendant is unable to secure raises considerable problems for the equal administration of the law.* We have held that *an indigent defendant is denied equal protection of the law if he is denied an appeal on equal terms with other defendants, solely because of his indigence. Can an indigent be denied freedom, where a wealthy man would not, because he does not happen to have enough property to pledge for his freedom?* [Italics added.]

It would be unconstitutional to fix excessive bail to assure that a defendant will not gain his freedom. Yet *in the case of an indigent defendant, the fixing of bail in even a modest amount may have the practical effect of denying him release.* [Italics added.] The wrong done by denying release is not limited to the denial of freedom alone. That denial may have other consequences. In case of reversal, he will have served all or part of his sentence under an erroneous judgment. Imprisoned, a man may have no opportunity to investigate his case, to cooperate with his counsel, to earn money that is still necessary for the fullest use of his right to appeal.

In the light of these considerations, I approach this applicant (for recognizance) with the conviction that *the right to release is heavily favored and that the requirement of security for bond may, in a proper case, be dispensed with.* . . . Further reflection has led me to conclude that *no man should be denied release, because of indigence.* Instead, under our constitutional system, a man is entitled to be released on personal recognizance where other relevant factors make it reasonable to believe that he will comply with the orders of the court."[6] [Italics added.]

Although Justice Douglas' thoughts have not yet been elevated to the level of settled, authoritative law, there are indications that the present Supreme Court might be sympathetic to his views in this regard. During the past decade the Court has been evolving through a line of cases a doctrine of constitutional law which demands equal justice for indigents. Though no court has decided so yet, it could well be that it will soon be held that hinging rights or freedom upon one's wealth, as bail does, denies due process of law or the equal protection of the law guaranteed by the Fifth and Fourteenth Amendments to the Constitution. And the Congress has turned its attention to this question, too. In introducing legislation aimed at improving this condition, Senator Sam Ervin, Jr., pointed out: "When pretrial punishment is determined on the basis of financial ability to pay for a bail bond, a question is raised as to whether this is an invidious discrimination between the indigent and those with financial resources."

Caleb Foote has noted that the due process clause of the Fifth and Fourteenth Amendments might properly be interpreted to protect defendants against the adverse deprivations of pretrial detention. If, as it has been indicated by recent research, the pretrial detention of poor defendants who go to jail simply because they cannot afford bail tends to affect adversely their future trial, sentence, and probation, this injury

---

[6] U.S. v. Bandy, 81 S. Ct. 197–8 (1960).

may well be considered to be one of constitutional proportions. The statistical proof of this charge, while not conclusive, is certainly persuasively suggestive.

Bail is mentioned only once in the United States Constitution. The Eighth Amendment states that, "Excessive bail shall not be required." With regard to the Eighth Amendment's prohibition against excessive bail, Professor Foote has also recently raised the question of "how to apply the concept of excessiveness to a criminal population which is at least fifty percent indigent." The rate of arrests is highest among the lower economic classes. Does then the requirement of bail create an economic or class discrimination against this class? Is bail of any amount excessive for the average American non-professional criminal? A converse question about the poor person's accessibility to bail can also be asked. If bail is reduced to what a poor man can afford, is it any deterrent to flight?

This leads to another important question: Are financial conditions of release, even if not unfair, inadequate for the chief end desired, that of assuring the presence at trial of the accused who does have money for bail? Whether or not money bail is fair to the poor, is it at least meaningful to the rich? If conditional release is our choice of treatment of defendants before trial, could there be other, more rational conditions than the payment of money? If so, what are they?

Is the bail bondsman useful? What valuable function does he serve? Does he in fact pervert the judicial process, as many have suggested? Is the commercialization of one step in the court's processes a valid example of our free enterprise system? The bondsman and all his ramifications are the subject of Chapter III.

How the rules of bail apply; if our system can be and is manipulated in practice and if so, by whom, against whom, and with what positive or negative results, these too are relevant inquiries about the status of our present bail system. These practical inquiries can show how the ideals work. They must be asked if a worthwhile appraisal is to be made.

To neglect the social climate and intellectual condition of society would be to examine a dynamic social process out of context, in an unrealistic laboratory-like atmosphere. Social problems cannot be properly treated this way. Thus it is important to observe that two phenomena of social action in recent years vitally bear on the subject of bail. One is a general rising recognition of the double standard of life and law encountered by the poor. Long an invisible, voiceless, but vast group, the impoverished one-fifth of the population is beginning to receive some significant attention. Both in terms of welfare legislation in general and law reform more specifically, steps are being taken toward equalizing the administration of the law by withdrawing the ingredient of wealth from the scales of justice. Whatever the general failings of the American bail system, the poor have special problems with a system that relies so significantly on one's wealth.

Secondly, focusing in particular on bail, the past decade has witnessed a growing awareness by some professional groups and by the press of the inadequacies and unfairness of our present bail system. Some programs of bail reform have taken place. These successful experiments are discussed in Chapter V. So, too, it is often helpful and enlightening to compare solutions by other societies to those of the American programs. Chapter VI discusses a number of legal systems abroad in terms of their treatment of persons accused of crimes.

There are, it should at least be mentioned, other forms and uses of bail. There is a form of bail in civil cases, that forces a man to put up a sum of money that will be the security for an amount which will be the subject of a forthcoming suit against him by another. This procedure is designed to prevent his secreting or spending the money which is the subject of the suit in order to frustrate the suit. The Supreme Court, as long ago as 1883, clearly described the difference between civil and criminal bail: "The object of bail in civil cases is . . . to secure the payment of a debt or other civil duty; whilst the object of bail in criminal cases is to secure the appearance of the principal before the court for the purpose of public justice."[7] There are also appeal bonds, which come into being after conviction and which allow a convicted defendant to remain free pending his appeal. In addition, material witness bonds force an individual to stay in custody, or to deposit a sum of money or a bond with the court adequate to insure his presence to testify at a forthcoming trial.

These bond situations raise interesting and perplexing questions. For example, ought an appeal bond be higher than an ordinary bond because theoretically the danger of flight is greater when a defendant has been convicted and faces immediate imprisonment; and, is the concept behind the material witness bond correct that a witness to a crime should be forced to remain in jail before a trial while the defendant himself may go free? This book will only tangentially deal with the varieties of bail, and will focus specifically on bail as the means for pretrial release in criminal cases.

History

Though the American bail system has been undergoing considerable re-evaluation recently, except for the past decade, there has been little literature on the subject. In fact, the origins of the modern American bail system lie in some uncertainty, caused in not the least part by historical inattention.

One theory has it that bail derives from the very ancient

[7] U.S. v. Ryder, 110 U.S. 729.

English institution of hostageship.[8] According to some German scholars, the institution of hostageship was developed in England by Germanic Angles and Saxons. This tribal custom of early systems was a war tactic; the hostage was held until the promise of a certain person was fulfilled or a certain consequence achieved. The personal responsibility of the hostage-surety in effect placed his body in a state of metaphorical hostageship. There is some difference of opinion among scholars whether the surety in the hostage relationship would really submit personally if the debtor defaulted, or whether he would only forfeit his property. There is historical evidence that the surety could have been made to suffer the punishment of the prisoner if the prisoner himself escaped.[9] It is more likely that the surety protected the debtor from the vengeance of the creditor by assuming his debt and then making the debtor responsible to him. By thus placing the debtor in a more favorable position, the surety substituted performance for bodily seizure.

Actual bodily seizure of the person putting up bail is, of course, absent in the modern bail situation. But, it has been suggested that the bondsman of today is no more than the extension of this older form of surety relationship. Both the old hostage and the modern surety assume responsibility for another, one by pledging his body, the other by pledging his material wealth. The classic condition of suretyship existed in the hostage relationship; that is, if the debtor failed to reimburse the creditor, the surety became responsible to the creditor. According to this theory, suretyship evolved from, and is no more than, a form of hostageship. Today's surety is responsible only for property liability and not bodily seizure.

[8] Elsa de Haas, *The Antiquities of Bail*, Columbia University, New York, 1940.
[9] Pollock and Maitland, *History of English Law*, Vol. 2, 3d ed., 1899, p. 590.

Money has replaced men. Liability for the responsibility of another is the common characteristic of both relationships.

Other scholars have suggested that modern bail comes from the old English laws governing debt, from the primitive concept of *wergeld*. Under this ancient scheme, one who was accused of committing a wrong had to guarantee a payment to reimburse that wrong, should he later be found at fault. Just as today's surety guarantees, at the risk of his own personal loss, the presence of the accused at trial under the modern bail system, so in primitive English society did a surety assure that a debtor would pay his *wergeld* to redress the victim of an injury. Victims of wrongs were assured of some compensation under this system without having to resort to feuds and personal vendettas. Instead, a third party would inject himself between creditor and debtor as a kind of trustee. By assuring performance he would avoid bodily seizure of the accused or other resorts to vengeance. The pledge of the surety warranted to the victim-creditor that the debtor would be presented and would pay his *wergeld* if fault were found. If the wrongdoer did not pay his just debt, the surety assumed that responsibility. This was a contractual relationship like bail.

In the period during the first thousand years A.D. in England, a bail system like the American system in use today began to develop, charted by the necessities of the times. Land was held in vast feudal baronies. Justice was administered by traveling judges whose visits to an area on the circuits of the realm were intermittent, often several years apart. The local sheriffs, who represented the Crown in their respective areas, were responsible for the custody of prisoners. Prison conditions were atrocious. Prison facilities were insecure and inadequate. They served no one, and they were a financial burden.

The sheriffs, executives for the administration of criminal justice until the judges arrived, were happy to have someone else assume the responsibility of maintaining custody of defendants. If someone would assume the personal responsibility of presenting a defendant for future trial, the sheriffs were happy to shift the responsibility to them. As the custodian of all those accused, sheriffs frequently relinquished defendants provisionally into the custody of a surety, usually a friend or relative of the accused. This system is referred to by some scholars as private jailing, "the Duke's living prison," the sureties being the private jailers.[10]

In their *History of English Law*, Pollock and Maitland described these early conditions:

If a man was arrested he was usually replevied or mainprised; that is to say, he was set free so soon as some sureties undertook or became bound for his appearance in court. It was not common to keep men in prison. This apparent leniency of our law was not due to any love of an abstract liberty. Imprisonment was costly and troublesome. Besides, any reader of the eyre rolls will be inclined to define a goal as a place that is made to be broken, so numerous are the entries that tell of escapes. The medieval dungeon was not all that romance would make it; there were many ways out of it. The mainprise of substantial men was about as good a security as a goal. The sheriff did not want to keep prisoners; his inclination was to discharge himself of all responsibility by handing them over to their friends.[11]

This rough and personalized system gradually developed in England into a more formal, institutionalized system in accommodating to certain changes in the administration of criminal justice from about 1000 to 1300 A.D. The primary changes in the nature of bail proceedings were set out in the Statute Westminster I, passed in 1275. There, for the first time, procedures on bail practices were made a matter of specific

10 *Ibid.*, pp. 584–590.
11 *Ibid.*, pp. 584–590.

articulated law. During early Norman and Anglo-Saxon periods, cases had been brought privately by injured parties.
Wrongs were private matters between the people involved,
the accused and the injured person or his relatives seeking
redress in his name. The state was not the prosecutor. This
factor probably contributed to the advanced theory of wergeld,
mentioned earlier. Under this system the accused was treated
as if he were probably guilty, and imprisoned without any
preliminary inquiry by a judicious third party. The sheriff was
custodian, but he was delighted to allow a private surety assume his responsibility and thereby release the accused from
custody.

With the passage of the ordinance called the "Assize of
Clarendon" in 1166, the system of individual institution of
prosecutions was replaced. The Crown took over the administration of all criminal jurisdiction. Crimes against the king
were defined, and procedures were instituted to deal with these
crimes. The forerunner of the present grand jury, the present-
ment jury, was created as the official means for beginning formal proceedings by the royalty against persons accused of
crimes. Since cases could be started on the basis of any claim
including hearsay and rumor, suspicion, and surmise, it became particularly necessary to devise a system to protect individuals from being unreasonably or improperly accused of
crimes. Under the earlier system, an accuser had to make his
accusation under oath, provide some security against fake
claims; he could be charged with malicious prosecutions (the
writ de odio et atia was created to charge one with having made
an accusation in spite and hate). Bail release became more
important once the criminal process was institutionalized
and made more formal. This was especially important, since
the judge often did not get to a place to conduct trials for long
periods of time. For most crimes, writs were available to secure

release before trial. But they were casually, often improperly, administered by the sheriffs, and bail became a matter of bargaining. No fixed formula or amount was required for bail; one got away with what one could, but could also appeal to the Chancery court for his release against the denial by the local sheriff of bail and release to sureties. Freedom was liberally awarded.

In 1275, as the result of an extensive inquest by a hundred jurors exposing many fraudulent and obnoxious practices in the administration of bail practices by the sheriffs, the first statute governing bail was passed. Extortions, bribery, improper releases, and improper incarcerations had been exposed in what became known as the "Hundred Inquests of 1274." It was pointed out that the poor suffered especially because they could not afford this game of payoff. One man remained in jail for eight years awaiting his trial for lack of the forty shillings necessary to secure his release. The Statute Westminster I of 1275, the first reform legislation dealing with bail, established which crimes were bailable upon the presentation of sufficient sureties and which were not. And it established penalties to ensure that the rules set up were observed.

A slow evolution of bail procedure is visible. At first the sheriff had unlimited discretion to release an accused. The common law built in certain exceptions based on necessity which denied the right to bail in the cases of certain serious crimes. Writs were developed so that individuals could appeal to the Crown for exceptions to the general rules controlling the sheriffs. Unfortunately, this practice became one of simple graft, with the Crown extending special privileges "for golden reasons." Local custom and common law were later regulated under Edward I, who had systematized the bail situation by the Statute Westminster I. Certain crimes became bailable as of right; others were not. Discretion in setting bail gradually came to rest in the judges of the lower courts. Their discretion was, however, limited by statutes and by common law considerations of the kind of case, the character of the defendant, and the risks of flight.

In 1688, the English Bill of Rights included a provision which forbade excessive bail. The United States Constitution contains a similar provision in its Eighth Amendment: "Excessive bail shall not be required." Even before the adoption of the Eighth Amendment, early lawmakers had passed America's first judiciary act in 1789. It guaranteed a right to bail in all noncapital criminal cases, and it made bail discretionary in capital cases, dependent upon "the nature and circumstances of the offense, and of the evidence and usages of law." That law, which has existed throughout this country's history, now finds expression in the rules of federal criminal procedure:

"A person arrested for an offense not punishable by death *shall* be admitted to bail. A person arrested for an offense punishable by death *may* be admitted to bail by any court or judge authorized by law to do so in the exercise of discretion, giving due weight to the evidence and to the nature and circumstances of the offense."[12] [Italics added.]

There is an interesting paradox in this general rule which has traditionally distinguished between capital and noncapital offenses for the purposes of the accessibility of bail. Historically, capital punishment was authorized for a shockingly great number of offenses. In 1765, for example, England had 160 capital crimes. Even some of what would now be considered petty or trivial offenses bore the potential ultimate sentence. The humanitarianism of the rule allowing bail in noncapital cases as a matter of right need not have been so extensive as it appeared. Actually, the rule was applied with a conservative interest in the public welfare. The

12 *Federal Rules of Criminal Procedure*, Rule 46.

famous historical commentator Blackstone wrote about this rule: "For what is there that a man may not be induced to forfeit to save his own life. And what satisfaction or indemnity is it to the public to seize the effects of them who have bailed a murderer if the murderer himself be suffered to escape with impunity." Today, on the contrary, capital punishment is authorized for few crimes, in some places not at all, and the trend is away from capital punishment. This being the case, the general rule for the availability of bail is now deceivingly liberal. Since so few crimes are punishable by death, most defendants ". . . *shall* be admitted to bail." The pragmatic result of the bail rule, then, may have changed considerably with the change in thinking about capital punishment, if not from any changes in the thinking about bail.

State rules on bail generally follow federal rules. All states provide for bail either by statute, constitution, or case law. Most states allow bail to sufficient sureties before conviction except for capital crimes, "when the proof is evident or the presumption great." A few states limit the power to deny bail in murder and treason cases. A few grant an absolute right to bail in misdemeanor cases, and a few allow the judge absolute discretion to grant or deny bail in accord with the common law.

It is unfortunate that the Constitution is not more specific or more extensive in its treatment of the law of bail. One has to turn to the accompanying laws and the general attitudes and policies of the times to gain any authoritative insight about the nature and extent of the law of bail. Ideally, one would hope that recourse to laws like the Eighth Amendment would be exceptional or unnecessary. The constitutional scholar, Story, expounding upon the simple constitutional direction against excessive bail, wrote:

The provision would seem to be wholly unnecessary in a free government, since it is scarcely possible that any department of such a government should authorize or justify such atrocious conduct. It was, however, adopted as an admonition to all departments of the national government, to warn them against such violent proceedings as had taken place in England in the arbitrary reigns of some of the Stuarts. In those times a demand of excessive bail was often made against persons who were odious to the court and its favorites; and on failing to procure it, they were committed to prison. Enormous fines and amercements were also sometimes imposed, and cruel and vindictive punishments inflicted. Upon this subject, Mr. Justice Blackstone has wisely remarked that sanguinary laws are a bad symptom of the distemper of any state, or at least of its weak constitution.[13]

Later cases and later laws have supported this philosophical attitude. Under modern federal law, the amount of nonexcessive bail is determined upon what is deemed necessary to insure the presence of the accused, considering the nature and circumstances of the charged offense, the weight of the evidence against the accused, the financial ability of the defendant to pay bail, and the defendant's character.

In a case decided by the Supreme Court in 1951, Chief Justice Vinson described what was the current American policy about bail:

From the passage of the Judiciary Act of 1789, to the present Federal Rules of Criminal Procedure, federal law has unequivocally provided that a person arrested for a non-capital offense shall be admitted to bail. This traditional right to freedom before conviction permits the unhampered preparation of a defense, and serves to prevent the infliction of punishment prior to conviction. . . . Unless this right to bail before trial is preserved, the presumption of

[13] Joseph Story, *Commentaries on the Constitution of the United States,* Vol. 2, 5th ed. 1833, p. 650.

innocence, secured only after centuries of struggle, would lose its meaning.

The right to release before trial is conditioned upon the accused's giving adequate assurance that he will stand trial and submit to sentence if found guilty. . . . Like the ancient practice of securing the oaths of responsible persons to stand as sureties for the accused, the modern practice of requiring a bail bond or the deposit of a sum of money subject to forfeiture serves as additional assurance of the presence of an accused. Bail set at a figure higher than an amount reasonably calculated to fulfill this purpose is "excessive" under the Eighth Amendment. . . .

Since the function of bail is limited, the fixing of bail for any individual defendant must be based upon standards relevant to the purpose of assuring the presence of that defendant.[14]

And in a dissent to that same case, Associate Justice Robert Jackson made the following, now-classic statement about the philosophy behind the American bail system:

The practice of admission to bail, as it has evolved in Anglo-American law, is not a device for keeping persons in jail upon mere accusation until it is found convenient to give them a trial. On the contrary, *the spirit of the procedure is to enable them to stay out of jail until a trial has found them guilty*. Without this conditional privilege, even those wrongly accused are punished by a period of imprisonment while awaiting trial and are handicapped in consulting counsel, searching for evidence and witnesses, and preparing a defense. To open a way of escape from this handicap and possible injustice, Congress commands allowance of bail for one under charge of any offense not punishable by death, providing: "A person arrested for an offense not punishable by death shall be admitted to bail . . ." before conviction. [Italics added.]

Admission to bail always involves a risk that the accused will take flight. That is a calculated risk which the law takes as the price of our system of justice. We know that Congress anticipated

[14] Stack v. Boyle, 342 U.S. 1.

that bail would enable some escapes, because it provided a procedure for dealing with them. [Italics added.]

In allowance of bail, the duty of the judge is to reduce the risk by fixing an amount reasonably calculated to hold the accused available for trial and its consequence. . . . But the judge is not free to make the sky the limit, because the Eighth Amendment to the constitution says: "Excessive bail shall not be required. . . ."

Congress has reduced this generality in providing more precise standards, stating that ". . . the amount thereof shall be such as in the judgment of the commissioner or court or judge or justice will insure the presence of the defendant, having regard to the nature and circumstances of the offense charged, the weight of the evidence against him, the financial ability of the defendant to give bail and the character of the defendant."

CHAPTER II

The Victims of the Bail System

THE POOR

The American bail system discriminates against and punishes the poor. The rich can afford to buy their freedom, and do; the poor go to jail because they cannot afford the premium for a bail bond. The average amount of bail is about $500, and the average premium for a bail bond—$25 to $50—is 5 per cent or 10 per cent of the amount of the bond, but many of the poor do not have a ready $25 or $50, and for lack of it go to jail while the rich or the comfortable go home.

The economic facts of the bail system go even further. When the defendant who cannot afford bail goes to jail before trial, he loses his present earning capacity, and often his job. His family suffers. Some people have been forced onto relief rolls as a result of lost earning capacity caused by pretrial detention. All of this happens before trial, without regard to their guilt or innocence. It is, in effect, punishment for the crime of poverty.

Not only is society unjust in condoning and fostering this system of unequal justice; it also loses money. The bail system is economically self-defeating. The cost to the public for the maintenance of these pretrial detention facilities, dismally stark though these jail cells are, is a staggering waste of millions of dollars a year. It yields no compensating profit. The bail system leads to economic fatuity and spiraling waste.

Even more disheartening is the fact that defendants who can afford bail are convicted less frequently, and receive lesser sentences when they are convicted, a flagrant violation of the basic American concept of equal justice.

Gertrude Samuels in the *New York Times Magazine* asked: "How can it be that members of Brooklyn's notorious Gallo gang, who were charged with murdering a policeman in the course of a gang war, were released on bail, while at the same time in that same city 17- and 18-year-old defendants were kept in jail over a year because they could not afford bail?" The two teenagers were acquitted.

Another poor defendant, described in the *Saturday Evening Post* by Don Oberdorfer, had been accused (on disputed evidence) of stealing $14.05 from a subway change-booth. He was jailed for six months awaiting trial because he could not afford the bondsman's fee of $105 required for his $2,500 bond. Ultimately, he was acquitted. Yet he had ". . . lost his job, his tiny apartment and an entire summer of his life," in a half-year in a jail cell in the company of a homosexual, a drug addict, and a veteran convict. Another case, reported by Oberdorfer, told of a twenty-one-year old accused of driving without a license (maximum sentence five days) jailed for fifty-four days for lack of $300 bail.

Former Attorney General Robert F. Kennedy testified about a similar case before Senator Ervin's Subcommittee on Constitutional Rights on August 4, 1964. "In Glen Cove, New York, Daniel Walker was arrested on suspicion of robbery and spent fifty-five days in jail for want of bail. Meanwhile, he lost his job, his car was repossessed, his credit destroyed, and his wife had to move in with her parents. Later, he was found to be the victim of mistaken identity and was released. But it took him four months simply to find another job." Kennedy told of another man in Los Angeles detained in

jail before trial for a minor crime because he could not afford
bail. He was in jail for 207 days, and then was acquitted.

James V. Bennett, former director of prisons for the United
States, told of other incidents. One thirty-five-year-old man,
charged with forging some money orders, spent 167 days in a
county jail before he was tried: ". . . we immediately found
him to be a mild and meek individual who could hardly be
considered much of a threat to the community, especially in
view of the fact that he had lived there all of his life and had
two children to whom he was very much attached." Bennett
gave other illustrations:

A 36-year-old man was held in his local county jail on a Dyer
Act charge for 126 days before he was released on two years'
probation.

A 22-year-old Selective Service Act violator was held in his local
county jail for 172 days before he was released on two years'
probation.

A 31-year-old man was held in his local county jail for 284 days
before being released on five years' probation. He had been charged
with the theft of government property and altering a Treasury
check.

A 38-year-old man was held in his local county jail on mail
theft charges for 213 days before he was released on five years'
probation.

And so it goes.

Examples of the long detention before trial of both guilty
and non-guilty defendants are legion. An eighteen-year-old
Marine was charged with robbery. After lifting a wallet from
a woman's open purse in a downtown market, he fled on foot
and was captured on the street nearby. He broke down crying
and confessed fully, claiming he had not eaten for several days,
had been sleeping in all-night theaters, and was AWOL from
Camp Pendleton.

The young Marine was a native of Oregon and his parents were unknown. His grandmother had talked him into going back to Camp Pendleton and turning himself in, but when he reached Los Angeles he decided he couldn't go back. Bail was set at $2,000. After 107 days in jail, he was found guilty, received a suspended 90-day sentence, and was put on probation for one year.

A bootblack was charged with burglary for allegedly taking clothing from a car. His prior record showed four gambling arrests and he had been in Los Angeles County eight years. But after 121 days in jail awaiting trial, he was found not guilty.

A woman was charged with burglary, accused of receiving stolen property. She contended that the allegedly stolen property in her possession had been taken from her. She was found not guilty, but she had already spent 102 days in jail.

A man was charged with grand theft of an auto. He maintained that he bought the car. He was found not guilty after 107 days in jail.

Another man was arrested for forgery in Los Angeles County, where he had lived for fifteen years. After 74 days in jail he was found not guilty.

One author, writing in *Parade* magazine about this scandalous aspect of our bail system reported two shocking cases:

[A 19-year-old boy] was recently jailed on a robbery charge in Des Moines, Iowa, because he could not raise $10,000 bail. Before the actual robber pleaded guilty, [the accused] spent two months behind bars.

In one horrifying case the boy arrested never had a chance to prove his innocence:

The most disturbing result of jailing young and impressionable defendants before trial is their contact with hardened criminals. In a case in St. Francois County, Mo., last June, [a 17-year-old boy], charged with stealing tools, was locked in a cellblock with eight or nine men, including an ex-convict. The deputy sheriff reportedly told [the boy's] family he would let them know if a bondsman was needed to raise bail. The family never had that chance. Two days later [he] was beaten to death by his cellmates.

Congressman McVicker recently addressed the United States House of Representatives and told this pathetic story. In Adams County, Colorado, last year a twenty-one-year-old with no criminal record was accused of assaulting an officer of the law. He was arrested, and bail was set at $10,000. Unable to afford the cost of this bail, he was imprisoned for eight months. Later the policeman confessed that he had falsely accused the defendant, who was then released. But, in the words of Representative McVicker, ". . . this twenty-one-year-old youth had lost much—his time, his good name, the companionship of his family, and the money he might have earned had the bail system in Colorado excluded an irrelevant but now controlling factor—namely, the financial status of the accused."

Such stories are not extraordinary. They are merely egregious examples of what is happening daily in the United States. Though universal statistics are not available, some investigations have made it possible to reach certain reliable general conclusions. Two telling and damning pioneer studies of the administrations of the bail systems of two major American cities were conducted in the 1950s—one in Philadelphia,[1] the other in New York City[2]—sponsored by the University of Pennsylvania Law School's Institute of Legal Research. These investigations were originated and led by Caleb Foote of the Penn Law School, the inspiring law professor whose early and

[1] 102 *University of Pennsylvania Law Review*, 1031 (1954).
[2] 106 *loc. cit.*, 685 (1958).

persistent interest and work has given impetus to bail reform. In Philadelphia it is the practice, not atypical, for United States commissioners to set bail in federal cases, and for state court judges to set bail for serious crimes; but by far the most cases are dealt with at the bail stage by magistrates. These cases are disposed of "in dingy station houses throughout the city" by magistrates who are not lawyers, where defendants have no defense counsel and where the attending crowd is mostly composed of prosecutors and police. Different magistrates set greatly varying bail for the same offense, and to judge by their comments, seem to be applying different and quite personal criteria. Most are unrelated to the only valid bail inquiry: Will this assure the defendant's presence for trial? Often the judges' decisions are dictated by the prosecutors. In the higher state courts, the recommendations for bail by district attorneys were followed 95 per cent of the time. The federal proceedings observed were more restrained and more sophisticated, and the bail determinations seem more reasonable.

The statistics gathered by this Philadelphia study, which compared the fates of bailed defendants with the fates of jailed defendants, are quite persuasive and pointed. During the summer of 1953, 752 defendants were held for trial. Three out of four who were charged with serious crimes for which the court did set bail were held in jail between arrest and trial. Of those charged with less serious crimes for which magistrates set bail, a little more than one out of four were not released. The detention cells were crowded with these pretrial detainees, who in 1952 had spent an aggregate of 131,683 days in jail awaiting trials. The public cost of this detention was over $300,000.

The fate of one thousand defendants who could not afford bail and who were therefore jailed before trial was charted.

Less than half, only 470 of them, were convicted and received jail sentences. Another 318 were convicted, but did not suffer any imprisonment after conviction. In other words, almost 32 per cent of those defendants were jailed before they were tried, yet *after conviction*, were considered for one reason or another to be worthy of going free. It is ironical and sad that these people—who exhibited enough mitigating circumstances or evidence of good character or reputation to warrant their not receiving executed prison sentences after their commission of crimes was proved—were thought so little of before trial that they had to suffer imprisonment because they could not afford bail. The remaining 210 defendants were not even convicted. This last group of 21 per cent of the thousand charted defendants served pretrial jail sentences, although they were subsequently found not guilty of committing the alleged crimes. Pretrial detention periods averaged thirty-three days, but some of the many who were not convicted served up to seventy-five days in jail before they were tried.

The disposition of another group of 946 cases was examined in order to compare the subsequent judicial treatment of the jailed and the bailed defendants. This comparison showed that defendants who came to court from jail received much less favorable treatment as to both the proportions of those convicted and those receiving prison sentences," reported the investigators. They added, conservatively, that ". . . the contrast between the disposition of jail and bail cases was so striking that it raises a strong inference that the handicap of jail status is a major contributing cause for the difference." Of 529 serious criminal cases where the defendants were on bail before trial, 275 were convicted; 254 defendants were not convicted. Of 417 similar cases where the defendants were in jail before trial, 340 were convicted and only 77 were not. To carry it further, of these 275 convicted offenders on bail before their trials, only 61 (22 per cent) were sent to prison after conviction. Of the 340 convicted defendants who were in jail before trial, 200 (59 per cent) received prison sentences after being tried and convicted.

It seems too obvious to be debated, though it is unprovable, that a defendant who is released before his trial and is able to maintain his family life and job would be likely to receive more favorable consideration for probation by virtue of his accomplishments on pretrial release.

Detention facilities prior to trial in these cases were moreover found to be quite unpleasant, and the untried defendants were treated like convicted criminals.

Equally frightening insights were provided by a similar, later study. In 1956, a second team of University of Pennsylvania law students surveyed bail practices in felony cases in New York City. It was first found that of 2,292 varied criminal cases where bail was set, in an average of only 49 per cent could bail be furnished. This average varied with the amount of bail required, from an average of 28 per cent who could not afford $500 bail up to an average of 86 per cent who could not afford $7,500 bail. Of one group of 3,038 cases examined, only 88 (2.9 per cent) were released on their own recognizance. Those forced to languish in jail before their trials were subjected to the same rules and facilities as convicted prisoners in maximum security penal institutions. The average daily census of inmates in pretrial detention was approximately 3,000. In the fiscal year 1954–1955 the operating costs of this city's detention services ran over $5 million.

Even more startling than the figures regarding the relationship between one's financial status and his ability to secure his freedom before trial are the figures that this study published regarding the effects of pretrial detention upon the later outcome of the cases and the fate of the defendants after trial. The

University of Pennsylvania study of the administration of bail in New York reported: "That being in jail operates to the disadvantage of a defendant at every stage of the proceedings is suggested by statistical comparisons of bail and jail cases at the grand jury level, in terms of court dispositions and at sentencing."

In one sample group of over two thousand defendants, the grand jury dismissed about 24 per cent of the cases where the defendant was free on bail, and only about 10 per cent of the cases where the defendant was in jail. Moreover, imprisoned defendants pleaded guilty about 90 per cent of the time while defendants on bail pleaded guilty about 75 per cent of the time. At trial, imprisoned defendants were acquitted about 20 per cent of the time, defendants who had been free on bail were acquitted in about 31 per cent of the cases. Jail, then, not only tends to cause one to plead guilty, but it also appears to lower the chances for a successful defense at trial. And for a coup de grâce, the study proved that jailed defendants who were convicted received suspended sentences about 13 per cent of the time whereas bailed defendants who were tried and convicted were given suspended sentences in about 54 per cent of the cases. One can reasonably conclude from these comparative figures that the inequality and unfairness of pretrial incarceration is not only bad in itself; it compounds itself and causes other consequential injustices which appear to be a result of the original wrong.

EFFECTS OF PRETRIAL INCARCERATION

A recent *Harper's Magazine* article, "The Poor Man in the Scales," described a study in one federal court in California showing that 94 per cent of the defendants who were not able to afford bail and were thus forced to be in jail prior to their trials were convicted. By comparison, only 71 per cent of the defendants free on bail before their trials were ultimately found guilty. And of those defendants who were convicted, 82 per cent of the defendants in jail before trial, because they could not afford bail, received prison sentences; 49 per cent of those convicted defendants free on bail before trial received prison sentences. As the authors of this article concluded: "Unless we choose to believe that guilt is inversely proportionate to wealth or that the federal judiciary operates with some kind of bizarre efficiency when it comes to indigent defendants, we are drawn to bitter conclusions. The explanations lie elsewhere, in the subtle handicaps placed on a man held in pretrial confinement."

What are these "subtle handicaps"? Frankly, these handicaps are not subtle except in their susceptibility to empirical proof. It is not at all surprising that these studies have shown that the defendant who can buy his freedom through bail does better at trial than his poor counterpart who awaits trial in jail. The jailed defendant is able to work with his attorneys, investigators, and witnesses only in limited ways and at limited times. He cannot try to make amends with the complaining witness and cause the charges to be dropped, as is often the case when the defendant is free before trial. He cannot help seek out evidence, witnesses, and generally aid his own defense. He is locked up in depressing jails with the dregs of society. His property is taken. He must wear either prison clothes or his own rumpled dirty clothes. His mail is opened. He can be visited only at certain times. He is taken away from all personal and enduring contact with his family. He cannot work to earn money to help his case or even to keep his income coming to his family. He is locked in a cell all day and night. He may be treated with greater restrictions in jail if the jailers presume from the denial of bail that this person is a risk. He enters court under guard, no doubt showing the strain of his experience. He can show little prospect for rehabilitation.

It would not surprise me at all if, as I suggested in a recent article,[3] an unbailed defendant is also prejudiced in the psychological tactics and strategies of trial. Although it would be difficult if not impossible to prove this, it is quite possible that a defendant who is brought into court from an adjacent cell, who has spent a long time in jail, who has not been as able to participate in his defense prior to trial, and who is publicly escorted in and out of jail by a guard, bears some stigma before the court and jury which is not the case with a defendant who casually enters the courtroom, well-groomed, and accompanied by his family and attorney.

And most important of all these disadvantages are not the pragmatic problems but the basic, spiritual loss to the imprisoned defendant. He loses man's most important asset—his freedom. And it is likely that this is compounded as his chances of attaining later freedom are lessened. "The glow of freedom apparently shines through."[4]

Is there some compensating feature to warrant these deprivations? James Bennett told the Senate:

> The typical jail has a destructive effect on human character and makes the rehabilitation of the individual offender much more difficult. There are some 3,000 county jails in this country, and several thousand more city jails. Our Federal jail inspectors have approved approximately 800 of these facilities for the confinement of Federal prisoners. These 800 jails by and large were not approved because they met *desirable* standards but because they met the *minimum* standards.
>
> The typical jail is dirty and overcrowded. The food is deplorable.

[3] Ronald Goldfarb, "The Bail Scandal," *The New Republic*, June 6, 1964.
[4] Wald, "Pretrial Detention and Ultimate Freedom: A Statistical Study," 39 *New York University Law Review*, 635 (1964).

Supervision is scant. And there are no programs for self-improvement or even for wholesome recreation. The typical jail has little to inspire the prisoner and much to demoralize him. The result is that he must spend his time there vegetating and degenerating. And worse.

By the time we get him he may be so embittered and so corrupted in spirit and character that it may take us several months—if ever—to get him in a receptive mood for our rehabilitation efforts. Unnecessary jail detention, in my opinion, is also a factor accounting for failure among those released on probation and even among those who are eventually freed on their current charges.

THE PUBLIC COST

Some figures have been quoted concerning the costs to the public of maintaining detention facilities in certain of the cities where bail investigations were conducted. The figures for the federal system are more complete, and they are even more persuasive. When the Constitutional Rights Subcommittee of the Senate Judiciary Committee met to consider pending bail legislation in August, 1964, James Bennett had some telling statistics to present for 1963. A total of 34,845 people was charged with committing federal crimes; of these, 22,343 were imprisoned awaiting trial. The average amount of time spent in jail awaiting trial was 29 days. Even worse were the figures underlying this average of pretrial detention. "On the average those who made bond spent 10 days in jail, those whose indictments were dismissed 37 days, those placed on probation 38 days, and those committed to prison 49 days." He also pointed out that there is a wide divergence in the practices of the different federal district courts around the country. In the 10 districts having the highest pretrial detention figures, the average pretrial detention lasted about 45 days. "Those who made bond spent from 6 to 30 days in jail on the average.

Those whose cases were dismissed spent from 20 to 68 days in jail, those who were placed on probation from 43 to 80 days, and those who were committed 53 to 96 days." And averages so often do not show the extremes. As Bennett noted for the Subcommittee: ". . . the offenders who may be held only a few days before their cases are disposed of cancel out in our statistics, so to speak, the cases of those offenders who remain in jail three or four months or longer before dispositions are made."

This practice of indiscriminate imprisonment before trial is costly to the government. The average daily population of federal prisoners awaiting trial in places of detention is 3,300. The government must pay $3.39 for each of them. "The total costs come to about four million dollars a year, and the trend is upward." In addition, the federal government often will not have facilities of its own, and will have to house its prisoners in local jails on a rental basis. These agreements cost the government more than its own prisons. According to Bennett, "In some instances we are paying as much as $7.50 a day for the care and custody of a federal prisoner, and for juveniles, it may run two or three times that high." It cost the federal government about $2 million to maintain only those federal prisoners who awaited federal trial in local jails in 1963, according to the former attorney general, Robert Kennedy.

Bennett's figures describing the numbers and types of federal crimes were also relevant to any appraisal of whether pretrial release would have endangered the community. Of the total of 34,845 defendants who were charged with federal violations in 1963, "5,042 were dismissed or acquitted, 12,047 were placed on probation, and 2,847 given fines only." And even of those who were ultimately sentenced to imprisonment after trial and conviction, "the vast majority do not eventually receive a sentence of sufficient length to warrant the imposi-

tion of substantial bail at the time they were apprehended."
Categorizing all federal offenses into types (robbery, fraud,
narcotics, liquor violations, etc.), Bennett expressed the opinion that experience proved that certain offenders could be released on their own recognizance prior to trial without risk to
society. "If the prisoner's ties to his parents or his wife and
children remain quite firm there is little chance that he will
attempt to escape. When a prisoner makes the decision to
become a fugitive, it means of course that he must give up all
contact with his family, in effect giving up the family itself.
Not many men are prepared to do that." Nor can many afford
to become and remain fugitives.

Women, he said, are good security risks: ". . . it is usually
a waste of effort and money to keep them in jail awaiting trial."
Yet Gertrude Samuels was able to report in the New York
Times Magazine that "the sordid, maximum security prison
for women in Greenwich Village held 760 girls and women,
though it was built to house 444. Those in detention had been
held from a few days to more than six months."

In New York City the cost of pretrial detention is higher
than that of the federal system. Judge Bernard Botein of the
New York Supreme Court reported that, in 1962, 58,000
people spent a total of almost 1,700,000 days in New York
City detention facilities awaiting their trials. The cost to the
city of boarding, lodging, and supervising these people was
more than $10 million that year. The costs of higher relief
expenses and lost employment are more difficult to calculate.
The costs in terms of human degradation and ignominy are,
of course, impossible to assess in terms of dollars and cents.

One writer, defending the charge that bail is a "rich man's
privilege" and thus an evidence of an unjust legal system, has
said: ". . . the courts and the judges did not bring about that
deplorable result. The law of bail brought it about and the

judges are bound by the law."[5] If that judicial helplessness is so then, if for no other reason, there is a significant cause to consider changing the law of bail. Almost two thousand years ago, Lactantius said: "Nobody is poor unless he stands in need of justice." In signing the Magna Carta centuries later it was necessary to agree that "To no one will we sell, to no one will we refuse . . . justice."[6] Do we need reaffirmation of this value again today?

THE UNPOPULAR: THE DOWN AND OUT

The University of Pennsylvania study of the operation of the bail system in Philadelphia disclosed another abuse of the bail-setting power. Though it is absolutely beyond their powers, and inconsistent with the whole system of justice that governs criminal trials, many judges use their bail-setting power to punish, to teach the accused a lesson, or to give expression to a personal point of view. Some judges feel that it is proper to set unattainable bail in order to break crime waves or "to protect society." Though their aim is commendable, their manner of attaining it is abusive. Again, the purpose of bail is to insure appearance. If there is a need to intensify police deterrents of crime, proper steps toward that end should be taken. Perverting the power to set bail is not the most proper or the most effective way to deter crime. Such official misconduct may well do more to breed disrespect for the law than it does to strengthen law enforcement.

Some judges consider high bail proper when it is deemed appropriate for the defendant to have "a taste of jail." One magistrate set bail in a larceny case, saying: "I'll make it $1500 —that will hold anybody." Another committing magistrate

[5] Longsdorff, "Is Bail a Rich Man's Privilege," 7 *Federal Rules and Decisions*, 309, 310.

[6] See dissent of Judge Jerome Frank, U.S. v. Johnson, 238 Federal 2d at 565, where he made this point in relation to an analogous issue.

said: "I disagree with you, Mr. District Attorney. I feel that the man should be punished and I don't feel that $500 is sufficient."

The Bar Association of the City of New York report included the following excerpts from a recent proceeding[7] in a New York Court:

The Court: The only thing I say is this: I'm going to insist that these boys are not to be bailed out. I'm going to set such bail that they will not be bailed out. If the parents will voluntarily agree not to bail them, I'll not set real high bail. But if they don't voluntarily agree, I'll set such high bail they won't be bailed out. Therefore, do you still want the 3rd? I'm giving them the earliest possible date. . . . Let them see what the inside of these jails look like. Maybe that will be a deterrent to them. I don't know.

* * *

The Court: All right. February 3rd. I'll give them that date. I won't be in jail and neither will he. Now, these boys, as I see it have gone beyond children's acts. This is something that shows they don't know when to stop. Maybe a couple of days in jail may solve the problem. I don't know. I'm going to set $5,000 bail on each. Now, I'm leaving word that if a bond is presented, the matter is to be sent back to me, and I'll tell you right now, if they put up $5,000 bail, I'll make it $10,000, and if they put it up to ten, I'll make it $25,000. I want these boys to spend one or two nights in jail. Maybe that is the answer. I don't know what the answer is.

* * *

The Court: . . . I think that the only way to teach these boys anything is to give them a taste of the inside of a jail. Maybe that will help. I don't know. I don't know what the answer is. It's a tough situation.

[7] People v. Ronald Garnett et al., docket #184, 185, 186 (Jan. 26, 1960), Magistrates Court, New York City, Felony Court, Queens County. Transcript pp. 4–5.

Some judges set excessive bail simply because they do not like the accused or what he is charged with having done. One was recorded as saying: "If you didn't bite the policeman I wouldn't be so hard. I would be lenient with you." One magistrate in Illinois was reported to have set $50,000 bail in a burglary case. At the time he said, "We do not like burglars in La Grange." This is a common attitude. Many judges feel that the bail-setting time is the time for the exercise of judicial leniency or severity. It is not. The only proper concern for a judge in setting bail should be assuring the defendant's presence at trial. Judging guilt or the likelihood of it, or the blameworthiness of it, is beyond the province of the judge at bail time. Yet, statements of the judges themselves show that this theory is not followed in practice. In one case, the judge said: "All right, I don't like hit and run drivers," and he set bail at $800. No one likes hit and run drivers, but at that stage of the proceedings all there was to indicate that the defendant was a hit-and-run driver was an accusation. A judge takes punitive action on the basis of a mere criminal charge when he sets onerous bail because he does not like people who are accused of certain crimes. Another judge was quoted as saying, "He is a Puerto Rican. What a bum." He set bail at $1,500 in an assault and battery case. A magistrate's remark sums up this kind of retributive attitude: "I'm going to make an example out of you." A judge said in setting bail: "I'm tired of seeing you in front of me; I'll hold you in $2,500 bail for court. Maybe that will keep you in for a while." Such judicial cynicism was captured in another exchange:

DEFENDANT: What do you mean, hold me without bail?
MAGISTRATE: That means that you will be kept in jail for two or
    three weeks until this case can be decided by a higher court.
DEFENDANT: You mean I got to stay here all that time?

MAGISTRATE: Are you kicking? Why, lots of guys jump ship just so they can stay here.

✱These judges at least stated their prejudices, but others, who are more careful, apply the same criteria for setting bail, but do not state their motives and reasons for the record. These practices, observed in the Philadelphia study and elsewhere, are probably more typical than unique. And they are unfortunate.

THE SUBVERSIVES

Another class of defendant against whom the bail system peculiarly sets itself is that accused of crimes of subversion and disloyalty. Although one lacks sympathy for these defendants, whose appeal is not the same as that of the poor or downtrodden (or of civil rights demonstrators mentioned earlier), one must consider that at the bail-setting stage of a case, the defendant is accused and not convicted; that this defendant has the same presumption of innocence as does one charged with price fixing or any other crime; and that he enjoys the same freedom from arbitrary punishment through abuse of bail. Despite these considerations, there are indications that the exercise of the power to set extraordinarily high bail is especially evident in subversion cases. This conclusion can be gathered from experiences in the lowest and the highest American courts.

In Cleveland, Ohio, the newspapers reported, a man was arrested for driving without a license. It became known to the judge in his case that he was a Communist. The judge set bail at $25,000, intoning this high judicial lesson: "This is how we treat Communists in this court." The Ohio Court of Appeals eventually reduced the bail to $200. There is a natural inclination to treat those whom we hold in the greatest disrepute in the most antagonistic manner. Yet, while there may be no quarrel with the utter contempt with which this judge personally viewed Communists, our noble traditions, for the sake of which we view Communism with such anathema, do not allow official, judicial injustices to be the evidence or manifestation of our distastes, or preferences, or even our hates. To abuse the power of any American court in order to espouse some disrelated moral viewpoint is wrong, at variance with the best traditions of our government (which traditions make our way of life and our legal system preferable to that of the Communists), and is in fact no more than an unnecessarily virtuous misproselytization.

In one case involving the propriety of high bail in the case of several defendants charged with subversion, Associate Justice Robert Jackson criticized the practice of using bail to punish those accused of being political undesirables. He wrote:

> . . . provoked by the flight of certain Communists after conviction, the Government demands and public opinion supports a use of the bail power to keep Communist defendants in jail before conviction. Thus, the amount is said to have been fixed not as a reasonable assurance of their presence at the trial, but also as an assurance they would remain in jail. There seems reason to believe that this may have been the spirit to which the courts below have yielded, and *it is contrary to the whole policy and philosophy of bail.* This is not to say that every defendant is entitled to such bail as he can provide, but he is entitled to an opportunity to make it in a reasonable amount.[8] [Italics added.]

In 1951, the Supreme Court dealt with this issue in the context of a unique case entitled *Carlson v. Landon.*[9] The United States attorney general had ordered four "active alien Communists" to be held in custody without bail pending

---

[8] Stack v. Boyle, 342 U.S. 1, at 10.
[9] 342 U.S. 524 (1951).

determination by the Immigration and Naturalization Service as to their deportability under the Internal Security Act. They appealed, questioning the validity of their detention without bail on two grounds: the Eighth Amendment, and the due process clause of the Fifth Amendment. The District Court judge upheld the denial of bail, and, somewhat like the Cleveland traffic court judge, was quoted as having said for the record:

> . . . there is nothing here to indicate the Government is fearful that they are going to leave the jurisdiction, [but] . . . I'm not going to release men and women that the Attorney General's office says are security risks. . . . I am not going to turn these people loose if they are Communists, any more than I would turn loose a deadly germ in this community. If that is my duty let the Circuit Court say so and assume the burden. . . . When there is a claim, and I don't know whether it is true or not . . . that these people are security risks and that their release is dangerous to the security of the United States, until that is either disproved or proved I am not going to release them. My first vote in that respect is for the security of the country. We have 42,000 casualties already.

The majority of the Supreme Court upheld the Attorney General's action, saying that the Eighth Amendment does not compel the allowance of reasonable bail in the context of this kind of case. In the words of Justice Reed:

> The bail clause was lifted with slight changes from the English Bill of Rights act. In England that clause has never been thought to accord a right to bail in all cases, but merely to provide that bail shall not be excessive in those cases where it is proper to grant bail. When this clause was carried over into our Bill of Rights, nothing was said that indicated any different concept. The Eighth Amendment has not prevented Congress from defining the classes of cases in which bail shall be allowed in this country. Thus in criminal cases bail is not compulsory where the punishment may be

death. Indeed, the very language of the Amendment fails to say all arrests must be bailable. We think, clearly, here that the Eighth Amendment does not require that bail be allowed under the circumstances of these cases.

Justice Black wrote a dissent in this case, sharply redefining the issues, entreating fairness especially in times of pressure, and stating about the defendants' Fifth Amendment argument:

The Fifth Amendment commands that no person shall be deprived of liberty without due process of law. I think this provision has been violated here.

Surely it is not consistent with procedural due process of law for prosecuting attorneys or their law enforcement subordinates to make final determinations as to whether persons they accuse of something shall remain in jail indefinitely awaiting a decision as to the truthfulness of the accusations against them.

And he stated about the Eighth Amendment argument:

I think Section 23 as construed and as here applied violates the command of the Eighth Amendment that "excessive bail shall not be required. . . ." Under one of the Government's contentions, which the Court apparently adopts, the Eighth Amendment's ban on excessive bail means just about nothing. That contention is that Congress has power, despite the Amendment, to determine "whether or not bail may be granted, or must be granted, and the Constitution then forbids the exaction of excessive bail. . . ." Under this contention, the Eighth Amendment is a limitation upon judges only, for while a judge cannot constitutionally fix excessive bail, Congress can direct that people be held in jail without any right to bail at all. Stated still another way, the Amendment does no more than protect a right to bail which Congress can grant and which Congress can take away. *The amendment is thus reduced below the level of a pious admonition.* [Italics added.] Maybe the literal language of the framers lends itself to this weird, devitalizing interpretation when scrutinized with a hostile eye. But at least until recently, it has been the judicial practice to give a broad, liberal interpretation to those provisions of the Bill of Rights obviously designed to protect the individual from governmental oppression. I would follow that practice here. The Court refuses to do so because (1) the English Bill of Rights "has never been thought to accord a right to bail in all cases . . ." and (2) "in criminal cases bail is not compulsory where the punishment may be death." As to (1): The Eighth Amendment is in the American Bill of Rights of 1789, not the English Bill of Rights of 1689. And it is well known that our Bill of Rights was written and adopted to guarantee Americans greater freedom than had been enjoyed by their ancestors who had been driven from Europe by persecution.

And finally, looking to the historical *raison d'être* of the bail provision in the Constitution, he said:

Prior to this Amendment's adoption, history had been filled with instances where individuals had been imprisoned and held for want of bail on charges that could not be substantiated. Official malice had too frequently been the cause of imprisonment. *The plain purpose of our bail Amendment was to make it impossible for any agency of Government, even the Congress, to authorize keeping people imprisoned a moment longer than was necessary to assure their attendance to answer whatever legal burden or obligation might thereafter be validly imposed upon them.* In earlier days of this country there were fond hopes that the bail provision was unnecessary, that no branch of our Government would ever want to deprive any person of bail. [Italics added.]

Crucial to one's thinking in these cases, as well as in all other criminal cases (perhaps the temptation to forget is greater here) is the notion that accusation is not proof. As Justice Black pointed out in his dissent:

Thus it clearly appears that these aliens are held in jail without bail for no reason except that "they had been active in the Communist movement." From this it is concluded that their association with others would so imperil the Nation's safety that they must be isolated from their families and communities. On this premise they would be just as dangerous whether aliens or citizens, deportable or not. Since it is not necessary to keep them in jail to assure their compliance with a deportation order, their imprisonment cannot possibly be intended as an aid to deportation. They are kept in jail solely because a bureau agent thinks that is where Communists should be. . . .

If these aliens, instead of awaiting deportation proceedings, were held for trial under a Smith Act indictment, they could not be denied bail merely because of the indictment. Membership in the Communist Party—the charge which is the foundation for the deportation proceedings—is surely not as great a danger as a leading share in a conspiracy to advocate the overthrow of the Government by force, which was the essence of the indictment in *Dennis v. United States.* And the opportunity for "the unhampered preparation of a defense" is quite as important to the alien arrested for deportation proceedings as it is to the Smith Act defendant.

The report on bail which was prepared under the auspices of the Vera Foundation and the Department of Justice for the National Bail Conference in May, 1964, noted that though bail is a matter of right in noncapital cases, "High bail or no bail has been the general rule in cases involving espionage and internal security."[10] Two reasons have been offered for this situation: one, that there is an unusually great danger of flight in this class of cases; and the other, that there is a "popular abhorrence of the crime." Another can be suggested: the fear of further crimes endangering the national security. Are either of these reasons valid grounds for setting "high bail or no bail" in these cases?

An answer to the "abhorrence of the crime" rationale was clearly stated by former Chief Justice Vinson in a case involving a number of Smith Act defendants who requested the

---

[10] Freed and Wald, *Bail in the United States: 1964.*

appellate courts to reduce the $50,000 bails which had been set in their cases.[11] He wrote in his majority opinion that, "To infer from the fact of indictment alone a need for bail in an unusually high amount is an arbitrary act. Such conduct would inject into our own system of government the very principles of totalitarianism which Congress was seeking to guard against in passing the statute under which petitioners have been indicted."

With regard to flight by subversives, two questions are relevant: Is there more danger of flight in these cases, and is astronomically high bail the answer if this is the case?

The American public was treated to the story of one of the most sordid and ugly episodes in bail jumping by the recent press coverage of the Soblen case. Dr. Robert Soblen was arrested and convicted of espionage. He was wealthy, old, and dying of cancer. No bondsman would cover his $100,000 bail because of the character of the defendant and his charged deeds. Ultimately, his wife and attorney posted bail for him. However, neither the high amount of the bail nor the personal relationship of the sureties served the purpose either of keeping Soblen in custody or preventing his running away. After his conviction was affirmed on appeal to the Supreme Court, he absconded to Israel, was arrested and extradited, and eventually committed suicide on an airliner returning under custody to the United States.

The Soblen case was not unusual. It only gave vast notoriety to the problems of law enforcement in the area of national security. In 1947, Gerhart Eisler was convicted for espionage. Two years later, after his appeals failed, he jumped bail and disappeared behind the Iron Curtain. In the famous Dennis case, the trial in New York City of several Communist leaders for violation of the Smith Act, four of the convicted de-

11 Stack v. Boyle, 342 U.S. 1, at 6.

fendants jumped bail: Robert Thompson, Henry Winston, Gil Green, and Gus Hall. They forfeited $80,000 worth of bail.

Further complicating the fact that forfeiture of money is not a likely deterrent in these cases is the fact that crimes involving disloyalty are considered political crimes and are therefore not extraditable. Thus the temptation to jump bail is greater, as is the likelihood of successful evasion. Communists are subject to Party discipline and may, with Party aid, cross our borders into Mexico or Canada, or even flee to more remote countries. Extradition treaties do not cover "political" crimes; thus it would be difficult to get them back for trial.

For these reasons, bail has been denied in some of these cases. In the celebrated case involving Colonel Rudolf Abel (the Soviet spy whom we eventually traded back to the Russians in exchange for U-2 pilot Gary Powers) and in the case of John Butenko, bail was denied. In the case of Igor Ivanov for conspiracy to commit espionage, at first bail was denied, but later it was set at $100,000. The Sokolovs were denied bail. And in denying bail in the case against the Egorovs for conspiracy to commit espionage, the Second Circuit Court of Appeals in New York wrote: ". . . The nature of the charges, the fact that the defendants are citizens of a foreign country, and all the circumstances of this case justify the position of the United States in urging that bail be denied."

And when bail has been granted, it has been high. According to a member of the Justice Department's Internal Security Division, the following bail was ordered before trial in the Smith Act cases. In the Dennis case in New York City, bail was set at $5,000 for each defendant; in the Flynn case in New York, bail was set at $25,000 for all citizen-defendants and $20,000 for noncitizen defendants; in the Frankfeld case in Baltimore, bail was set for different defendants at sums from

$5,000 up to $20,000; in the Schneiderman case in California, bail was set at $5,000 and $10,000; in the Fujimoto case in Hawaii, bail was set at $7,000 and $8,000; in the Mesarush case in Pittsburgh, bail was set at $15,000 and $20,000; in the Huff case in Seattle, bail was set at $5,000 and $10,000; in the Wellman case in Detroit, bail was set at $5,000 and $20,000; in the Forest case in St. Louis, bail was set at $5,000, $10,000, and $15,000; in the Kuzma case in Philadelphia, bail was set at $10,000 and $20,000; and in the Brandt case in Cleveland, bail was set as $5,000, $7,000, and $20,000. These amounts are not extraordinarily high; but they are high.

The federal government often asks for high bonds in security cases, even though the effectiveness of bail seems to have an inverse relation to the notoriety of the defendant and the risk of his flight. The more important the defendant, the more likely it is that he will have financial support from the party organization's funds; thus the less effective a deterrent to his flight is the money put up for bail. The unimportant defendant may be left on his own by the party to be sacrificed. For him, high bail would be an effective deterrent to flight, but we would have gained less in the bargain.

Another special reason why we may need the pretrial control of defendants in security cases is that generally there are no natural ties to the community to keep the defendant from running away. Quite the contrary: The defendant (who is in fact a spy or subversive) will be antagonistic to the local community and will be likely to flee to another country more compassionate to him and his conduct, where he can avoid trial. Thus the usual natural unlikelihood of flight is not prevalent in these cases, and the elements in the judicial balance are differently weighed. The FBI generally has been successful in catching these defendants. Two bail-jumpers who were Communist Party officials were caught in a mountain camp in the

Sierra Nevadas. But in a number of cases, defendants fled and remained away for years without being caught.

For these reasons, and to satisfy one of the inadequacies in the old system, a bail-jumping statute was recently passed, making flight from trial while on bail a crime. The statute arose out of the confusion following the famous New York Communist trials of the early 1950s. One of the defendants in that case, Green, was tried, convicted, and sentenced to five years in prison. He was ordered by the court to appear on a set date for the execution of his sentence. He disappeared. Several years later, he voluntarily returned. The court summarily sentenced Green to an additional three years imprisonment for contempt of court. The case was appealed, and a divided (five to four) Supreme Court upheld the contempt conviction. However, the problems of using the contempt power to deal with this kind of situation gave rise to the promotion and eventual passage of a statute in 1954 making bail jumping a crime.

The same argument can be made in these cases as in all other criminal cases that modern means for detection have been so well developed and refined that few can evade the inexorable pursuit of the law. More so in subversion cases than in others is the FBI trained, prepared, and effective in its detection and surveillance work. It is not likely that many would escape permanently. And for those who flee abroad, though their punishment is avoided, the country is well rid of them and the danger implicit in their presence.

Aside from the risk of flight (a legitimate fear) and the unpopularity of these defendants (ideally an irrelevancy), is there a danger that they would commit crimes endangering the national security if released prior to trial? In those cases involving more than advocacy, and in time of war, this factor should be a real consideration in determining the pretrial status of defendants in subversion cases. But perhaps these cases would be so few and so extreme that some special procedure could be devised to deal with them alone. For example, no one could reasonably question the outright denial of bail or any other pretrial release in cases involving overt acts of treason.

The argument is persuasive that the salutory nature of liberal bail practices should not apply in cases involving an organized subversive conspiracy directed by a hostile foreign government and employing violent means. Some of these subversion cases then may well involve special circumstances and certain dangers against which this country would be foolish not to protect itself. However, acceptance of these conclusions need not mean that our control of defendants through bail, such as it is, is the best way to protect ourselves. In the concluding chapter, a suggestion will be offered for a procedure which would not pervert present judicial practices but which also would not leave the courts helpless in protecting society from the real dangers in these cases.

CIVIL RIGHTS DEMONSTRATORS

Defendants who are poor, as we have seen, are victims of the money-bail system itself. Nothing has to be added to the system to prejudice them. The unpopular defendant is also a victim of our bail system, but for far different reasons. While the system per se does not operate against the unpopular defendant, he may be constantly prejudiced by easily managed abuses of the system. It is the receptivity of the bail-setting power to perversion by the legal power structure (judges, prosecutors, police) to achieve special ends that works to the disadvantage of defendants who are out of favor. Whereas the bail system may appear to be operating openly and normally in these cases, there is often a silent or tacit conspiracy within society to use the system in special ways prejudicial to certain classes of defendants. In these cases it is not the bail system itself but the susceptibility of the system to simple but subtle subversion which tends toward corruption.

The cases arising out of the civil rights demonstrations during the past several years are a prime example of this phenomenon. The established order of the South, including judges, police, lawyers, bondsmen, unwilling to countenance civil rights demonstrations and dead-set upon supporting the white supremacy system, has often combined to fight the freedom movement and has used bail as one powerful weapon to win that fight. Much more completely and graphically than the scattered cases involving other unpopular groups, the civil rights cases are a classic study in the varieties and extents of the misuse of the bail system for ulterior purposes.

Although it is arguably tangential to the recent civil rights movement as such, bail has played a significant role in the freedom demonstrations of the last five years, in an utterly negative sense. The power of those who are so disposed to manipulate the bail procedure in ways that frustrate or economically choke civil rights demonstrations, and which punish the demonstrators, is as manifest as it is difficult to do anything about or to prove. However, all the people centrally involved in the civil rights struggle agree that bail has posed a specially difficult and in many cases insurmountable hurdle to both the sponsoring organizations and the persons participating in these demonstrations.

John M. Pratt, the legal counsel to the Commission on Religion and Race for the National Council of Churches, and one who has been personally involved in much of the Mississippi litigation arising out of the recent demonstrations, had this to say on the subject:

Responsible civil rights leaders will not begin demonstration activities in a city without having an adequate war chest to cover the bail they know they will incur. Groups whose leaders do not take this point of view have repeatedly created situations where long and onerous jailings took place for want of sufficient funds to make bail. This has happened several times. This kind of failure results in the breakdown of morale among indigenous Negroes. They will not participate in civil rights demonstrations in some cases for fear of long internments. There is no question that the use of excessive bail to deter the demonstrations, which are constitutionally protected activities, illustrates the worst aspects of the American bail system.

The problem of proving and doing something about the unjust application of bail powers is compounded by the sometimes competing interests of the victims of this injustice. Jack Greenberg, chief counsel for the NAACP Legal Defense and Educational Fund, points out that the problems raised by bail practices are complex: "This problem really cuts two ways. Some of these defendants do not want to get out of jail even if they can. Their purpose, and it is a legitimate one, is to operate upon public opinion by the very act of being in jail." So, actually the absence of bail may not impair the effectiveness of some demonstrations. Some defendants may want to get out of jail and cannot; others may actually want to stay in jail. The withholding of bail may, in a given situation, be good or bad for the civil rights movement. One important aspect of the problem, according to Greenberg, is whether or not there is a mass of demonstrators or a lone individual. "If it is just one person, then as a matter of humanity it might be best to get him released. On the other hand, a large number of people in jail may really reach national public opinion and accomplish an important purpose of the demonstrations." This conflict poses a difficult problem for those who are administering the civil rights movement. "Who are we," Greenberg asks, "to decide for these people what they should do." He also points out that "this same issue also poses difficult problems for the very people we are trying to impose upon. They may lose the battle by keeping demonstrators in jail and thereby coming under critical public pressure, or they might also lose face in a given case by letting them out."

Assuming an intent to stay out of jail, and to seek a just redress of legal grievances, civil rights groups have found bail a singularly vexing problem. Carl Rachlin, the chief counsel of CORE, says that his group must always face the question of bail before thinking about getting involved in any demonstration. "Bail has a very serious effect upon us. We must always ask how much this or that project is going to cost us and where we can get the money to get past this hurdle and thus be able to get to the more important things we are aiming at. Often we cannot undertake a project simply because we are short of the money which we know we will need to meet the bail problem."

The broad, discretionary power of lower court judges and local prosecutors to control bail proceedings and to manipulate their bail-setting powers in ways that defeat civil rights demonstrations or hurt the demonstrators themselves can take one of many forms and can arise in one of many ways.

THE DENIAL OF BAIL

The most obvious and the most extreme instance of abuse is the outright denial of bail. A judge may arbitrarily deny bail and get away with it until the case is successfully appealed. Often the lower court's ruling is not appealed. And there is no reversal of this action unless some redress is sought. Unless the demonstrations are organized and assisted by sophisticated collaborators, the judge is likely to get away with imprisonments which stop demonstrations simply by denying bail. This is not always the case. In one Alabama town about a thousand people demonstrated and some two hundred were arrested for violating an injunction against civil rights protests. Bail was refused. After the trial of a habeas corpus petition filed by the defendants, bail was allowed. When a judge's hand is forced legally he cannot get away with an outright arbitrary denial of bail. However, when a judge has a case involving a lone individual, one not in the public eye and one without effective legal counsel, he can deprive him of his freedom by denying bail with relative impunity. Once a conviction is gotten, bail pending appeal can usually be denied with legal sanction since this issue lies in the sole discretion of the court. After a quick conviction in a lower court, a defendant can be denied bail while he appeals for ultimate release.

The denial of bail may also be caused by the invocation of some purported legal theory, no matter how outrageous, in a particular case. An extreme example was the charging of civil rights demonstrators in some cities with nonbailable offenses, thus foreclosing the possibility of their release on any bail. This was the case in one Georgia town, when in the summer of 1963 several SNCC demonstrators were arrested leaving a church meeting and rally. After some shouting and jostling between the demonstrators and the police, several were indicted for a capital offense—attempting to incite an insurrection. Bail was refused. Bail need not be set in capital cases. The prosecutor publicly announced that this was done to teach these people their place. He was quoted as saying: "The basic reason for bringing these charges was to deny the defendants bonds. . . . We were in hopes that by holding these men we would be able to talk to their lawyers, and talk to their people and convince them that this type of activity is not the right way to go about it."

Eventually, several months later, a Federal court held the

state insurrection statute unconstitutional and lowered the bail to $500 for the alleged misdemeanors and $1,000 for the alleged felonies. Bail was made. This ruling was no surprise, since the Supreme Court of the United States had ruled the same statute unconstitutional in a similar situation in 1939.

The same technique of avoiding bail by indicting for non-bailable offenses was used in one Georgia town. In August, 1964, several people attempted to distribute leaflets protesting several recent shootings of Negroes. The petitions asked the chief of police for help. The leaflets were prepared by some of the individuals involved in the local rights movement. Three days after the petition was delivered to the chief of police, several people were arrested on a warrant of the chief of police. Two were charged with attempting to incite an insurrection, a nonbailable offense. This device had just been found unconstitutional in the other Georgia case. Yet, one defendant was jailed for thirteen days before this charge was dropped. He had also been charged with circulating insurrectionary materials, a noncapital felony upon which bail was then set at $2,500.

In Louisiana, the same tactic was used, but the charge there was criminal anarchy.

One legal defense fund attorney has suggested that bad faith charges are really the essence of the bail problem facing the civil rights organizations today. By the time the bail situation gets straightened out, the original and more significant problems, those actually giving rise to the demonstrations, may have been mooted, and the demonstrators may have endured their punishment.

Exorbitant Bail

A nuance of the technique of denying bail outright is the tactic of setting bail but setting it exorbitantly high. The defendant will either fail to make bail, and consequently will be forced to serve some prison sentence regardless of the outcome of his case, or, on the other hand, in paying the exorbitant bail, the individual or the organization behind him will be needlessly put to great expenses and will ultimately go bankrupt. In effect the power to set exorbitant bail is the power to stop demonstrations by bankrupting the demonstrators.]

This awesome power has been exercised. In Chester, Pennsylvania, the Rev. Clayton K. Hewitt, the rector of the Episcopal Church of The Atonement, protested against segregation in the school system of his home town. He was arrested and charged with inciting to riot, unlawful assembly, and conspiracy. His bail was set at $26,500.

One southern judge was catapulted into the national news when he tried to single-handedly end public civil rights protests in Atlanta. According to a report to the National Bail Conference, he required appearance bonds of $3,000, $4,000, and $7,000 for some demonstrators charged with trespass. He reset two of these bails, which had originally been set at $300 and $500, raising them on his own motion to $3,000 and $7,000. In one case involving a motel sit-in, when the judge set bail at $4,500, the defendant wound up in jail for two weeks because he could not afford the cost of bail.

The judge also used his power to set bail in a way which effectively held a minister in jail for seven months. The minister, a white clergyman from California in his seventies, was arrested for and convicted of interfering with religious worship in an attempt to protest against segregation in the First Baptist Church in Atlanta. He was held in this prolonged detention pending his appeal. His bail was set by the judge at $20,000 pending the appeal of his conviction and sentence to one year on a public works project, six months in jail, and a $1,000 fine.

This decision was appealed to the highest court of Georgia on three occasions. The bail of $20,000 was ruled to be exorbitant and was reduced to $5,000. Even when The National Council of Churches raised the $2,000 necessary as collateral to secure the $5,000 surety bond, the judge refused to accept it and allow bail. Eventually, the Supreme Court of Georgia ordered him to accept the cash.

In another similar case in the fall of 1963, two women, one pregnant, were arrested for demonstrating near a segregated restaurant. The judge set bail at $20,000 each. The case was removed to a federal court, which ordered the bail reduced to $500. The judge refused to comply. The federal court then took over the custody of the two women and reset bail at $500. Eventually, after first refusing to release these women to the custody of the federal courts, he finally did release them.

In some of the Georgia cases in the fall of 1963, aside from the nonbailable capital offense of inciting an insurrection, the defendants still had to make bail of $12,000 for combined charges of riot, assault with intent to murder, unlawful assembly, and attempting escape, all arising out of a few arrests after a church meeting. This amount was eventually lowered to $1,000 for the felony charges and $500 for the misdemeanor charges (as opposed to $5,000 and $1,000 as they had been originally set).

In one case the legal maximum amount for bail for certain offenses was raised undoubtedly so that it could be especially applied in civil rights cases. In Alabama the state legislature raised the maximum bail through a law that applied only to the city of Birmingham. This special bill allowed a police court judge to set bail up to $2,500 on misdemeanor charges. Previously, the maximum had been $300. At the time of the Birmingham demonstrations maximum bail was set on some rights leaders who were charged with misdemeanors.

Multiplied Bail

[Another technique, and possibly the one that has played the most significant role of all in crushing civil rights demonstrations, is the multiplication of bail. This problem usually arises in the case of mass arrests resulting from large demonstrations. Here, bail can be multiplied in three ways: by arresting a large number of people and making each put up separate bail; by charging defendants with numerous crimes arising out of the demonstration and setting separate bail for each crime; and by requiring separate bail at each separate stage of the proceedings]

Mass Arrests

If there is a mass arrest, even what ordinarily might have been a reasonable amount of bail can be made unattainable, since there are such large numbers of defendants who must each raise bail separately. If one hundred demonstrators were arrested for trespass and bail was set at $500 each, someone would have to contend with raising $50,000 worth of bail. For students and poor people, who compose a large percentage of the demonstrators, even $500 is unattainable; $50,000 is more than any of them have ever dreamed of. Even for the national organizations sponsoring these demonstrations, this amount of money is often beyond their means. These organizations are not in the business of raising money to keep bondsmen or southern courts rich, or even to bail out protesters. Such a task would be too diversionary from their real aims and goals. The civil rights groups have little enough money even to carry out the important substantive work for which they were created. Mass bail has been a crushing impediment to all civil rights demonstrations.

Perhaps the two most extreme examples of mass arrest arose

at the times of the Jackson, Mississippi, freedom rides of 1961 and the Birmingham demonstrations of 1963.

In December, 1960, the United States Supreme Court declared racial segregation in public interstate transportation facilities unconstitutional. In May, 1961, large numbers of freedom riders began to arrive in Jackson, Mississippi, to protest against continued segregation in the local bus stations, railroad stations, and airport. The demonstrators continued their protests throughout the summer. A large number of Negroes and whites was arrested. The federal government had tried to enjoin these arrests, but unsuccessfully. Some of those arrested chose the Ghandian alternative and went to jail. Hundreds of others chose to fight the charges lodged against them. But for those who chose to fight their cases and who wanted to stay out of jail while their cases were appealed, appeal bonds were necessary. The average cost for this was $1,500 each (guilty verdicts brought four months' sentences and $200 fines). To appeal these cases from the City Court to the County Court, $500 bonds were needed for each case; to appeal from the County Court to the Circuit Court, $1,500 per case ($500 for a cost bond, and $1,000 for an appearance bond). To pursue the appeal of these cases, then, would have cost $372,000. No corporate sureties would handle these cases. CORE, which was providing defense assistance, ran out of money. Private appeals were made and several hundred thousand dollars of bail was eventually raised through collections from private sources. The NAACP Legal Defense Fund later took over the legal defense of the cases. The matter is still pending, so the bail money has been tied up for about four years.

In one Virginia town approximately $400,000 worth of bail was reportedly required for the release of civil rights demonstrators in that city alone. The exhaustion of funds for bail in these demonstration cases caused the termination of civil rights demonstrations in that city. Here, then, is the classic example where the requirements of bail ended demonstrations.

In New York City in the summer of 1964 more than three hundred people were arrested for picketing at the World's Fair. They were charged with breach of the peace, trespass, sitting on the grass, and similar "crimes." Bail was set at $500 a person without regard to whether they were students, celebrated personalities, out-of-staters, good or bad bail risks, poor or wealthy people. CORE raised the money through private sources to provide bail for these people. But in one night more than $10,000 was tied up in bail.

In Tuscaloosa, Alabama, civil rights groups demonstrated in the late spring of 1964 against general segregation practices in that city. Seventy-four people were arrested in one afternoon as they marched away from a church meeting. The charges varied: resisting arrest, parading without a license, disturbing the peace, unlawful assembly, and more of the typical charges that are customarily made in these cases. The total amount of the bonds required in the cases arising out of that afternoon's demonstration was $75,900.

In Itta Bena, Mississippi, in southern LaFlore County, in the early summer of 1963, from fifty to seventy-five local Negroes, most of whom lived in Itta Bena and worked at the local cotton farms, held a mass meeting in a small church. The facts are disputed, but a brief of the Civil Rights Division of the Justice Department represents the story as told by the Negroes who were present and by one of the Department's own attorneys who was also there at the time: During the meeting something was released into the church which had the noxious effect of tear gas. The people inside streamed out; some were sickened, others were coughing and their eyes were tearing; one was treated at the hospital. The people gathered outside the church and marched into the nearby town of Itta Bena en masse to seek the protection of the deputy sheriff from such assaults during their voter registration work. This was about 11:00 P.M. As the group entered the small business district of the town, they were assaulted with a barrage of bricks and bottles thrown by a small group from town. Soon a truck arrived bearing a special deputy sheriff and several citizens who were specially deputized. They asked the Negroes to go home. Some started to drift away. Then the full-time deputy sheriff for Itta Bena came and arrested all the Negroes (there were fifty-seven of them) for conduct designed to provoke a breach of the peace. They were locked up in the county jail for the duration of the night. Their ages ranged from fourteen to seventy-nine. The next morning the juveniles (approximately a dozen) were released to their parents. The others were tried in groups of twelve by the local Justice of the Peace.

The apparent reason for holding the trials twelve at a time was that there were twelve seats in the small courtroom. Each defendant was found guilty and the men were sentenced to $500 fines and six months' imprisonments; the women were sentenced to $200 fines, and four months' jail sentences. The distinction, one can cynically assume, was based on some atavistic Southern chivalry that recognizes the extra attention which the delicacy of womanhood warrants. Bonds were set at $750 for each man; $500 for each woman, even though they were all local people with no place and no inclination to go. Since none of them had any money, they all were sent to the county penal farm. After they had spent two months there, the National Council of Churches was able to arrange for their bonds through a New York insurance company. The case is now on appeal.

Bail for Many Charges and at Many Stages

Another form of multiplying bail so as to make costs unattainably high is the separation of charges. Suppose, for example, that a demonstrator is arrested for picketing a store. If he is charged with disorderly conduct, resisting arrest, trespass, breach of the peace, and several other unique "crimes," bail can be set separately for each crime. Thus one act of protest, or one course of conduct, whether or not it is ever proved to be a crime, could, at $500 a charge, give rise to the need to raise thousands of dollars worth of bail. This pyramiding of charges has been a typical tactic in almost all cases arising out of civil rights demonstrations. In his report to the National Bail Conference, entitled "Bail and Civil Rights," Assistant to the United States Solicitor General Louis F. Claiborne pointed out a "most dramatic illustration" of this tactic, a "barrage of charges heaped on demonstrators at a New Orleans theatre in March" 1964. Most of these defendants were required to post $4,500 worth of bonds on eight charges: trespass, resisting arrest, disturbing the peace, refusing to move on, criminal mischief, blocking an entrance, and two counts of contributing to the delinquency of a minor.

As well as multiplying charges, courts can also multiply the times bail is exacted. A person charged even with one crime for one act of protest can be made to put up bail first to appear at trial, then again to appeal his case, and still again to go through the other appellate processes that are often necessary to obtain ultimate justice. Since each appearance at each step of the proceedings can cost the defendant a separate premium for a new bond, one $500 bond could be reiterated as many as four times, thus costing in premiums an amount ordinarily required for a $2,000 bond.

BAIL AS PUNISHMENT

The manipulation of bail to punish civil rights demonstrators can be illustrated by many examples. One large group of civil rights demonstrators in Mississippi was arrested on relatively minor charges in 1963 and sent to a county penal farm. Protesting the conditions there, a smaller group of them refused to eat or to work. They were then sent to the maximum security facility at the State Penitentiary in Parcksman, Mississippi. The National Council of Churches was able to arrange to bail out the few women defendants. But the men were, according to their later reports, subjected to inhuman, barbaric, and gruesome treatment. It was a while—an ordeal—before they could be bailed out. Money had been raised by the National Council of Churches from one of its constituent members, the Board of Homeland Ministries of the United Church of Christ. Fifty-eight bonds were then prepared by representatives of the National Council and the Lawyers Committee for Civil Rights Under Law. After several days of attempting to find the proper authorities and meeting the technicalities regarding the bonds, the prisoners were ordered released. The story they tell about their incarceration sounds like a study in the grotesque.

In one Georgia town some of the demonstrators in the summer of 1963 were imprisoned in condemned buildings and ex-army camps with terrible facilities after their arrests during a SNCC voter registration drive.

In the St. Augustine lunch counter sit-ins in the summer of 1963, four children were arrested for refusing to leave certain privately owned but publicly operated lunch counters after being told by the proprietor that he would not serve Negroes. They were arrested on July 18, 1963, and tried and adjudicated delinquents on July 23. They had no counsel, but their parents were present. They were sent to the Florida State School after refusing to consent to a condition of probation that they would not participate in further picketing or other forms of demonstrations. They appealed and asked for the right to go free on bond pending their appeals. This request was denied on the ground that bail was not available in a juvenile proceeding that is not a criminal proceeding. This was a strange and perverted construction to put on the distinction between juvenile and adult criminal proceedings. Actually, most courts treat juvenile cases specially in order to avoid the ordinary harshnesses and psychological disadvantages present in criminal trials. But to deny one of the reliefs of the regular criminal trial process on the ground that courts give special consideration to juvenile cases is an illogical and perverse misapplication of two purposeful rules to come out with one bad one. This practice is not uncommon, and since so great a percentage of the civil rights demonstrators in the south are children, the practice has had a serious punitive effect. The only consolation for these children is that, like many of the original labor leaders of earlier decades, they will someday be able to wear their arrest and prison records as badges of courage. The children appealed their cases and their imprisonment.

A year later, the Supreme Court ruled that convictions for arrests like these were unconstitutional and therefore void. However, it was not until six months after their imprisonment, on January 16, 1964, that these children were released. And then it was not until numerous court proceedings had been brought, newspapers had begun to publicize the situation, and even the governor had to intervene. A local statute specifically provided that the appeal on the merits of an adjudication of delinquency should be heard in thirty days (in this case, that would have been August 24, 1963).

In one Louisiana town in a well-known parish, near Mississippi in location and in attitude, Negroes comprise the majority of the population, but traditionally they have not voted. In the summer of 1963, CORE attempted a voter registration drive with the town's Negro population. In doing so they incurred the ire of one southern district attorney. Progress toward racial understanding and equality was very slow, and in September, 1963, a young CORE volunteer prepared a letter which was sent to the local mayor and district attorney, signed by twelve elders of the Negro community. It was a proposal for the creation of a biracial commission to study and discuss the causes and cures for racial tension in the area. Such commissions had done a lot of good in other areas of the country, and in fact they were praised and their increased use was called for by President Kennedy. The letter requesting this commission urged (among other things) that without some step like this toward understanding and accommodation, local racial problems were likely to get worse and could lead to public disturbances. One southern district attorney responded by publicly promising an open probe of CORE and the letter writers, who were, he said, criminal conspirators. In December, 1963, the twelve Negroes who signed the letter were indicted for public intimidation and conspiring to commit public intimidation, based on the letter. The twelve were arrested, and their bonds were set at $4,000 each. They were able to post property bonds and were released.

Next, one of the young CORE workers, a white man from California, and the one who had actually written the letter in question, was arrested as a material witness to the conspiracy and public intimidation. Nonresident witnesses to crimes may be arrested if there is a reasonable belief that they will not be present to testify. His bond was set at $14,000.

The basis for arriving at this figure was that each of the twelve letter signers committed a criminal act and therefore Vickery witnessed twelve separate criminal acts for which $1,000 bail for each was set, and $2,000 more was thrown in for witnessing the conspiracy. Vickery could not get the necessary property for his bond and was jailed. The local statutes allowed depositions to be taken of his testimony within forty-eight hours. After three weeks in jail one deposition was taken from Vickery, but he was not released. The authorities insisted on twelve depositions, a separate one for each signed letter. Eventually, after Vickery was severely beaten by fellow prisoners, he was finally released.

One southern judge, who presided in this case, an avid segregationist and a well-known official in the state White Citizens Council, denied all the defendants' pretrial motions. After a year, the case is still pending. There is no telling when that case will ever come to trial. However, the property upon which the bond was posted is all tied up.

FRIVOLOUS ARRESTS, CHARGES, AND REQUIREMENTS

[Still another way to use bail to defeat demonstrations or to punish demonstrators is to arrest the demonstrators on frivolous charges. The people involved in civil rights demonstrations ordinarily cannot afford bail and will have to sit it out in jail until the charges are later dismissed or until their appeals are made and recognized by some appellate court. And there is a paradoxical twist to this technique. Once the demonstrator is in jail awaiting trial or appeal he may be subtly advised that he can get out of jail by pleading guilty or by forfeiting the bail and waiving his appeal. The cost of bail is usually the same as (sometimes more than) the fine following a guilty plea.] However, to succumb to this temptation would be, in essence, to admit guilt and to dissipate the very motive for having been a demonstrator in the first place. If this alternative is chosen in order to avoid the hardships of prolonged incarceration, then the local government not only gets the bail money but also wins the moral and legal points as well.

Bail procedures can be manipulated so that the defendants receive a maximum imprisonment either before their trial or pending their appeal. It is rare that this class of defendants is ever acquitted until they have exhausted the long appellate process. They may be forced into choosing between long incarcerations or the payment of separate bails throughout the appellate process. One could conclude that this reality adds a pyrrhic quality to any ultimate victory that may be attained. The demonstrators, by that time, would have gone to great expense and sometimes would have suffered physically.

In one city, for example, those convicted demonstrators who appealed their cases sat in jail pending appeal from forty-five to sixty days. Those who pleaded guilty went to jail only for a few days, or not at all. The assertion of legal rights to appeal, then, was in effect what was being punished. The requirements for bail negated the efficacy of appeal.

Paradoxically, the social system in which this all takes place has replenished its coffers at the expense of its antagonists, people who can little afford this luxury. One public official told a lawyer who has been active in the representation of civil rights demonstration defendants in Mississippi that the bail which was put up for the demonstrators has gone to pay for the costs of hiring special police and for the general extra charges of coping with and stopping these demonstrations. In refusing release on recognizance in a group of cases involving several ministers, one Mississippi official summed up the situation with the comment: "The NAACP has lots of money!" In effect, then, the civil rights demonstrators are paying their own way to prove their points.

Frivolous charges, or charges for trivial, if legitimate, offenses have proved to be successful devices to exact bail ransoms or to force retreats from demonstrations.

Most cases arising out of civil rights demonstrations give rise to such vague charges as disorderly conduct, trespass, resisting arrest, contributing to the delinquency of a minor, loitering, parading without a permit, obstructing a sidewalk, refusing to obey a lawful command, and other similarly nebulous catch-all offenses. Whether or not appellate courts later throw out these charges, they fulfill their subverting purposes of stopping demonstrations, punishing the demonstrators, and enriching the local administrations on the bail charges.

In one Alabama town in June, 1963, CORE sponsored some demonstrations protesting segregation in local buses, lunch counters, and several other facilities. The local sheriff made wholesale arrests of several hundred people for violating a local injunction against marching in the streets. These people were jailed without formal charges or committing papers, and bail was denied. After they had been jailed for more than a week, the NAACP Legal Defense Fund secured their release.

In a Mississippi town, in the summer of 1962 some people gathered for a voter registration meeting. Occupants of those cars with out-of-state license plates were arrested for violating a twelve o'clock curfew. Their cars were towed away, for which unsolicited service they were liberally charged, and they were jailed. Property bonds were required because they were out-of-staters.

In one city, some individuals who were in town to help the indigenous civil rights protesters were arrested for cooking in their rooms. In another city a Negro working on a voter registration drive was arrested for driving with a bad headlight and having an improper license. Bond was set at $2,000. In an Alabama city, a demonstrator was charged with carrying a concealed weapon, a knitting needle in her pocketbook. In a city in Louisiana, a Negro registration worker was arrested for disturbing the peace while sitting quietly in an office waiting for another Negro to complete registration tests. Bond was set at $2,000.

Another gimmick lies in changing the requirements made for security for the bonds in civil rights cases. If a person has the cash to put up bail the judge will sometimes require property security. If property is available and cash is not, cash will be required. If both are available, unencumbered property may be required. Though property that is owned free and clear is sometimes available, there is not a lot of that around and it can be easily and quickly dissipated. Other rigid technicalities can be applied to avoid freeing defendants even when bail could have ordinarily been made. There are usually only a few persons in the community who will provide the collateral security for bail. Their security can be easily used up if there are a sufficient number of cases and separate security is required for each case. Certain kinds of disclosures or requirements can also be exacted from those who put up the bail, conditions that will cause some people to become ineligible or reluctant to provide the bail. The following are some examples.

In one South Carolina town several hundred demonstrators were arrested for violating city ordinances. At first, the court would not allow property bonds. Then the court allowed property bonds but adjusted the valuation of the bonds by requiring sureties to be many times the assessed valuation of the property instead of the ordinary requirements in that state. The property available for use in securing bonds was cut to a fraction.

In one Georgia town a Negro who owned about $300,000

worth of property offered to use it as surety for bonds in some cases arising out of the demonstrations. Unencumbered property bonds were required. In Savannah, Georgia, when a Negro attorney offered $10,000 in cash for bond collateral, the court ruled that only property was acceptable.

Sometimes in cases when property was available, cash was required. Thus judges can nullify what is a proper tender of bail or collateral in ways which will defeat the attainment of bail in the few cases in which it is available.

In Savannah, when local people tried to meet the requirements for peace bonds, the court was able to frustrate their tender by applying rigorous technicalities. Ordinarily, only one piece of property is provided for several bonds where the combined value of all the bonds equals the value of the property. Here, the court ordered each bond to be secured by a single piece of property even if the value of the property far exceeded the amount of the bond it secured. Thus, all property available to be used for bonds could be easily tied up and wasted. In one case, a separate piece of property was required for each of eleven peace bonds demanded against one person. And the court assessed the available property offered as security for these bonds at its assessed valuation, which is only a quarter of its real value.

By requiring rigid, technical specifications to be met, courts can also impose at least some imprisonment during the time when arrangements are being made to meet these ad hoc requirements. It takes some time just to arrange the mechanics of providing bail, time during which the defendant must languish in jail.

In Baton Rouge two Negroes were jailed for minor offenses arising out of their picketing of a store for jobs. Each time bail money was raised, the authorities would place additional charges on them (while they were in jail and obviously doing nothing) so that more bail was required. Eventually the charge was elevated to criminal syndicalism, bail went up to $1,500, and though the defendants were never tried, they spent seventy-six days in jail.

Not only are the crimes charged maximized; so also are the amounts of bail charged for a given offense maximized when the charge arises out of a civil rights dispute. Some cases involving Judge Pye and the Birmingham riots provide extreme examples of this fact. More typical is the case of Chapel Hill, North Carolina. There, in 1963, when hundreds of civil rights demonstrators were arrested for trespass, disorderly conduct, and obstructing the sidewalk, bail was set at $175 instead of the customary $25 which usually prevailed in cases like these. The amount of bail itself may not be exorbitant but the difference in the charges and the multiplication of the costs can cause the prejudicial discrimination. When this difference is multiplied by the numbers of all the cases, the money differential reaches significant proportions. A lawyer who was active in the Chapel Hill cases said: ". . . it cost us $18,000 in fees and court costs for three months' demonstrations. There will be second thoughts before there is a repeat."

In Selma, Alabama, about fifty people were arrested for demonstrating on a Fourth of July weekend. The NAACP Legal Defense Fund could not determine who set bail—the sheriff, the chief of police, the circuit court judge. Most of the defendants were herded into one bullpen at the local jail. At first bail was set at $300 cash bond on each charge. The attorneys were prepared to make this bail. Then the amount was raised to $500 cash. Again, they were prepared to make bail. And when $500 surety bonds were allowed, that, too, was raised to $800 surety bonds as new charges were added. Eventually the NAACP Legal Defense Fund went to a federal court to seek an order requiring the state officials to stop changing the standards for bail. Finally, the federal court took control over the matter and the defendants were released on reasonable bail, after having been in jail during all these back and forth proceedings for ten days.

PEACE BONDS

[Another device that has been used by some judges and which has worked to frustrate civil rights demonstrations and to punish the demonstrators is the requirement of peace bonds. The peace bond is an archaic device which has been used in the past to deter family fights, domestic disputes, and neighborhood arguments. However, it has been reincarnated recently in some places to imprison demonstrators, especially the leaders of the demonstrations, the so-called troublemakers. The unique aspect of the peace bond is that it is applied before any alleged crime or misconduct takes place. One can be made to put up a peace bond just to assure that he will not do a certain act in the future.]

This technique was used in Savannah. In the summer of 1963, Hosea Williams led the demonstration movement in Savannah. A local white woman swore out a complaint asking the court to issue a peace warrant against Williams on the grounds that Williams' conduct presented a future threat to her person, property, and security. He was required by the local court to put up a bond to assure his good behavior. When the money was raised for this bond, another similar warrant was sworn out by another person who also alleged that she feared that Williams was a threat to her. Successive peace bonds by different individuals followed. Eventually, in one day there were twelve warrants successively sworn out. For each one, a $2,500 peace bond was required. Needless to say, Hosea Williams ran out of money and ended up in jail.

Some of these complaints made against Williams were

made by people who never even saw him but who had heard that the night demonstration marches from the Negro district to the center of town were led by him. Williams spent almost two months in jail until eventually his bond was reduced from $30,000 to $15,500. This was posted and he was released.

The same device was used in Selma, Alabama, in the fall of 1963, to squelch a SNCC voter registration drive. About a half-dozen persons, some local SNCC workers and some other "outsiders" and "troublemakers," were arrested for picketing the local courthouse, charged with contributing to the delinquency of a minor, breach of the peace, or disorderly conduct. They were convicted of these charges and given an additional penalty of $1,000 each, constituting a peace bond, prospectively to keep the peace for the ensuing twelve months. The local statute allowed this as part of the sentencing power in certain cases. In all, seventy-six such bonds were required against the leaders of the demonstrations and certain out-of-state defendants. Eventually, the Alabama Court of Appeals held that the state peace bond statutes did not allow peace bonds in these particular instances. Only then were the bonds discharged.

BAILABILITY

One must recall in considering this special class of cases that there is an even greater likelihood that these defendants will appear for trial than exists in the ordinary criminal case. Since it is with the very purpose of being tried and provoking litigation and ultimately being vindicated by the courts that most of these demonstrators demonstrate, it is quite unlikely that they would not show up for trial after they are arrested. In fact, almost all demonstrators want to be tried, and go to great lengths to be present at trial.

In Tulsa, Oklahoma, for example, several hundred individuals were arrested in the course of a civil rights demonstration. All were released on their own recognizance. One Monday morning when their cases came up for trial, every one of them showed up and voluntarily presented himself to the court.

Rachlin, the general counsel for CORE, says that in his experience it is rare that there are bond forfeitures or that civil rights demonstrators jump bail. He tells the illustrative story of the "freedom riders" in Jackson, Mississippi, as an outstanding example of this point. Hundreds of individuals from all over the country were convicted in 1961 in the course of the freedom rides in Jackson. They appealed their convictions from the city court and had to await a new trial in the county court. Even though it was impossible to try all these individuals at the same time, the judge ordered all to be present at a certain date. Several hundred thousand dollars worth of bail was riding on their appearances. On the appointed day, over two hundred people showed up from all over the United States and some even came from as far away as Europe to answer the calendar. This was obviously done at great and, under the circumstances, wasteful expense and personal difficulty to all the individuals involved.

In February, 1964, a group of Itta Bena citizens who had been convicted and who were released on $23,000 worth of bail was ordered to appear for sentencing. Only forty-eight hours' notice was given to their lawyers to have all the defendants in court. Forty-four of these forty-five defendants appeared for trial, many having traveled day and night from as far away as Florida and Chicago in order to be present. The man who did not appear said this was because his life had been threatened if he ever returned to the county.

If the purpose of bail is to insure that defendants show up for trial, then the greatest majority of the defendants in the civil rights cases would uniquely qualify for release on their own recognizance or on minimal bail. But this has not been granted.

Bondsmen

As elusive as the availability of bonds and security can be made to be, the unavailability of commercial bondsmen can be even more frustrating. Bondsmen are typically businessmen who are in the business to make money. The recent civil rights demonstrations have posed a windfall opportunity which any bondsman would ordinarily have found irresistible. But with only some exceptions, bondsmen have not handled cases arising out of civil rights demonstrations. It has also been observed that in some instances where bondsmen did provide bail services in civil rights cases, they charged a higher fee. No one motive can be ascribed to all bondsmen; however, it is likely that two reasons motivate their general aloofness from this potential bonding bonanza. No doubt some bondsmen refuse to provide bonds for civil rights demonstrators because they are in sympathy with the local practices or the local individuals demonstrated against. Therefore they do not want to encourage the demonstrations and may even enjoy seeing the demonstrators go to jail. Others, who might ordinarily take these cases, their commercial interests outweighing their social or political commitments, or even possibly out of sympathy for the demonstrators, have not provided bail bonds either because pressures have been put on them not to or because the message had been made too clear that those who cash in on these cases by providing bonds for the civil rights demonstrators will lose the rest of their local business. Local bondsmen are usually receptive to local pressures. National bonding companies must use local agents and are therefore indirectly subjected to these pressures.

In one case an agent in Mississippi countersigned fifty-seven bonds in cases arising out of civil rights arrests. The local district attorney prepared a memorandum disclosing this fact and then released the defendants. Later, that agent received mail from his other customers threatening to cancel their business because of this incident. The Mississippi Methodist Ministers and Layman's Association also distributed a circular reporting the facts in the district attorney's memorandum verbatim. That agent refused to countersign any more bonds in civil rights cases. In one later situation involving mass arrests in a nationally celebrated demonstration, the NAACP Legal Defense Fund wrote letters systematically to every one of the over three hundred companies licensed to do bonding business in that state, asking for help. Few even answered; none was available.

The National Council of Churches has attempted to meet this problem by creating a special bail fund to be used wherever necessary to avoid the harsh results of lack of bail money in civil rights cases. Arrangements were made with one bonding company under which the insurance company issued bonds upon authorization from the Council that payment would follow. The Council then would hold the company safe from risk of forfeiture. Yet the Council's money has been quickly used up.

Several major civil rights groups have considered the possibility of participating in the creation of a common bail project, including the establishment of a special bonding company to be devoted to providing bail in these cases. So far, sufficient funds to support such a notion have not been accumulated.

Not only is this kind of undertaking economically impossible for civil rights groups, but it is also so diverting of time and money as to be self-defeating even if it were possible. And there is some question about the legal propriety of rights groups taking such action. This kind of undertaking is likely to be outside the powers with which these groups have been created.

As Greenberg, chief counsel of the NAACP Legal Defense Fund, points out, "Raising bail is not the function of this group. We need our money to hire lawyers to do our main work. And the administrative problems surrounding such an undertaking would make it impossible. We discussed the idea of setting up our own program by creating a bonding fund composed of loans, property of Negroes in various communities and locally raised money, early in the rights movement, but so far it has proved impracticable and nothing has yet come of it."

Some private groups or individuals have raised money which was donated for this purpose. For example, Dick Gregory conducted a benefit show for the purpose of raising funds for the bond fees needed to secure the release of a group of Florida A & M students who were arrested in Tallahassee during a civil rights demonstration. Ad hoc arrangements like this have had to fill the gap left by the failure of bondsmen.

One noble attack at the misuse of bail and the irresponsibility of bondsmen arose out of the series of demonstrations in Birmingham, Alabama. On Good Friday in 1963, Martin Luther King led a protest march from a church to a courthouse in Birmingham, Alabama, for a public prayer meeting. As he left the church, he and twenty others were arrested by the local police at the direction of "Bull" Connor. These arrests, along with those previously made, aroused the anxious Negro community and mushroomed into a series of subsequent protest marches in Birmingham over a five-week period. This was the time when the stories of the dogs and the hoses and the mass arrests occupied the front pages of newspapers of America and the world. At the end of this infamous siege, approximately three thousand people had been arrested. Most were charged with parading without a permit. Some were charged with such crimes as disorderly conduct, trespass after warning, loitering after warning, and resisting arrest. Most were local citizens. There were few outsiders, some students and soldiers. About one-third of the defendants were juveniles. Some were under sixteen (for them no bonds were required), most of them were high school students aged sixteen to eighteen. A few were older people—sixty-five, seventy-three, one was eighty. They were tried quickly in the Birmingham Recorders Court.

The procedure is that this conviction can be appealed and a new trial can be had on the same charge in the circuit court where a jury trial can be had. In order to make such appeal, an appeal bond had to be raised for each defendant. Most bonds were set at $300, though some were higher and one was for $1,500. A special statute was passed during this period allowing a maximum bail of $2,500, and a few bonds were set this high, according to one report. The one Negro bondsman in town, and the only one who would bail out these defendants, soon ran out of the necessary collateral to be able to post all the necessary bonds. Some defendants were able to afford bail or to have someone do so for them. But 840 demonstrators were still in jail. Most were awaiting trial and over 200 were appealing their convictions.

In the meantime, behind the scenes, Burke Marshall and Louis F. Oberdorfer, two key assistants to Attorney General Robert Kennedy, were dispatched to Birmingham to try to make peace, to ease the situation, and to attempt to find a solution that would appease the leaders on both sides of the issue. It soon became apparent that the organized Negro community would not be satisfied until all demonstrators were let out of jail. The negotiators called Attorney General Kennedy and asked what he could do. Kennedy called Walter Reuther, who in turn sought the advice of Joseph Rauh, a well-known Washington attorney who is counsel for the United Auto Workers Union. Rauh conferred with Walter Reuther and the following plan was proposed and accepted: The AFL-CIO, the United Steel Workers Union, the Auto Workers Union, and the Industrial Union Department of the AFL-CIO each raised $40,000. All agreed that the necessity caused by these events raised a problem of national importance and warranted the unions' assistance. This took place on May 9. Hurriedly, the $160,000 was wired to Birmingham in the morning, May 10. The local Negro bondsman used this money to provide the city with the security he needed to write the rest of the bonds. Within the same day, May 10, he had written 840 bail bonds totaling over a quarter of a million dollars. The bonding fees were over $8,000; the tax charges were over $2,500. Most of this money put up by the unions will probably be returned eventually, although to this day it is tied up pending the disposition of these cases.

Aside from the question of the morality of these practices or the propriety of what these judges are doing, there are serious questions about the legality and the constitutionality of these misuses of the bail power. One former southern judge at the National Bail Conference in Washington in May, 1964, candidly asked: ". . . are we not in the South presently in the civil rights cases both exercising preventive detention on bonds and using excessive bonds? For example, is not a $500 bond for what would ordinarily be a $50 bondable disturbing the peace charge for a Negro college student who is sitting-in more excessive than a $25,000 bond for a professional criminal?" His very appropriate question only scratches the surface of potential questions that should be asked about the legality of these bail practices.

It could be argued, for example, that in the civil rights cases, bail is excessive and therefore in violation of the Eighth Amendment, not only when it is exorbitant but even when a student or a poor farmer is required to make $50 bail, or upon failure to afford the cost of bail when they are made to suffer prolonged incarcerations far out of proportion to the crimes with which they are charged.

The suggestion could also be ventured that the planned and persistent special treatment in these cases is an unconstitutional deprivation of due process of law or a denial of the equal protection of the laws. It should not be too difficult to show that one set of rules is being applied in these cases while a separate, more lenient set of rules is applied to the bail-setting practices of many courts in all other cases. A good example could lie in the Birmingham situation if the special new $2,500 maximum bail is used by lower courts in misdemeanor cases arising out of civil rights demonstrations, but not in the cases of other more serious misdemeanors.

Another question that should be asked, and might be litigated, is whether arrests for petty state crimes, or local ordinances like blocking a sidewalk or failing to disperse, are a violation of the First Amendment. If citizens are punished for speaking or associating or petitioning for the redress of their grievances, the arrests and incarcerations may well be unconstitutional burdenings of the exercise of First Amendment rights protected by the Constitution. Of course this issue is really tangential to the bail problem.

Peace bonds could also be questioned as unconstitutional

because they result in imprisonments without any of the accompanying constitutional protections relating to the trial process and which protect defendants in all other cases involving the exaction of criminal imprisonments. Where a person is incarcerated under some peace-bond practice, he is deprived of the presumption of innocence, and in fact is presumed guilty prospectively. And he is denied the customary trial hearing with all its procedural protections that would ordinarily apply.

Sending juveniles to jail before convictions and pending appeals also could be considered to be a deprivation of due process of law which so shocks the conscience of the ordinary reasonable man that it would warrant constitutional protection.

The trouble is that few of these issues have been litigated; nor are they likely to be because of the unusual nature of the cases, the defendants, and the circumstances out of which they all arise.

The wide discretion that judges have under the current bail laws, along with the lack of litigation on the important and complex constitutional questions raised by modern bail practices, makes these techniques difficult if not impossible to change. Rarely can a judge's motivation for setting bail in a particular way or at a particular amount be determined. Though one could easily guess the obvious, one will usually find it impossible to prove the kind of prejudice or wrong motive that would warrant reversal of a ruling. Few judges spell out on the record their intention to manipulate bail this or that way in order to defeat a demonstration or to punish a demonstrator. Even when a judge is so candid as to make this kind of admission, the appellate process necessary to be exhausted before the lower court judge can be overruled is slow, expensive and painful.

The danger arising out of the breadth of the judge's discretion in setting bail is compounded by the lack of judicial temperament or sophistication of many judges who have this far-reaching power. Bail, it must be remembered, is set by the judge at the lowest level of the judicial ladder. Sometimes it is not even set by a lower level judge, but is originally set by a police official.

When and if a test case does get to the Supreme Court, one predictable, far-reaching decision could go far toward ameliorating this extraordinarily unusual and unfair situation.

This review has not even attempted to list all examples of egregious misuses of bail that have been used to punish civil rights demonstrators and to frustrate and stop the demonstrations. It should already be clear that this simple device has been a major problem for those involved in the civil rights movement. It has been estimated that, to date, well over a million dollars are tied up in bail in cases arising out of the civil rights movement. And, as we have seen, there is much more to the problem than money alone.

Burke Marshall has aptly summed up this situation: "The manipulation of bail to maintain white supremacy and to keep up the caste system, wherever it exists in America, is an extreme and clear example of the misuse of the administration of justice by state agencies. There is no question in my mind that these practices are unconstitutional and immoral."

CHAPTER III

The Bondsmen: The Beneficiaries
of the Bail System

Charles Dickens, a perceptive and pungent critic of the foibles of the law, referred to bondsmen in *The Pickwick Papers* as a "Curious trade . . . these men earn a livelihood by waiting about here, to perjure themselves before the judges of the land, at the rate of half-a-crown a crime!" Mr. Pickwick was talking about the practice of falsely vouching for a defendant as his bailor for a fee. Since Dickens' time, most bondsmen have gotten no better, no less crass, no closer to candid. Supreme Court Justice Arthur J. Goldberg has criticized the bail system as "capital punishment for the poor" and the bonding business as "checkbook justice." Recently, one leading New York bondsman was quoted in a magazine article as saying of his avocation: "It's a crummy business—I wish they'd outlaw it." And writing in the May 30, 1964, *Rocky Mountain News*, Richard Starnes made this unsentimental statement about the bail-bond "profession": ". . . the typical bondsman is a cynical, hard-bitten resident of the half-world peopled by untalented lawyers with their offices in their hats, process servers, and others who fatten on the awesome difficulties of people in law trouble."

Who are these bondsmen? What do they do? And how did they get this reputation?

EVOLUTION OF THE BONDSMAN

The American bail system, like most of our legal traditions and practices, was modeled after the common law of England. However, the change in the nature and proportions of Colonial American society wrought a change in the workings of our bail system. The young nation was not property-oriented as England had been. There, fear of the forfeiture of land was a strong incentive against jumping bond and fleeing. Outlawry (banishment from the country) and confiscation (the loss of land and status) were the consequences of flight in England. No such built-in immobility as a predicate for the bonding system existed in America. In fact, conditions quite the contrary existed here. America was a young nation, geographically far-flung, possessed of broad and relatively unknown frontiers, and a potential haven for fugitives from justice. The economic basis of American society was not land-based like that of the English feudal system. And the fear of savages and other unknown dangers of the frontier might well have seemed a better course than succumbing to the often cruel sentences assured under Colonial law.

The comparative intimacy of the limited, established, homogeneous English country was not prevalent in America. People often did not know each other or each other's backgrounds. Officers of the law could not judge the trustworthiness of citizens on the basis of their familiarity with their established reputations or their past conduct. In this respect, the American situation was quite different from that in England; it was a new land inhabited by many new people with no roots or long-standing relationships with each other. In this one sense the bondsman filled a valuable role. For many people without personal friends or relatives to help them secure their freedom through bail, the commercial bondsman was a welcome substitute (if one could afford his aid). If one had no money or property or friends to help him to secure his own release, but could afford a premium, he had a means to secure pretrial release. It was the commerical bondsman.

For these reasons, the personal surety relationship that had been the essence of the original bail system as it developed in England changed, and the newer American bail system also changed to meet these new conditions. Money security came to take the place of personal sponsorship. As the *Yale Law Journal* described it:

> In America . . . emphasis on the individual's absolute right to bail led to practical difficulties in a large country whose frontier territories beckoned invitingly to those with a dim view of their chances of acquittal. The initial judicial reaction was to remind the party furnishing bail that he was a quasi-judicial officer with powers of a jailer, and that he was responsible for procuring the accused's attendance at trial. But since private sureties could not effectively conduct nationwide searches for their itinerant charges, their promise to produce the accused gradually became a promise merely to pay money should the accused fail to appear. This development ushered in the professional bondsman who saw an opportunity for financial gain. In return for the payment of a fee, the bondsman would post a bond on behalf of the accused.[1]

The bondsman was born to fulfill this one need in the gradually developing commerical bail system. As the personal responsibility of the original surety changed to one of financial responsibility under our money-oriented system, a void was created for the large class of defendants who could not raise the amount of the security required but who could afford the fee to pay the bondsman for assuming the full financial responsibility. In a system so money-oriented, something like the bondsman was needed. While judges undoubtedly accom-

[1] 70 *Yale Law Journal* 966 (1961).

modated to the bail-bond system by setting bail at $1,000 instead of $100 when they meant the defendant to put up only $100, there is no way of determining how common this subjective juggling is, or whether this factor is the cause or the result of the institution of the bondsman. Probably it is mostly the latter. Theoretically at least, the bondsman grew out of this system. His purpose was to help the poor and the friendless. In fact this is not the case today.

The bondsman eventually took over control of the bail process. For a fee (a premium in the insurance argot), he would guarantee the presence of the accused at trial. If the defendant failed to appear for trial, the bondsman could lose his money. He, in turn, would require indemnity or collateral from the defendant to protect himself. Thus a full-fledged business arose out of this simple device of judicial control of prisoners who were charged but not convicted. But, as the *Yale Law Journal* observed recently, the evolution of our bail system ". . . seems to have occurred without any clear perception of the functions bail ought to serve, with the result that the institution of bail currently consists of an incoherent amalgam of old and new ideas serving more to defeat than to achieve the aims of the criminal process.[2]

✳ THE MODERN BUSINESS STRUCTURE

The structure of the modern bonding business, which developed out of these historical phenomena, is a straight line beginning with the large national insurance companies and running down through regional subadministrators and eventually to local agents (the bondsmen) who camp around the local courthouses and actually hustle the business. By describing this business structure as a straight line, it is meant that there is little real business interplay among these three levels.

[2] *Ibid.*

The business functions begin at the top; and the responsibilities and risks increase on the way down, while inversely the profit risks also increase on the way down. The insurance company on top sets the public image of a respectable business and within the working scheme of its bail setup takes no risk with its agents. The agents go about their business in their own fashion, and for this privilege agree to retain only a small percentage of the profit. The company cannot lose money, and neither can the bondsman if he plays it safe and smart. The insurance companies require indemnity from their agents, who in turn require indemnity from the bondsmen, who in turn require collateral from their clients. If run right, no one from the bondsman up needs run any risk of loss. While the insurance companies in the bonding business can get the collateral from the bondsmen or refuse to accept a bond, the agents who are hustling the bail bonds get what collateral they can, but do not always operate with the absolute protection enjoyed by the companies. Nevertheless, together they enjoy what Robert F. Kennedy when he was attorney general described as a $250 million a year business in bail bonds.

One prominent bond-business figure, an insurance executive, has reported that all companies in the country that are writing bail bonds make a total profit of $4,500,000 a year. The agents writing the bonds make a total profit of $22,500,000. And it could well be much more. For example, one estimate has it that ten to twelve million Americans need bail bonds each year (for other than traffic cases). One high estimate states that of all the misdemeanor cases in the country, 90 per cent of the defendants get bail bonds; of all the felony cases, 70 per cent get bail bonds. And at that, an estimated 1,500,000 defendants went to jail in 1963 for lack of money to afford the costs of bail bonds. The bondsmen simply turned this business away.

Recently a committee of the Association of the Bar of the City of New York conducted a study that pointed out many of the shortcomings of the current administration of bail in the criminal courts of New York City.[3] The study findings presented a very clear and thorough picture of the structure of the state's bail-bond business. The description was "based on existing published studies, grand jury presentments and interviews with those familiar with the day to day operation of the courts and the detention system."

This report began by pointing out that in New York County, a jurisdiction with the greatest population density and the most criminal court business in the country, almost half (43 per cent) of the bail bonds were written by one insurance company, and that 99 per cent of all bonds were covered by only five insurance companies. These companies are regulated by the State Insurance Department which mostly concerns itself with the companies' financial stability. Yet, the report points out, the insurance companies really only lend their names to the bail business, and rarely suffer any losses from their coverage. The report describes why:

The miracle of the safe assumption of liability can be attributed to the operation of the insurance company's general agent, the kingpin of the bail bond business, and his requirement for collateral. This functionary needs no license and need not write any bonds, but is at the heart of the administration of bail, for it is the general agent who selects the agents and subagents of the insurance companies who in fact write the bulk of the bonds. This power of selection is a life and death power over the industry. The general agent is authorized by the insurance company to arrange for the writing of a certain dollar amount of bonds. It is the general agent who determines the volume and success of a company's business. Before that authorization is granted, however, the agent must have

[3] "Bail or Jail," Journal of the N.Y. Bar Association, Vol. 19, No. 1, January, 1964.

in hand a certain percentage of the authorized amount as collateral for the insurance company with the understanding that in the event of a forfeiture and payment by the insurance company, this collateral will be drawn down accordingly to cover the loss.

Below the general agent is the executing agent, "the bondsman," selected and approved by the general agent. It is he who maintains the office near the Courthouse, and it is he who actually signs the bonds that are submitted to the Court and fills out the affidavit required. . . . He too is given a financial limit within which he is authorized to write bonds, this time by the general agent, and he too must deposit collateral but with the general agent in an amount proportionate to his authority, also with the understanding that in the event of a forfeiture, this collateral will be drawn down accordingly. Roughly 184 agents are licensed as bondsmen in the City of New York by the Department of Insurance.

The bondsman earns his money through commissions at the legal rate, and retains half of the commission as income. The remaining half is turned over to the general agent of the insurance company. A portion is credited to the bondsman to build up his "float," the collateral which he is required to deposit, and what is left is split between the general agent and the insurance company, usually fifty-fifty. Thus, out of the $25 premium on a five hundred dollar bond, the executing agent (or bondsman) retains $12.50, the general agent gets $10 which is split with the insurance company and $2.50 is deposited to build up the bondsman's fund for future forfeitures. Any employees, runners, typists, etc., of the bondsman must be paid out of his retained fifty percent.

The ultimate decision as to detention is therefore left with the bondsman—not by virtue of the legally fixed premium, but through an unfettered decision as to the amount of collateral he will demand. . . .

Once written, the bonds are those of a particular company licensed by the State Department of Insurance. . . . In all of these companies the writing of bail bonds is a relatively minor part of their entire business. The financial stability of the Companies is carefully reviewed by the Insurance Department and a questionnaire must be completed by them which is quite comprehensive. There is little doubt as to the financial responsibility of these approved companies. Yet such a company lends merely its name to the administration of bail, for although it is on the bond, it runs no risk. Indeed, it has been stated that the insurance companies have never suffered a financial loss through the writing of bonds, or hardly ever.

It is quite apparent that the insurance companies have nothing to lose, and everything is gain. They give nothing for this windfall but the patina of sophisticated business formality lent to the bail process by the use of their names. The companies' conformity with any state insurance laws does not have any coherent relationship with the state's efficient control of the bonding business. The local bondsmen are free to go about their business relatively unhampered, openly acting as partners-of-sorts with the public officials involved in the bail-bonding process, and as quiet, disassociated working partners with the rich law-abiding insurance companies.

The local agents, the actual bail bondsmen, are themselves subject to few legal regulations. Usually, they must pay a small fee, prove their authorization from the insurance company to write a bond; sometimes they will have to conform with local rules of court, but these matters are simple, insubstantial, and easily circumvented.

Even in the federal court system where the quality of judicial procedures are often best, there are minimal controls over bondsmen. For the most part, the problem is left to the courts. One Treasury Department official in the surety bond division told me that he knew of no federal regulations of the bail-bond business even though the insurance companies are subject to regulation and several of the companies deal exclusively with bail bonds. The only control, he said, is in the courts. But courts do not have the time or personnel to allow involvement in the policing of bondsmen, if they have the inclination. In one recent article read into *The Congressional Record* on May 14, 1964, the author wrote:

Although States like New York limit the premium fees he [the bondsman] can charge, at least ten States have no legal check on his operations. He haunts the courts, paying off lawyers and tipsters for business secured, charging what the market will bear for his bail bonds.[4]

There are some meager fiscal regulations on most bondsmen, but they are without much effect. The rates that bondsmen are supposed to charge for their services are regulated by executive officials of the government. But these regulations are formalities which are frequently and easily circumvented. Bondsmen get around these set rates by various machinations. Some charge a minimum fee, no matter what the amount of the bond may be. This assures a profit for the mass of small bonds which are written. Some charge extra for night service. Others tack on extra charges for service fees, adding this charge to the regular fee on the ground that they are doing something special, above and beyond what they are paid to do. Others are in the loan business, and sell bail bonds on credit, making added profits from the interest they charge for the loans they make. Moreover, although premiums are regulated, there are no controls over the limits on the collateral that a bondsman may require. The typical rule is "get what you can." Bondsmen try to get 100 per cent collateral, thus erasing any risk of loss. This makes good business sense. However, sometimes this requirement for maximum collateral reaches heartless and humorless proportions, as in two instances when bondsmen took a wedding ring and a set of false teeth as collateral for their bonds. It all adds up to the fact that there are few effective regulations on the character of bondsmen or the

[4] Lawrence Lader, "The Bail Scandal," *Parade Magazine*, March 1, 1964.

finances of their practices, and these purported restrictions are ineffective.

Not only is little required of bondsmen legally, but also they actually do very little in terms of service. Often bondsmen lose track of defendants, maintain minimal contact with them before trial, or merely send a reminder note to the defendant to assure his presence for trial. They do very little work for their money. Criticizing bondsmen for forgetting even to advise their clients to appear for trial, one Rhode Island Superior Court judge accused them of "wallowing in wealth" and being "too busy collecting money to be bothered carrying out their obligations." The bondsman is hard-working mostly when his money is involved; he *is* available night and day to sell a bond, and he will sometimes go far to find a defendant when forfeiture is imminent. In these cases he serves a distinct function. Police may not have the resources to chase minor criminals. And without the omnipresent bondsman a phone call away from the police station, many defendants would be exposed to incarceration for some avoidable hours. Whether these services compensate for the wrongs bondsmen commit is, however, questionable.

Who is this quasi-public servant for whom the law has created this sinecure? Many, too many, agents are undesirable persons, former felons, and generally repugnant characters. Some bondsmen are colorful Runyonesque characters. Some are legitimate businessmen. But too many are "low-lifes" whose very presence contaminates the judicial process. The character of bondsmen is rarely well regulated. And when a bondsman is so bad that he is outlawed from the bonding business, he can simply get some unknown associate to take over his work nominally as his alter ego. The undesirable bondsman can continue his profitable business with no effective censure.

In fairness it should be mentioned that there are some

men in the bail-bond business who are decent people. They
suffer the indignities or injustices of their work much like
other businessmen, and it should be borne in mind that general references to bail bondsmen are not intended to include such men. But very frequently, if not generally, the
bail bondsman is an unappealing and useless member of
society. He lives on the law's inadequacy and his fellowman's
troubles. He gives nothing in return, or so little as to serve no
overriding utilitarian purpose. Society must share the blame for
this creature. Our system created him. Bondsmen are products
of our uniquely commercialized administration of justice, just
as prohibition created the racketeers who preyed on the
society that gave them birth. It is our national disgrace that
our system of justice should allow a group consisting of so
many undesirables to thrive and profit from its inadequacies.

The escapades and machinations of bondsmen who have
eluded control and exploited their roles could fill books. Some
examples should be illustrative.

CRIMINAL INFILTRATION OF THE BAIL-BOND BUSINESS

One chief fault of the bonding business is that criminals and
the criminal element have found it to their tastes and have
taken it over in many places. The easy-buck aspect of the
business, along with these peoples' natural contacts among
prospective clientele and courthouse riffraff, no doubt made
bonding a natural business for them. Some of society's worst
characters have been drawn to the bail-bond trade. The business has been a boon and a magnet to racketeers.

In 1959 and 1960 the *Indianapolis Star* ran a series of
articles about the infiltration of a major bonding company
by a gang of Cleveland hoodlums. Fascinated by this business
phenomenon which they unearthed, two correspondents of
the *Star*, Edward H. Frank and Carolyn Pickering, continued
their probe and found that this condition also existed in other

major cities around the United States. They found that nation-wide crime syndicates had infiltrated the bail-bond business in major cities across the nation. Then they went on to conclude that ". . . underworld domination is rapidly turning the once-legitimate and still vital bail bond business into 'the bail bond racket.' . . ." In their words:

Pay-offs to policemen and judges, the use of fake and counterfeit bonds and collusion between lawyers and prosecutors are but a few of the everyday practices of unsavory bondsmen.

In cities where the investigation could find no evidence of syndicate control, the bail bond business is saturated with exconvicts, convicted gamblers and men of questionable background.

Evidence revealed that these gangsters, making a mockery of the law, will stop at nothing to extract exorbitant bond fees from the poor and uneducated.

NOT ONLY is bail bonding a highly lucrative field, but it also provides crime syndicates with perfect springboards to freedom for their members.

Indiana law does not require out-of-state surety companies to post collateral with the state in order to transact business.

This makes it possible for the underworld to "spring" a gangster on bond without any intent of producing him for trial. The bond is declared forfeited. . . .

With this vast power resting in the clutches of notorious hoodlums, convicted gamblers and mob bosses, bail bonding no longer can serve the administration of justice.

Instead it becomes an obstruction to justice.

These intrepid reporters found that, in Cleveland, racketeers had organized a twenty-three state bail-bond syndicate that wrote $8 million worth of bail in an eight-month period. This syndicate was reportedly run by "a big time hoodlum" and convicted felon, and a convicted arms smuggler who it was said spared no efforts to gain a monopoly over the bonding business.

As the reporters continued their investigation, they found that in city after city around the country the bail-bond business was commanded by exconvicts and similar unsavory characters.

In one major city, a reputed high rackets figure was reported to be associated with a major local bondsman, said to have the bail-bond business for almost all local hoodlums. He had a large network of agents working for him; together they were recorded as having done over $7,500,000 worth of bonding in one year recently.

In one city in Louisiana, the reporters found that the bail-bond business was dominated by two racket-related characters who molded a highly profitable bail-bond operation through close alliances with police, judges, and well-placed public officials. The local crime commission had many records of charges and complaints against these bondsmen for unethical and alleged illegal bail-bonding practices.

In a midwestern city, they reported that an exconvict with a forty-year police record had control of the bail-bond business. In a southern city, they found that the man who ran the bail-bond business had been convicted for accepting bribes while in state office. The *Indianapolis Star* concluded:

The crooks, the thugs, the bums, the mobsters and their associates stand ready today to take over part of the United States Constitution. Unless they are checked soon, the syndicate and the Mafia will be able to wring millions in profits from the basic rights of every American.

The criminals and their "clean" front-men can do this if they are successful in capturing the bail bond business.

The mob is close to making that seizure. The *Star* has shown how the mob moved in on a legitimate business here, and how the big dealers were thrown out only by strenuous effort on the part of sincere, honest businessmen. In other cities over the nation, the story isn't the same. In too many states, the mobsters are sitting squarely on top of the right of every citizen to be free on bond until proved guilty of criminal charges.

Other newspapers have run similar exposés. The story always seems to be the same. In one major midwestern city, hoodlum-run groups are supposed to control 90 per cent of the bonding business. In Chicago, one bondsman's license was taken away after he was arrested as a member of a counterfeiting ring. Another was recently arrested for a $100,000 swindle arising out of a fraudulent gold scheme. And the Illinois Insurance Department took away the certificate of one bondsman because he was allowing himself to be used by bosses of a criminal syndicate. The bondsman had gone into debt to the "juice men" of the local Cosa Nostra, according to the *Chicago American* newspaper. These were the local loan sharks and enforcers. To pay off, the bondsman would bail out certain defendants specified by the racketeers, who would demand of the released person payments on these "juice" loans. If the person could not pay, the gang would send him out to commit further crimes in order to get the money to pay them off.

Some bondsmen are loan sharks themselves. Their business lends itself to this kind of financial exploitation. One bondsman bailed out a defendant charged with stealing a car. The bond was $5,000 and the premium would have been $500. When the defendant said that he did not have the $500 to pay for the premium, the bondsman kindly offered to lend him the $500—if he paid $200 interest on it. Some resourceful bondsmen have circumvented the new Illinois law that allows defendants to avoid paying a bondsman by depositing the amount of the premium with the court in place of the ordinary bail bond. To get around this new law, they make loans to defendants who do not have the 10 per cent to deposit with the court, and charge exorbitant interest fees for this "social service."

Again and again this relationship between the underworld and the bail-bond business has been found in one major city after another. And no laws have been able to prevent it, yet.

William Hundley, the chief of the Justice Department's Organized Crime and Racketeering Section, recently summed up the relationship between racketeers and the bail-bond business as a frequent and natural liaison that grew out of a flaw in our legal system. The phenomenon is there, he says, and one can see it time and again as one looks through the literature and reports about racketeering.

CRIMINAL SUPPORT OF THE BAIL-BOND BUSINESS

Racketeers often run and profit from the bail-bond business, and are catered to by it and supply much of the nonracketeer bondsman's business. In return for this, the racketeer is treated like a special client and given the courtesies of the trade. In the famous Appalachia case, one of the defendants was released on $100,000 bail. A bondsman is supposed to have provided this bail at no charge to him and with no collateral. It was done as a favor. In another case in New York one bondsman put up $35,000 bail without security for a well-known racketeer defendant in a narcotics case. The defendant jumped bail. The insurance company paid the forfeiture and collected from the bondsman. He, in turn, was paid off by the racketeers who all along had expected this to happen.

This occurrence is not uncommon. The highest bails seem to be most easily made. The big operators either own bondsmen or are such good sources of business that they themselves can get extraordinary bonds perfunctorily.

More significant than the casual favor is the long-term working arrangement which often brings together the racketeer and the bondsman. An example of this situation came to light when a New York grand jury conducted an investigation for the General Sessions Court to determine if lawyers and bondsmen were combining to aid local lottery operators. It issued a report in March, 1960. The grand jury found insufficient evidence to indict, but nonetheless did reveal practices by these groups which the grand jury uncovered and characterized as ". . . improper, unethical and detrimental to the interest of justice."

What the grand jury found was a typical pattern in organized lottery and numbers and gambling procedures all over the United States. These vast and highly profitable gambling kingdoms are reigned over by a few overlords who remain behind the scenes. They manipulate the business, often "fix" local officials, and leave the actual, open, physical bet taking to local street agents. In the "numbers" or policy business, for example, the "writers" and "collectors" do all the outside leg work, that is, make the bets, gather the slips, and turn it all in to the bosses. It is understood that for thus exposing themselves to frequent arrests, the boss, who is rich and who stays apart from the actual outside operation and is therefore insulated from these arrests, will take care of his employees when they get in trouble. In the words of this one grand jury:

The testimony of more than seventy-five collectors and runners clearly established that they had received this "protection" in fact. Referring to more than one hundred and fifty separate arrests, these seventy-five witnesses testified that they were promptly released on bail by bondsmen whose services they had not requested and were represented by attorneys whom they had not retained. They paid neither the bondsmen nor the lawyers.

. . . Furthermore, certain controllers testified that they made advance arrangements with bondsmen in order to facilitate the prompt release of collectors who might be arrested. The bondsmen agreed to provide bail immediately when notified by phone of the arrest of any collector employed by the controller.

. . . the established controllers were able to obtain credit for bail and legal services. Certain lawyers and bondsmen even went so far as to call at the controllers' places of business to collect their predetermined fees. One lawyer periodically received from a bondsman his list of clients which the bondsman's clerk had prepared for the lawyer. In another instance, lawyers and a bondsman shared an office and took each other's calls.

. . . this service furnished by lawyers and bondsmen on a "mass production" basis was highly advantageous for both the controllers and the collectors. Frequently collectors were back on the street taking bets again a few hours after being arrested. Not only was the inconvenience to the collector minimized, but also there was hardly any interruption of his service on behalf of the controller.

The grand jury report continued, pointing out how

. . . the bondsmen, who were hired by controllers to provide bail on behalf of collectors, engaged in various deceptive practices in order to conceal their arrangements with the said controllers. In executing bail bond affidavits as required by law, those bondsmen repeatedly stated that their fees were paid or promised by the defendants. However, the great majority of defendants who testified before the grand jury stated that they neither paid nor promised to pay the fees and had not dealt with the bondsmen at all. This testimony was legally insufficient to provide a basis for an indictment in the absence of corroboration.

In many instances, the bonds were executed not by the bondsmen who had the arrangements with the controllers but by other bondsmen. These "substitute" bondsmen, who executed affidavits, claimed before the grand jury that they did so at the request of and on the basis of information given to them by the principal bondsmen. In this manner, the bondsmen who dealt with the controllers evaded the obligation of stating what they knew to be the fact under oath.

Another irregular practice . . . revealed controllers acting as indemnitors for bondsmen. Certain controllers testified that they assumed the risk on policy bonds, despite the fact that their names did not appear on the bonds as indemnitors. It was understood that, if a collector failed to appear in court, the controller would either produce him or pay for the forfeiture.

In providing bail for unknown defendants who did not hire them, certain bondsmen have sometimes been unable to obtain the signatures of the defendants as required by the insurance companies on applications for bail bonds. These bondsmen have flagrantly disregarded the company rules by submitting the applications unsigned and sometimes completely blank. In a few instances the bondsmen made the pretense of complying with company rules by signing the names of the defendants without their permission.

Under arrangements like these, the arrested bookie or numbers writer is quickly sprung and can be back on the streets in a few hours plying his trade. The whole process of the law is made a mockery of, and the lawyer and the bondsman who play a role in this sham procedure are guilty of subverting the law which unfortunately plays into their hands. For the organized gambling world this setup is a kind of "socialized law"; the bondsman is a fringe benefit for the bookie who works for "Big Crime."

CORRUPTION CAUSED BY THE BAIL-BOND BUSINESS

Misconduct with outsiders is not the only indictment which can be made against many bondsmen. The history of the bail-bond business is also replete with examples of misconduct involving "insiders." Collusion with the various officials who are involved with the administration of criminal law has been uncovered in numerous investigations of the bail-bond business. Lawyers, judges, court officials, and police have at some time succumbed to the enticements offered by unscrupulous bondsmen.

In Louisville, Kentucky, jailers are paid on the basis of how many defendants are in jail—the more the better for them.

They have joined bondsmen in objecting to bail reform. It is to their benefit to have bondsmen refuse to provide bail for the poor, who populate the jails for the lack of bail. In Lexington, Kentucky, magistrates and justices of the peace write bonds for defendants as long as they are in courts other than their own—a suspect practice, or one exemplifying less than a rigorous restraint on professional ethics.

In 1961 a grand jury in Jackson County, Missouri, conducted an investigation and reported that most bondsmen were quasi-partners of certain policemen. Some police on the scenes at the times of arrest would steer defendants to these bondsmen. The bondsmen in return would kick back 20 per cent of their fees to the referring cop. This arrangement could lead to a monopoly on the local bail business, since the police are at the sources of all early criminal proceedings and all jailings. Therefore they can be the first to contact all potential clients for bail. Their peculiar position also lends an aspect of coercion to the transaction. Some police have been known actually to fill in a particular bondsman's name on the required forms.

In Brooklyn, one investigation of the local bail-bond business led to the removal of one magistrate, twenty-eight police captains, the disciplining of a number of lieutenants and sergeants, and the conviction of others for bail-bond fraud and irregularities.

A few years ago in Cincinnati it was discovered that some municipal court clerks were getting referral kickbacks from bondsmen of up to 30 per cent. For this split of the fee, the clerks called in their cohort bondsmen at the right times and also helped the bondsmen avoid full forfeitures when their defendants fled.

Bondsmen have been so brash as to appear as attorneys for clients. Sometimes at preliminary proceedings, a bondsman will act in court for his client defendant as if he were a member of the bar. Their action can be quite freewheeling. In Birmingham, Alabama, a bondsman was convicted for appearing in court with a substitute defendant. The real defendant who was out on bail had fled. However, the cost of the fine was less than the price of forfeiture, so this bondsman came to court with someone else who pretended he was the real defendant.

Collusion between bondsmen and jailhouse employees is common and has taken many forms. In some places, low-level nonjudicial officials set bail, and this can lead to collusion. In one state it was discovered that police, who had the power to set bail in noncapital cases, were in collusion with bondsmen. Aside from direct involvement in the bonding process, police can also be useful sources for the referral of business. In San Bernardino when it was disclosed that the names of six bondsmen were listed at the jail, their competitors from a nearby town complained to the governor. In Denver, the state insurance commissioner suspended one bondsman for making gifts to officials of the sheriff's office. He had also given $50 bills to some court employees. At first, when other local bondsmen complained of the practice to the former State Commissioner of Insurance, he ruled that this was proper as long as no wrongful deals were involved. The law specifically forbade bondsmen from attempting to influence officials by gifts. It was later learned that the former insurance commissioner had received a gift of three cases of scotch and a generator for his mountain cabin from the same generous bondsman. The commissioner said that the bondsman had asked no consideration in return for these gratuities.

Bondsmen have even consorted with judges. When, for example, a judge indicates that he does not desire a defendant to be released, a bondsman may refuse to provide his bail. Bondsmen need the court's cooperation in numerous ways from time to time and will try not to offend a judge before whom they have frequent business. A judge can effectively see to it that bail is denied in a given case without subjecting himself to criticism for denying bail.

One occasionally hears from a candid and outspoken bondsman how other bondsmen have certain courts "all tied up" and get all the work there. Such a practice can raise the suspicion of collusive fee splitting. A Missouri magistrate turned down an offer of bond because the defendant had "the wrong bondsman."

A dramatic example of the way in which some courts indulge bondsmen was illustrated in Maryland recently. A United States congressman, while residing in Maryland during a session of Congress, was arrested. Bail was set at $200. The representative offered $200 cash to the court. The judge refused the money and insisted on the use of a bondsman. The legislator refused to satisfy what he considered a ridiculous requirement and instead, as a matter of principle, went to jail for two days. He was applauded by his colleagues upon his return to Congress for the strength of integrity he had displayed.

One chief favor that judges can offer bondsmen comes at forfeiture time. It could be argued that forfeiture practices themselves bespeak the breakdown of the bail system. When a defendant who is free on bail fails to appear at trial, the very essence of our money-based bail system is that the bond shall be forfeited. This inevitability should be the very inducement that underlies the system. Yet, in practice, it is rare that bail money is in fact forfeited. Judges will often give the surety some time to make good on his assurance by finding the defendant and presenting him for later trial. Failing that, courts will often remit forfeitures on one ground or another even though the bondsman has failed to fulfill his role if the defendant disappears. Often judges will remit forfeitures even in cases where the defendant does not appear, late or ever. Where the bondsman shows due diligence in pursuing the disappearing defendant or pleads extenuating circumstances to account for his failure to produce a defendant, courts will often excuse his failure.

There have been cases where it appeared that the judge's leniency with or remission of forfeitures by bondsmen might have suggested some interest in the matter on the part of the judge.

In one midwestern city, the newspapers criticized a judge who had vacated $300,000 worth of forfeited bonds. As a result, the forfeitures were reinstated and five bonding companies went out of business. The frequently imperfect forfeiture practice is a perfect example of the phoniness and failure of the bail system. One can easily imagine what it might be worth to some bondsman who does a vast business to be able to avoid big forfeitures—and to some venal judges.

It has also been found that bondsmen sometimes abuse their arrangements with judges or prosecutors in order to secure periods of grace during which time they can find and return a missing defendant. Defaults frequently occur because the defendant is angling for a more receptive judge. If there is no danger of forfeiture, a defendant can wait for the judge he prefers and then show up for trial.

Enforcement of forfeitures has become so lax that bondsmen will sometimes operate without sufficient funds to support forfeitures which could arise from their bonds. They offer the courts no insurance at all. One bondsman wrote $670,000 worth of bonds on $20,000 worth of pledged property. The proportions of this practice can be great. A state lost approximately $10 million in uncollected forfeitures over a ten-year period because small surety companies wrote more bonds than they could afford and then went bankrupt when called upon to pay up. Collection rates on forfeited bonds in city after city are a mere fraction of what they should have been.

Some bondsmen have come to expect this sinecure. At times, when district attorneys or judges have called for stricter enforcement of forfeited bail bonds, bondsmen have threatened to strike. On some occasions they have struck, forcing acute overcrowding in local jails and the needless incarceration of helpless individuals, including minors.

Of course the worst and at the same time probably the most frequent collusion by bondsmen is with lawyers. As the New York City Bar Association reported:

. . . a frequent condition of the granting of bail is the requirement by the bondsman that a particular attorney be selected to defend the case. It is said that this attorney will frequently kick back part of his fee to the bondsman, and that a failure to split fees in this manner will eliminate the attorney as a recipient of business from the disappointed bondsman and from his colleagues as well. The amount of such fee-splitting ebbs and flows and has been in the past the subject of investigation and grand jury concern.

In 1960, a special bar committee in Baltimore made a study of the relationship between bondsmen and attorneys and issued a report with similar findings. Certain bondsmen solicited for a small number of attorneys. Some bondsmen would urge defendants to appeal their cases, then charge them again for the appeal bond. Unauthorized people solicited business for some bondsmen. Some bondsmen even attempted to get into the jails to solicit business from defendants in distress. But the relationship between many of the bondsmen and the attorneys was clear. Aside from the unethical aspect of collusion between lawyers and bondsmen, there is a further serious question as to the effect of this type of deal upon the defendant's case. Several years ago, Vergil W. Peterson, director of the Chicago Crime Commission, pointed out that, where this collusion and fee splitting exists ". . . in most instances the accused does not get the best representation for his money."

These grand jury disclosures are not unique. Time after time, place after place, collusions have been found between attorneys and bondsmen. Each refers cases to the other; each kicks back to the other; each stoops to the other's unprofessional level. Grand jury after grand jury, newspaper after newspaper, reformer after reformer, all have been shocked at the operation of this and all other faults of the bail-bond business and have called for change. Little has come.

The Bondsman's Role in the Administration of Justice

A cardinal flaw even with the legitimate aspects of the bondsman's present role, and it could be argued that this is in and of itself a fatal flaw, is his power to singlehandedly inject himself into the administration of justice and impede or corrupt it. Once a judge sets bail in a given case, one would hope that the issue of the bailability of a defendant was settled. But because of the absolute power of the bondsman to withhold his services arbitrarily, the matter is not settled by the judge. In fact the judge's ruling can be defeated by the caprice of the bondsman, who can refuse to provide bail for good reasons, bad reasons, or no reasons. Bondsmen frequently exercise this mighty prerogative. This omnipotence and power of control over judicial proceedings was recently criticized in an opinion of Judge J. Skelly Wright of the District of Columbia Circuit Court:

Certainly the professional bondsman system as used in this District is odious at best. The effect of such a system is that the professional bondsmen hold the keys to the jail in their pockets. They determine for whom they will act as surety—who in their judgment is a good risk. The bad risks, in the bondsmen's judgment, and the ones who are unable to pay the bondsmen's fees remain in jail. The court and the commissioner are relegated to the relatively unimportant chore of fixing the amount of bail.[5]

For similar reasons, the *Missouri Bar Journal* once referred to the professional bondsman as "our jailer-at-large, our warden-without-portfolio.[6]

This power to frustrate judicial rulings is truly shocking. And it is not merely a theoretical possibility; it is all too often the case in our criminal courts today. One survey has disclosed that bondsmen accept only a fraction of the potential cases they could handle. Sometimes the percentage of cases refused has been as high as 50 per cent and more. This power to refuse bail is the power to negate the whole bail system as it is conceived as part of our administration of law. And if the statistics drawn from the Vera experiments mentioned in Chapter V are true, the bondsman's decision to decline bail may not only sentence a man to jail before his trial but also may affect the disposition of his case thereafter.

Judge Wright is not the only member of the bench who is repulsed by this unwitting partnership with bondsmen. Judge John Murtagh of New York City has said: "Bondsmen have done more than any other group to lower the prestige and destroy the integrity of the criminal court system." Others have voiced similar criticism about the bondsman and his unofficial partnership with the courts. But the partnership is yet to be dissolved.

The veto power over a defendant's bailability is not the only example of the intrusion of bondsmen into official, hitherto exclusively, governmental roles. The bondsman also has certain police powers of arrest and extradition over bailed

5 Pannell v. U.S., 320 Federal 2d. 698 (1963).
6 *Missouri Bar Journal*, January 1964, p. 13.

defendants who have fled. Justice Swayne described this unique role in an opinion for the United States Supreme Court in 1872.

When bail is given, the principal is regarded as delivered to the custody of his sureties. Their dominion is a continuance of the original imprisonment. Whenever they choose to do so, they may seize him and deliver him up in their discharge; and if that cannot be done at once, they may imprison him until it can be done. They may exercise their rights in person or by agent. They may pursue him into another state; may arrest him on the Sabbath; and, if necessary, may break and enter his house for that purpose. The seizure is not made by virtue of new process. None is needed. It is likened to the rearrest by the sheriff of an escaping prisoner . . . it is said: "The bail have their principal on a string, and may pull the string whenever they please, and render him in their discharge."[7]

These powers would be far-reaching and abusable enough in the hands of proper and responsible police authorities. The same powers in the hands of bondsmen is shocking and frightening. The bondsman is subject to less controls and is possessed of greater powers than is the law enforcement officer who would exercise counterpart functions. Hence he can act as a de facto state agent without being subject to the usual safeguards ordinarily surrounding the conduct of those officials.

When a defendant who is free on bail flees from the jurisdiction of the court under whose control he is, no matter how metaphysically, the bondsman may pursue, arrest, and return the truant. The bondsman's powers conflict with the traditional safeguards that protect all criminally accused during the process of extradition. He can arrest and return a defendant in a summary manner beyond the powers of peace officers

[7] Taylor v. Taintor, 83 U.S. 366, at 371, 2.

who must follow the procedures of extradition. And yet he is acting as part of the administration of the official criminal law apparatus of the state when he is doing this.[8]

Bondsmen have used crass and at times brutal methods in exercising this quasi-police power for their private and commercial ends. Four persons were convicted in the United States District Court in Toledo in June 1963 on charges of impersonating FBI agents. The evidence showed that the four forced a couple into their custody at gunpoint and, representing themselves as FBI agents, held them captive for eleven hours, questioning them about the whereabouts of a bail jumper. Two of the imposters were bail bondsmen who were responsible for $50,000 and $25,000 bonds which they had posted for defendants. In another case, a deputy sheriff was indicted for doubling as a special investigator for a bonding company and arresting a $50 bail jumper who had fled. He exceeded his powers as a cop by assuming the second role as a bondsman's agent.

Bondsmen pursue their quarry with diligence for two reasons. The first and obvious reason is that the profit motive of their business demands vigilance. A caught escapee is a loss erased from the ledgers. Secondly, some bondsmen have said that they pursue, even in cases where they have adequate security, to protect them from any losses due to absconding. This is, they say, because relentless pursuit gives them a reputation which deters flight on the part of their clients. Such a reputation is good for their unique business image.

Aside from examples of brutality and overbearing conduct, aside from the idea that at whim the bondsman can "go off a bond" and arrest a defendant without returning his fee, the very idea of a kind of partnership between this less than exemplary group of private citizens and the police, combined

[8] 73 Yale Law Journal 1098 (1964).

with the fact that in some ways the bondsmen have even greater powers than the police themselves, is utterly repugnant and condemnable.

IN DEFENSE OF BONDSMEN

What is the bondsman's side of this story? Recently the bonding business has been called upon with graduating intensity and publicity to rationalize its purposes and to defend its right to exist in the face of the general criticism which has been consistently and is increasingly leveled against it. Its response has been a dull cry for laissez faire and a reincarnation of the standard shibboleths of conservatism. On August 4, 1964, George L. Will, the executive director of the American Society of Professional Bail Bondsmen, testified before the Constitutional Rights Subcommittee of the Senate about the *raison d'être* of the commercial bondsman. In the belief that no summary could do justice to his plea, that statement in full, as it was publicly released at the time of Mr. Will's testimony (with some brief suggested answers following in brackets), is presented here verbatim:

Bail bondsmen have been in the Insurance Business for over 100 years. They more than anyone else have "Insured" that the American Citizen receives "Equal Justice Under the Law" by his enforced attendance in the Courts to Answer to the Charges placed against him. [Questionable; but allowable introductory puffing.]

The Bail Bond System is the Very FOUNDATION OF JUSTICE because if Those Released on Bond did not appear in Court, the Machinery of Justice would break down. It is the task of the Bondsmen to release "good risks" Citizens so that while they are Free on Bond they may prepare their cases, support their family, and continue their normal way of life pending Trial. [Fact is that frequently they do not perform this task.]

The Bondsman operates a Service Business, his Service is available 24 hours a day, seven days a week, 52 weeks a year. His Service is available to Every Citizen Regardless of RACE, COLOR OR CREED. For his Service he receives a Fee for every Bond underwritten and when he makes a mistake by Releasing a defendant who does not appear for Trial he pays for his mistakes by payment of Forfeited Bond to the Court. By this System of Release before Trial the Taxpayer has saved MILLIONS OF DOLLARS for pre-Trial Custodial Care of Defendants. [It is true that bondsmen save the courts some administrative costs.]

It has Been Charged that thousands of citizens are in Jail because they cannot "Buy their Release." We charge that This Statement is a LIE. The Bail Bond Business is so highly competitive that Any Person who is a "good risk" is Released on Bond. ONLY THE BAD RISKS REMAIN IN JAIL. [Utterly at war with fact.]

They Charge that only the Wealthy can afford to Buy their Freedom and that we discriminate against the "poor indigent." This is a LIE. Certainly the financial condition of the defendant is an important qualification for Bond. But the facts and Records prove that the majority of Bailees are in the Middle Income Bracket. It is Unfortunate but TRUE (the Bondsmen have found out from bitter EXPERIENCE) that the "poor indigent" is the poorest RISK and that Is Why He Remains in Jail pending Trial. [The suggestion of a shocking general notion based on a *possible*, unproven half-truth.]

They cite in magazine articles and in the Readers Digest (see exhibits A and B) the case of a "poor indigent" who though later proved to be innocent languished in Jail for months because the Bondsman refused to underwrite his Bail, however it is not the Bail Bondsmen who hold these "poor indigents" in Jail awaiting Trial but it is the COURTS WHO VIOLATE HIS CONSTITU-TIONAL RIGHTS BY DENYING HIM A SPEEDY TRIAL. The Courts only have to initiate a System of Immediate Trial for Indigents giving them Preference over those Released on Bond. However ever mindful of being re Elected the Judges and Courts are operated for the benefit of the Wealthy and Politically powerful, not for the poor indigent citizen. [Speedy trials would help;

but speedy trials can only be so speedy without converting a defendant's privilege into a punishment. And no matter how speedy the trial, what about the interim period?]

It is Charged that Bondsmen associate with Thieves and Crooks, it is unfortunate but true as we do not receive our business from Priests and Bishops. However because three apples in a barrel are bad you do not condemn the whole barrel. The average Bondsman is a Home owner, Tax payer, family businessman who operates his business in a Professional Manner. [The charge referred to is not that the clients are crooks, but that the bondsmen and their associates frequently are. At what point do enough bad apples adequately prove the unacceptability of the barrelful?]

Under the provisions of Bill S. 2840 they would Have the United States Government operate as a BONDING COMPANY. [Not so.] They would RELEASE ANYONE by the deposit of 10% of the Bond with the Court. Under this System Thieves, Crooks, Sexual Perverts, Prostitutes, Counterfitters, Spies, Bank Robbers, Rapists and Kidnappers would be released Without Supervision or Control to Prey Upon the Public again merely by the deposit of 10% of the Bond. [The same people who buy bonds now.] To EXCLUDE CERTAIN TYPES OF CRIMES WOULD BE THE HIGHEST FORM OF DISCRIMINATION, and would Certainly Violate Equal Rights, Justice and Opportunity Under the Law. [Less so than the present system.] This Plan is UN-WORKABLE AND IMPRACTICAL as it has been our EX-PERIENCE that it is very difficult to enforce the attendance of Traffic Offenders in Court (see exhibit C, Metropolitan Traffic Bench Warrant Book). YET THEY WOULD RELEASE ANY PERSON ACCUSED OF A FELONY merely upon Deposit of Premium on Bond with the Court. Under this System the number of Forfeitures on Bail would Increase by the THOUSANDS and Turn this Country into a NATION OF FUGITIVES (see exhibit D) [doubtful], as it is Only COMMON SENSE that if a defendant can be Released on a FELONY CHARGE merely by Deposit of a Percentage of the Bond, the INCENTIVE TO FLEE the Jurisdiction of the Court will be considerable when he knows that by his Appearance he Jeopardizes his Liberty or His Life. [How does the bond premium alter this motive?]

Under provisions of Bill S 2838 they would Release "good risk indigents" in their Own Recognizance WITHOUT BOND. We charge that there is no such person as a "good risk indigent" [WOW!] the qualifications for Bond are the same for everyone and certainly if a man although indigent has family and friends he will be able to raise the Bail Bond Premium. Less than 10% of all Bail Bonds written have any type of cash collateral to back up the Bond.

We believe this ATTACK UPON THE FOUNDATION OF JUSTICE is indicative of a great change in the Social Policies of our Government. We regret using "Cliche"; but sometimes they are the only way to definitise a Philosophy of Government namely "from the Cradle to the Grave." Under this role the Citizen is Guaranteed Employment, "free" medical care, "free" Legal Counsel, "free" Release from Jail. All of these "free" programs are totally foreign to the original concept of Government as practiced by our Forefathers. It is Ironic that these "free" Release Systems have been financed by TAX FREE foundations whose basic wealth was originated by men who believed and made their fortunes under Our Free Enterprise economic System. The very personal and individualistic traits that made these men Millionaires are being used to Destroy our Way of Life and Beliefs that have made this Country the strongest and wealthiest Nation on the Earth.

The question is Who Will Control the "Keys to the Jail"? the independent businessman or the Social Parasite who infiltrates the Government and lives off the fruits of another's labor and business. If they Successfully Attack our System of Justice by seizing the "Keys to the Jail" under the smokescreen of helping the indigent they will have a tremendous political advantage to foister their sociological changes in our government.

We say that Russia is our Mortal Enemy and its Economic and Social Systems are the exact opposite of our individual Liberty and Free Enterprise Systems. However Russia has "free" Medical Care, "free" Legal Counsel, Guaranteed Employment and "free" Release from Jail Systems.

Today our Leaders are giving "Lip Service" to our Individual Liberties and quietly "selling us down the river of Socialism."

If the Government can Seize a Business that has been Serving the Public for over 100 years [???] they Can and Will Socialize Every Business and Profession Tomorrow. When this happens we will not have to cross an ocean to witness the POLICE STATE AND OMNIPOTENT FACELESS GOVERNMENT.

It is doubly Ironic to note that if the present Socialistic Trend continues to its logical conclusion (where our life is regulated from morning to night, from Cradle to Grave) the only individuals left will be the Criminals who by their anti-social activities will refuse to live in a Nation of ZOMBIES.

> Respectfully Submitted
> George L. Will
> Executive Director

On a somewhat more constructive plane, if equally as unrealistic and guilty of the "old saw" resort to cries against the socialization of business (this time the whole insurance business is said to be in jeopardy), Frank Wright spoke out in defense of bondsmen at the 1964 National Bail Conference. Wright recognized at once the need to reform the administration of modern bail practices as a parallel to the equally compelling need to maintain the bail-bond business. He suggested such superficial reforms as the policing of bonding agents (something which supposedly goes on under present conditions) and the creation of an assigned risk bonding pool to cover poor defendants, and financed from forfeited funds (a good idea if forfeitures were enforced and if the institution is to continue without more radical changes).

This view expressed by Wright, that any faults with the commercial bonding business are intramural only and should therefore be the concern of the business itself, or at the most poses a problem of regulation rather than reform, is the view of the elite of the bonding business. The view is expressed in the Uniform Bail Bond Law which the National Association of Insurance Commissioners, along with some states, has adopted. The intent of this law is that adequate controls over bondsmen will eliminate the few bad ones and leave a useful and worthwhile profession. To accomplish this self-regulation the Uniform law seeks to eliminate undesirables, equalize rates, avoid federal control, control licensing, prevent any bad agents from moving from one state to another, gather information, and tax premiums and raise money thereby. Wright confessed that the companies cannot themselves regulate their agents.

Wright is a sincere and articulate spokesman, who attempts to be constructive in his estimations of the bail-bond business. He represents that better part of the bonding business which sees the bail system as part of the legitimate business world of insurance, and which tries to maintain some self-discipline and respect commensurate with their unrealistic, but sincere view of the value and utility of their own "profession."

When Wright spoke at the National Bail Conference, he attempted to rationalize the bail-bond business on grounds of public service, regulation, and free enterprise. Bondsmen investigate cases, he pointed out, and save men from needlessly going to jail. Some are innocent men, he reminded us. Thus the presumption of innocence is preserved by the intervention of the bondsman. And this service is at no expense to society or the taxpayer. Bondsmen are better custodians, he argued, because they have their money invested in a defendant's stability. What greater motive? Mr. Wright then called for the bondsmen to clean their houses, cure corrupt practices, and help find relief for the poor. Finally he, too, made his pitch for the sanctity of business and the danger of government:

We must not forget that in this country we have the free enterprise system. We do not expect everyone to own the same priced automobile or to have the same priced home, and we do not expect all workers, whether labor or professional, to receive the same pay.

Bail bonds are surety bonds. Surety bonds are insurance. Therefore, bail bonds are insurance.

Shall we say that if a man cannot afford a life insurance policy to protect his family, the Government should pay for it? Shall we say that if a man cannot afford fire insurance, the Government should pay for it? Shall we say that any of the benefits that the middle class or the wealthy have should be provided by the Government for the poor?

This is not the free enterprise system. This is socialism. And if the Government can move in on a small fraction of the insurance industry and socialize it, they can also socialize the whole insurance industry. And if they can do that, they can socialize all industry.

Thank you.

One can safely attack both the foundation premises and the bizarre reaches of Wright's arguments. He recognizes the need to control the bad elements in the bonding business and to aid the poor who have special problems making money bail. But he also admits the traditional inability of his business to do anything about it. He does not treat any of the numerous other problems that cast doubt upon the value of bondsmen. Nor does he solve the problems he does recognize. But even more essentially he assumes a natural right of bondsmen to their role, and this assumption flies in the face of fact, history, and reason. Bondsmen graduated into their role for reasons of at best questionable necessity and expediency. And while they have abused their questionable position, time has stolen their utility. Experience has amply shown that the bondsman's few legitimate functions can be filled better by other agencies. Once recognizing these facts, then the government is taking nothing from the business world that belongs by nature with business. Government is merely ending a questionable partnership which it created, and ending it for good cause. In the face of this reasoning, Wright's shibboleths about the sanctity of business and his bugaboos about overprotecting the disadvantaged are unconvincing.

The paradox of the bondsman's arguments is that at one moment he is asserting the rights of free enterprise while at other times he feels perfectly free to use public facilities and play the role of a public utility. Bondsmen want to have the benefits of both a public agency and a private enterprise, but they satisfy the responsibilities of neither.

CHAPTER IV

Preventive Detention: Society's Need for Self-Protection

The bail system keeps many innocent persons in jail. So, too, ironically it permits the freedom of many dangerous persons who threaten society. The price of a bail bond or the ability to afford a bail bond has no relation to society's need to protect itself from the accused person who threatens its safety. And yet, before trial, the only judicial control of criminal defendants rests in the bail system. In the cases of many of the worst and most dangerous criminals, this amounts to no control at all. The "big shot" racketeer can afford bail, if in fact he is not a bondsman himself or if he does not have one under his thumb. The bail system cannot cope with the need to detain before trial some who would flee before trial or those who are dangerous. The bail system does not provide for detention and, in addition, any suggestion that it does so provide can be challenged on legal and constitutional grounds.

Often, under the guise of denying or setting bail too high to be met, judges exercise preventive detention in cases where they themselves feel strongly that the person indicted should not be freed, or that the crime for which he is charged is so heinous as to compel detention, or in cases where community pressure is so great that the release of the prisoner would be condemned. In many such cases society must have a way to confine these defendants whether or not they have the money for bail.

The previous few chapters have dealt with the problems of those many defendants who ought to have been freed before their trials, but who were imprisoned. Is there a counterpart group of defendants who ought to be detained but who are often released pending trial? Wise observers would agree that there is such a group. The treatment of these defendants presents very strained and perplexing problems, for the resolution of which we have no clear, fixed procedures. These defendants ordinarily are dealt with through the practice loosely labeled "preventive detention." The practice is not so much a recognized part of our bail system as it is an inevitable by-product of the system's failure to deal openly with the problems these defendants pose.

Preventive detention is the practice of either denying bail or setting bail at an unattainably high amount in order to imprison a person who presents a particular danger to society if left free before trial. This practice is commonly (if unofficially), unadmittedly, and often improperly used to detain a defendant who presents a clear danger of harming people, destroying evidence, or committing more crimes. This is distinct from the cases (discussed in Chapter II) where a defendant's pretrial incarceration is ordered to punish him or to teach a lesson. Fear of flight may or may not be part of the problem in these cases. The main motive for preventive detention is self-defense.

The idea of preventive detention is traceable to the historic peace bonds authorized under English law at least as far back as 1360.[1] Under this procedure a court could oblige one whose past record or general behavior created probable ground to

[1] 34 Edw. III, 3.

suspect his future misbehavior to stipulate and give assurances to the public that the apprehended offense would not occur. The person charged would have to assure this by giving pledges or securities to keep the peace. The bond was forfeited to the king if one misbehaved during the term of the bond. If one failed to provide the required peace bond he was sent to jail. These bonds were available against people of a reputation which made it likely that they would commit a crime, those "not of good fame," and those who menaced the peace by threatening to commit a specific crime.

About this fearsome and extremely questionable procedure, Blackstone boasted in Book IV of his *Commentaries* that ". . . really it is an honor, and almost a singular one, to our English laws, that they furnish a title of this sort since preventive justice is, upon every principle of reason, of humanity, and of sound policy, preferable in all respects to punishing justice."[2] Blackstone rationalized this preference upon the dubious distinction between *preventive* as opposed to *punishing* justice. This very questionable theoretical difference was predicated on the argument that preventive justice was ". . . intended merely for prevention, without any crime actually committed by the party, but arising only from a probable suspicion that some crime is intended or likely to happen; and consequently it is not meant as any degree of punishment, unless perhaps for a man's imprudence in giving just ground of apprehension." Apparently, to Blackstone, the noble motive of the state was more important than the actual ignoble result to the individual. A month in jail is, after all, a month in jail. And it is little consolation to the person imprisoned (whether he is ultimately adjudged innocent or guilty) that his pretrial incarceration was "not meant as any degree of punishment." In fact, if there are gradations of punishment, imprisonment

2 *Commentaries*, 4th ed., p. 251.

as punishment for a proven crime is more tolerable than imprisonment to assure that one will not commit a crime in the future. The latter is a frightening, abusable power, one inconsistent with the American way of conducting official affairs. Even Blackstone realized the sweeping nature of this power:

. . . a justice may bind over all night-walkers; eaves-droppers; such as keep suspicious company, or are reported to be pilferers or robbers; such as sleep in the day, and wake in the night; common drunkards; whore-masters; the putative fathers of bastards; cheats; idle vagabonds; and other persons whose misbehaviour may reasonably bring them within the general words of the statute, as persons not of good fame: an expression, it must be owned, of so great a latitude as leaves much to be determined by the discretion of the magistrate himself.[3]

Nonetheless, even in modern England, this broad power of magistrates is preserved on the ground that the public interest requires it. (And as we shall see in Chapter VI, some practice of preventive detention is common in all other countries of the world.)

This drastic power of crime prevention was transferred to the United States and adopted with the English common law. Yet, this power to demand a peace bond, and upon failure to provide it to incarcerate a man not for some act which he has done, but to prevent his doing some act in the future, seems flagrantly to violate our basic constitutional guarantees of trial by jury and due process of law. Still, the authority for this power does exist. Though it is exercised rarely, it does have a clear historical common law source, and every once in a while it is reincarnated for some special reason like that described in Chapter II in the discussion of the recent civil rights demonstrations.

The power to commit for preventive detention lies with the

[3] *Op. cit.*, Book IV; p. 256.

lowest level of the judiciary, the justice of the peace, and the courts of first instance. This practical factor compounds the dangers of abuse inherent in the very existence of the broad power itself. Though it was warned long ago that this "ounce of prevention" philosophy of criminal law cannot and should not be expected to accomplish what our general system of law cannot do, the practice of preventive detention is common today.[4]

In modern times, the peace-bond technique for deterring potential crime is itself rarely used. However, the concept of preventive detention lives on, not in the form of any specific bonding procedure, but as an off-the-record attitude reflected in the exercise of discretionary powers by many prosecuting and judicial officials. This attitude finds expression in the manipulation of the bail-setting procedure to accomplish the general aims of preventive detention. If the judge feels that a defendant's freedom before trial would create a public danger, he can and often will set bail at an amount that is too high for the defendant to afford, or he may deny bail altogether. The laws of the different states vary with respect to the discretion that judges have to deny bail. In most places the trial judge does have a broad, general discretion to deny bail in certain cases or to set it unattainably high, while still avoiding the claim of excessiveness. But this power is really exercised for improper, or at least unauthorized, reasons where the aim is not to deter flight but to prevent future crime. The motive may be right, but the grounds are wrong.

There is a special class of cases in which the argument for preventive detention is quite compelling. This class includes cases involving organized crime and racketeering, recidivists, the criminally insane, and subversion. Although the purpose of bail is theoretically limited to securing a defendant's attend-

4 "Preventive Justice," 88 *University of Pennsylvania Law Review* 331.

ance at trial, it is hard to criticize a judge who, because of a sincere and rational concern for society at large, accomplishes preventive detention in these extreme cases through the manipulation of his power to set bail.

Imagine yourself to be a judge confronted with the following situation: A defendant is before you for arraignment. He requests to be released on bail until his trial. You are convinced that he will appear for trial. However, the district attorney advises you that bail should be denied and the defendant should be locked up because otherwise the witnesses will be endangered, or the evidence or some part of the prosecution's case would be put in jeopardy, or because the nation's security would be endangered if he were released. As a judge you feel that the law is clear—the only proper or legal purpose for setting bail is to assure the defendant's presence at trial. But, though you are convinced that this defendant will not flee, you are equally convinced that the fear expressed by the district attorney is reasonable. What action do you take? Do you let the defendant go free on bail and thus endanger society because you are inhibited by your concept of the limited, proper purpose of bail, a concept that may restrain you from taking any other action? Or do you pervert your bail-setting power and restrain the defendant without a trial because you *think* the safety of the public is endangered and that this danger is more important than the absolute rights of any one man? Does not the choice of either solution create an unsatisfactory quandary?

CRIMINAL CASES

Preventive detention on the ground that the defendant is likely to commit another crime creates the most difficult theoretical and practical problems.

The theoretical legal problem is that if you imprison a

person on the mere speculative possibility that he might commit a crime at some future time, you are denying him any presumption of his present or future innocence. Not only would this action presume his guilt of the crime for which he is charged, but it would also presume him prospectively guilty of the crime which, it is argued, that there is a tendency or likelihood that he will commit. Either step is in the direction away from traditional American values of freedom and human dignity. To prejudge a person may be a natural inclination, but one man's prejudgment ought not to be the basis for the exercise of official punitive power. What might be appropriately decided by a person as an informal personal matter may not also be the predicate for official action in the more circumscribed official judicial arena. Such a totalitarian power, aside from being awesome in itself, would be too susceptible to the kind of abuse that our system of government was designed to avoid—too violative of our values and our way of conducting the affairs of state.

The practical problem arises out of the fact that if certain people are free at certain times there would be a real risk of immediate danger to specific members of society. Where there is a crime wave or a particularly shocking crime, there will often be strong public sentiment that demands some official control over the defendant. Whether or not there is a specific procedure to deal with these cases, there is a specific and real need for some power to cope with these important situations.

When an informal study was conducted recently by the Ramsey County, Minnesota, district attorney's office it was found that on about thirty occasions in a period of only a few months persons who had been arrested and placed on bail were rearrested for committing other felony offenses, all crimes of violence. These repeated crimes between arrest and trial are often serious, as was the case reported in the March 18,

1964, *Baltimore Sun*. A twenty-eight-year-old man was indicted for attempted murder (he shot a policeman in the head) and attempted robbery. These charged crimes took place while the defendant was a fugitive, having jumped $5,000 bail in connection with deadly weapon and barbiturate charges.

Another egregious example, this one involving a defendant harming a victim-witness, was related at the 1964 National Bail Conference:

[A young man] was, at the age of 19, convicted of rape and sentenced to the Illinois State Penitentiary for three years. Approximately one year after his release, [he] was suspected as being the individual responsible for a wave of robberies of pensioners. Bits of information came to the attention of the police that a number of old men had been attacked and threatened with bodily harm if they complained to the police. Detectives identified one of the victims and from him obtained sufficient information to identify [the suspect] as the perpetrator of these crimes. A warrant was signed and [he] was arrested and charged with robbery. Shortly after being arraigned and released on bail, [he] broke into the apartment of a 71 year old man, beat the victim about his head, kicked him numerous times and left him in an unconscious state. He then ransacked the apartment, taking approximately $3,000 in currency and a .38 caliber revolver. The victim required seven stitches in his head and suffered a possible concussion. [The suspect] was identified by the victim and apprehended. He was arrogant toward the arresting officers; threatened to shoot them on sight after his release; *and boasted that he would be on the street immediately after his appearance in court.* [Italics added.] Most of the currency and the revolver were found on his person. While in custody, he was identified by another pensioner as having robbed him and threatened him with bodily harm if he complained to the police. He was indicted on two counts of robbery and released on bail of $1,500.

Upon his release, [he] returned to the home of the victim and again assaulted the old man in an overt effort to dissuade him from testifying. He was again apprehended and charged with aggravated battery. Bail, was, at the initial arraignment, set at $50,000 and the case scheduled for the grand jury within twelve days. On the scheduled date, a request for continuance was granted and the amount of bail was reduced to $5,000—enabling [him] to be released.

On October 15, 1963, *The Philadelphia Inquirer* printed this moving editorial, which graphically pointed out the need and argument for preventive detention in general.

He Was Free on Bail

The man who shot and critically wounded a young policeman in West Philadelphia early Sunday, and was then shot and killed by another patrolman, was free on bail in the razor slashing of a 19-year-old boy only three weeks earlier.

His companion was free on parole after serving a short sentence in prison for beating a policeman.

If one wants a brief lesson in the shortcomings of law enforcement in this city in the face of widespread criminality, he can find it in the fact that these two thugs were on the loose on Sunday morning, heading in a stolen car for Officer Norman Jones' rendezvous with tragedy.

The man who shot Jones had a police record of five arrests in 2½ years. He had never served time. When he was picked up the last time, for cutting a boy with a straight razor for refusing to give him a cigarette, he was charged with assault and battery with intent to kill, aggravated assault and battery and carrying a concealed deadly weapon.

Magistrate Thomas Marotta ordered him held in $10,000 bail. But two weeks ago the bail was reduced to $2,500 by Common Pleas Court Judge Charles L. Guerin and the slasher, Emanuel Roulhac, was released.

If the higher bail had been continued, it is possible that Roulhac would still be in custody and the young cop, who is the father of two small children, would not be at the edge of death today.

At a time when South Philadelphia is in a state of crisis over racial violence, it seems particularly outrageous that a young man charged with slashing another with a razor should have been allowed to go free on virtually nominal bail.

What was the Judge thinking of to make this gesture of leniency to someone so undeserving of it?

What are other Judges thinking of when they so casually fix bail, in cases of violence, at figures permitting release of prisoners awaiting trial or grand jury action? [Italics added.]

It seems evident that they are not thinking too much of the policemen who are beaten up and killed by criminals out on bail or parole.

Emanuel Roulhac came out with a gun in his hand when the policeman ordered him from the car for a routine check. He knew that possession of the gun and the stolen car would send him back to a cell.

He should not have been there, and *he would not have been there if the courts had done the same job of protecting the public from the criminal as Officer Norman Jones had done in the gun duel with Emanuel Roulhac that left one of them dead and the other critically wounded.* [Italics added.]

Notwithstanding how common this problem is, it is still unsettled whether and when courts may imprison to deter crime prospectively. Some courts have taken it for granted that they have this power. In one murder case in Minnesota recently, bail was set at $100,000 at the request of the District Attorney, who represented to the court that it was likely that the defendant would hinder the prosecution if he were set free on bail. In an appeal questioning whether the bail was arbitrary, discriminatory, and excessive, the United States Circuit Court of Appeals held:

While it is inherent in our American concept of liberty that a right to bail shall generally exist, this has never been held to mean that a state must make every criminal offense subject to such a right or that the right provided as to offenses made subject to bail must be so administered that every accused will always be able to secure his liberty pending trial. Traditionally and acceptedly, there are offenses of a nature as to which a state properly may refuse to make provision for a right to bail. . . . It has always been accepted that, beyond the purpose of assuring presence at trial, a state court may in a particular situation make denial or postponement of the general right to bail where this rationally appears to be necessary to prevent a threat or likelihood of interference with the processes of investigation or the orderliness of trial as to the matter involved.[5]

This court's viewpoint goes to the heart of this issue. The court's holding was based on the idea that ". . . there are offenses of a nature as to which a state properly may refuse to make provision for a right to bail." This is indeed so. However, that class of case is usually specified by law to be a capital offense. What about noncapital offenses of a violent or shocking nature? Usually there is no law providing for the denial of bail in these cases, though the social need for some self-defensive power may be even more demanding than in some capital cases.

Justice Douglas has voiced an opinion different from that of the court in the Minnesota case just quoted. In his opinion, and indeed in a commonly accepted point of view, a defendant's evil reputation or community sentiment against an individual are not in and of themselves proper grounds for the denial of bail.[6] It is in these cases that courts must succumb to frustrating self-restraint, or manipulate their power to set bail in such a way as effectively to deny it. We do not have a satisfactory procedure to deal with these cases. Recently Chief Justice Warren ruled that on appeal bail may be denied in situations in which there is a strong showing that release

[5] State v. Mastrian, 326 Federal 2d 708.
[6] Carbo v. U.S., 825. Ct. 662.

would be abused in such a way as to threaten the community.[7]
Should this theory be articulated and applied to these criminal
cases, prior to trial? Or is it better to deal with the problem
outside the framework of the traditional bail system?

The cogent argument has been made that the strictly traditional purpose of bail should not bog down or eclipse a judge's
thinking; that rules are created only for general usefulness and
not as absolute strictures; and that the best test for this and
any judicial action is what is best in the balance of competing
interests and values in each specific case. Herman Goldstein,
who was then the executive assistant to the Chicago super-
intendent of police, articulated this sophisticated argument at
the 1964 National Bail Conference in these words:

> The use of the bail system to serve a purpose quite different from
> that which it was designed to serve has frustrated the efforts of
> those concerned with introducing some logic into our bail policies.
> Obviously, their problems would be greatly simplified if the use of
> bail were restricted to assuring the reappearance of the defendant
> for trial. But *employing a procedure designed for one purpose to
> serve quite a different purpose is not unusual in our criminal justice
> system. Rather, there is a pattern of adaptation of the system
> which, in a somewhat awkward manner, often fulfills socially
> acceptable goals which are not provided for by the legal system.
> The purpose which bail has come to serve may be without founda-
> tion in law, but they cannot be rejected for this reason without at
> least examining the needs which they fulfill.* [Italics added.]

One solution which has been used in cases presenting the
problem of the likely intimidation of witnesses is the material
witness bond. Here, to avoid dangers, we lock up the witness.
If you cannot *protect* the endangered party, then do the next
best thing and *detain him.* Leave the threatener alone, and
punish the likely victim. This is often done in important cases.

[7] Leigh v. U.S., 82 S. Ct. 994 (1962).

It is akin to, but essentially different from, protective custody. But the technique is somewhat self-defeating. If it is wrong to deprive the liberty of an accused, why is it less so to hold a witness or victim in protective custody? The answer that the latter person would go into custody voluntarily and out of his own self-interest is not accurate. Certainly, neither form of these types of detention would be the voluntary choice of any person. It is an ugly experience, and many cannot endure it long. Some would rather take their chance and run the risk of harassment than live in the fearful, unnatural custody of the police. As a stopgap measure in extreme cases, this material witness bond may be appropriate. As a general rule it is an obnoxious practice.

Though we have no adequate procedure for directly dealing with any of these difficult criminal cases, preventive detention is frequently practiced by judges through their denial of bail. To make this matter worse, it is very difficult for a defendant who has been abused by being incarcerated for preventive detention, or who wants to dispute whether he should have been imprisoned with or without good reason, to ever be able to prove this and seek redress. A clever judge will not articulate for the record why he has set bail at a certain unattainable amount or even why he has denied bail. Since his judgment is discretionary, the appellate courts will not upset his decision by reversing him unless the abuse is clear, far-reaching, and beyond reasonable allowance. This is very difficult to prove. Not only may the record be silent about his reasons for setting bail as he did, but it may also be deceptive. His true reasons can be shrouded in generalities apparently conforming with the rules governing discretionary bail. The criteria for setting bail are vague and general anyway, and only in the most extreme case could reversible abuse be proved.

The judicial dilemma created by the competing interests of

public safety and individual freedom are particularly perplexing in the context of the disposition of defendants before their trials in these certain kinds of criminal cases. It is presently impossible for judges to protect the public and the defendant adequately at this pretrial stage without abusing their bail powers in the process. It is a critical commentary upon our system of justice that this should be so. A suggestion for a more accommodating alternative will be made in Chapter VII.

THE ORGANIZED CRIMINAL

This problem of the dire need for a technique of preventive detention does not arise in the majority of the criminal cases in this country. But the issue does arise in a notably significant number of cases and, to make matters more difficult, in a large percentage of the most important and most notorious criminal cases.

A three and a half year experience as a prosecutor in Attorney General Kennedy's Organized Crime and Racketeering Section of the Department of Justice brought home a clear awareness of this frightening fact. Hovering over the prosecutor's preparation of most major racketeering cases is the real and serious concern that some person essential to the case is in danger. In some cases, witnesses are threatened; in some, they are injured; evidence may become unavailable or be destroyed. Many cases could never be brought to trial because prospective witnesses were too afraid to tell what they knew. Indeed, here lies a standard technique of the bigtime mobster. He creates a reputation that deters citizens from taking any action against him out of fear that he will take retaliatory action against them. This is the law of the jungle. In the history of almost every major racketeer's background is a series of charges which had to be dropped because witnesses backed down at the last minute out of fear or because witnesses disappeared or died before the case could be brought to trial.

One case which an associate tried is illustrative. A man was indicted in a large midwestern city for selling narcotics. While he was free on bail, the chief government witness was shot and seriously wounded on the steps in front of his house. The defendant and three others were indicted and tried for obstructing justice, based on the shooting of the witness. Though all were convicted, on appeal the conviction of the chief defendant was reversed. Eventually he was convicted of the original narcotics offense; but the wounded and terrified witness did not testify.

This type of problem is very serious, since the bigtime racketeer, the organized criminal, has both the money necessary to afford bail and the organization effectively to persuade witnesses not to testify. In one case in New York several years ago, a notorious defendant jumped bail in a narcotics case. He was caught and brought back. Very soon his codefendant, who was going to testify for the government, was found strangled. The case had to be dropped and the defendant released. In another narcotics case a codefendant, whom the mob suspected was going to testify for the government, was found strangled and burned in gasoline. The defendants were free on bail, but the victim was discovered many cities away. As usual, no proof existed to tie the other defendants to this crime. In one case in Minnesota the codefendant in a murder case confessed to the crime charged and in doing so implicated two other people. While he was free on bail he was told to recant his confession and exonerate the two others he had involved in the case. He refused. He was kidnaped and murdered. These examples are not unusual. Experience with these cases leads to the conclusion that one recurring characteristic of the worst racketeers is their ability to evade conviction and avoid trials by seeing to it that the incriminating witness or evidence becomes unavailable.

What is the judge to do in cases like these? Charges that a

defendant is too dangerous to let loose are rarely susceptible to empirical proof. And clearly anything less than the strongest evidence of prospective wrongdoing should not be the basis for pretrial imprisonment. That quantity or quality of evidence can rarely be shown. Yet, though incarcerating a bigtime racketeer does not guarantee that his organization will be deterred from harming witnesses, it is a step in the direction of protecting the public and the administration of justice.

The Cyclical and Recidivist Criminal

Another pertinent problem in many criminal cases is that the injection of extra financial demands in terms of bail and lawyers' fees upon certain kinds of criminals only causes them to commit further crimes to catch up economically with their expenses. The professional burglar, for example, will often ply his trade to make legal expenses. A district attorney in New York City described one stark case involving a young man with approximately twenty-five arrests for crimes involving burglary. He was arrested in June, 1963, for crimes involving five burglaries. He was indicted and freed on $7,500 bail. In September he was arrested again and held for possessing burglar's tools. He posted bail for $10,000 and was released. In October he was again indicted for burglary. He made bail of $5,000 and he was released. In November, he was charged with another similar crime. Bail was set at $10,000; he made bail and was released. In December, it all happened again, and bail was posted at $3,500. All these cases are now pending. Obviously bail served no purpose at all. But no procedure existed for proper deterrence of the on-going crimes of this young man.

Narcotics cases often give rise to cyclical crimes, too. A retired New York City police detective whose career had been in the narcotics bureau pointed out that since judges usually give concurrent sentences for repeated crimes, the "pushers" sell all they can while on bail because they need the money and they feel that they really have nothing to lose. Since they may go to jail anyway, and since their sentence would probably be the same for one or several illegal sales, they feel that they can, with impunity, continue their criminal activities.

The burglar will steal and the narcotics pusher will sell more "junk" to pay for his bail or his lawyer. Thus bail may create a cycle of crimes.

In other cases a defendant may commit crimes compulsively while free on bail. Similar to the cyclical criminal, but presenting still a different problem, is the recidivist criminal, the kind who may compulsively continue his criminal conduct whenever he is free. This person may be a pathologically irresponsible character for whom only diagnostic and medical incarceration would be proper, or a professional criminal who candidly is in "business" all the time he is free. The former cannot resist crime; the latter is so deeply enmeshed in the life of crime that he has nothing else to do and nothing to lose. At the National Bail Conference in 1964, the case of Anthony Massari was described as an example of a recidivism case properly calling for preventive detention:

Massari was released from the Illinois State Penitentiary upon completion of a three-year term for burglary and armed robbery in 1961. On July 8, 1963, Massari was apprehended in the act of committing a burglary. He was indicted and released on bail totalling $7,500. On August 24, 1963, while free on bail, the subject was apprehended in the commission of a second burglary and was found to have in his possession the proceeds of still another burglary committed earlier in the day. He was indicted on two counts of burglary and released on $4,500 bail. The subject was again arrested on November 18, 1963, when he was found to be in possession of a loaded firearm and burglary tools. On January

16, 1964, he was arrested in the act of committing a burglary and found to have the proceeds of two other burglaries in his possession. He was indicted the following day and released on $15,000 bail, only to be again arrested on the same afternoon while committing still another burglary for which he was indicted and bail set at $5,000. Subsequently, he was arrested on February 8, 1964, with release on bail set at $10,000; again on February 21, 1964, with release on bail of $5,000; and again on March 5, 1964, when bail was set at $5,000.

On April 24, 1964, when Massari went to trial, he had been arrested nine times in the period from July 8, 1963, to March 5, 1964, indicted on ten counts, and was free on $48,500 in bail. He entered a guilty plea to the 10 indictments and was sentenced from five to fifteen years in the penitentiary on each count—the sentences to run concurrently.

A case involving the question of possible pathological recidivism was described in a spring, 1964, issue of the *Baltimore Sun*. A twenty-two-year-old man was convicted of possessing stolen mail matter. While free on bail before his trial and conviction for that crime, he was arrested for passing a stolen check. Freed again on bail for that second charge, he passed a series of checks using a stolen credit card for identification. He was arrested a third time. It was discovered that he had stolen other checks, too, and used them to open accounts upon which he wrote subsequent checks. A presentence medical report suggested that he was in need of psychiatric treatment. Indeed, in many of these cases of repeated offenses while on bail, it later develops that psychiatric confinement originally would have been proper. This kind of consideration is an aspect of the bail hearing which is nonexistent today. Its incorporation as part of the pretrial process will be discussed fully in the conclusion of this book.

In another case in March, 1964, a man was indicted for

kidnaping, raping, and robbing a twenty-two-year-old woman. In November, 1963, only five months earlier, he had been indicted for robbery, larceny, and burglary, and was freed after making bail of $15,000. A month later he was accused of making indecent phone calls to prominent women whose pictures he allegedly cut out of local newspapers. The judge in that case set bail at $2,000 for each of seventeen charges. The defendant appealed and bail was reduced from $34,000 to $10,000. He put up this amount of bail and was released. A few months later he was charged with rape, kidnaping, and a $10 robbery. Investigation showed that he had been court-martialed in the past for attacking a woman. A psychiatric evaluation showed that he possessed long-standing deviant sexual interests. Again, some alternative other than jail or bail ought to have been available, both from the standpoints of the defendant and society.

The cases of the benign and kindly kleptomaniac or the vicious pathological rapist, and many others between these two extremes, call for some pretrial control. Release is certain to lead to further crime; imprisonment may be cruel and useless. There must be a better way to deal with these cases than we have used so far. The denial or granting of bail is clearly not the best answer.

SUBVERSION CASES

The problem of preventive detention arises in the subversion cases, too. A number of these cases were discussed in Chapter III, but the problem these cases raise is again pertinent here. It is unrealistically simple to suggest that withholding bail or making it unattainably high in loyalty cases is beyond the legal power of the court. In the past, prosecuting officials in subversion cases have often argued that it was of the utmost national importance that defendants in this class of case should be incarcerated before trial. In reply it has been argued that these prosecutors are vindictive, and feel the way they do because they harbor paranoid fears and fantasies about the nature of the Communist conspiracy. To evaluate the accuracy of this charge is to enter into speculation which should be less the subject of inquiry than the propriety and legality of their proposal. It is time the problem was faced in a judicious way.

One must recognize that in these specific cases there is a unique dilemma facing the court because there is a basis for special worry. Experience has demonstrated that some defendants in subversion cases will jump bail and flee to political sanctuary. It is no wonder that they do. The usual natural deterrents to flight do not exist in subversion cases. These defendants have no natural ties to the community. Quite the contrary. And the loss of some money is not likely to keep them either. Their political party often will pay the bail. The prospect to these defendants of an American jail is probably viewed with a special anathema. Moreover, some of these defendants might be capable of conduct that would be seriously dangerous to the national security of this country. And to allow them freedom is to increase their opportunity to continue their work. Examples of these cases were offered in Chapter III.

Denying bail in these loyalty or subversion cases can rest on one of two general grounds: that the defendant is likely to commit other similar crimes (similar to that with which he is charged, though not yet convicted), or secondly, that the defendant will jump bail and run away to a country from which he could not be extradited (extradition treaties ordinarily do not provide for political crimes). In this latter case, bail could be denied or set extraordinarily high on a proper, legal ground. It is the accepted predicate for bail that the amount of bail should relate to the inducement to return for trial. If in these cases it is necessary to set bail extraordinarily high, or to deny bail because otherwise there would not be a defendant at the trial, this would be consistent with the very fundamental purpose of bail. If this kind of pretrial detention worked some hardship on a defendant, that could be written off as an inevitability of the system.

However, in the former case, where the fear is that the defendant will commit more crimes, the answers become more complicated. All the arguments for and against detention to deter crime, which were expressed earlier in this chapter, would apply again here in equal force. They are, in fact, complicated both by the emotional content of these cases and the fantastic proportions of the potential crimes of treason or sabotage.

In a case entitled *Williamson v. U.S.*,[8] which Justice Jackson decided while he was sitting as circuit justice for the Second Circuit Court of Appeals, the issue of preventive detention came up in the context of a subversion case. Certain Communist leaders had been convicted for Smith Act violations, for conspiring to advocate and teach violent overthrow of the United States government. They appealed the case to the Supreme Court and asked to be allowed to go free on bail pending their appeal. The prosecution asked that the court deny the request and revoke their pretrial bail on the ground that the defendants while at large had continued to pursue a course of conduct and activity that was dangerous to the public welfare, safety, and national security. The misconduct feared by the government attorneys involved the making of speeches and the writing of articles for the Communist *Daily Worker*. (One can envision cases where this issue would be more difficult, such as where the conduct feared was physical

[8] 184 Federal 2d. 280, 282–3 (1950).

rather than intellectual, and more clearly and imminently dangerous to the nation.) Justice Jackson considered the issue of preventive detention under these circumstances and ruled:

The Government's contention is that defendants, by misbehavior after conviction, have forfeited their claim to bail. Grave public danger is said to result from what they may be expected to do, in addition to what they have done since their conviction. If I assume that defendants are disposed to commit every opportune disloyal act helpful to Communist countries, it is still difficult to reconcile with traditional American law the jailing of persons by the courts because of anticipated but as yet uncommitted crimes. *Imprisonment to protect society from predicted but unconsummated offenses is so unprecedented in this country and so fraught with danger of excesses and injustice that I am loath to resort to it,* even as a discretionary judicial technique to supplement conviction of such offenses as those of which defendants stand convicted. [Italics added.]

The agonizing intellectual rigor demanded of a patriotic and conscientious judge like Justice Jackson in a case like this was evident in the Justice's concluding words in his opinion in this case:

My task would be simple if a judge were free to order persons imprisoned because he thinks their opinions are obnoxious, their motives evil and that free society would be bettered by their absence. The plea of admitted Communist leaders for liberties and rights here, which they deny to all persons wherever they have seized power, is so hypocritical that it can fairly and dispassionately be judged only with effort.

But the right of every American to equal treatment before the law is wrapped up in the same constitutional bundle with those of these Communists. If in anger or disgust with these defendants we throw out the bundle, we also cast aside protection for the liberties of more worthy critics who may be in opposition to the government of some future day.

To have decided this issue any other way, Justice Jackson stated, could have a "disastrous effect on the reputation of American justice," for what would happen if the conviction were reversed on appeal? "Under no circumstances," he concluded, "must we permit their symbolization of an evil force in the world to be hallowed and glorified by any semblance of martyrdom. The way to avoid that risk is not to jail these men until it is finally decided that they should stay jailed."

Not all subversion-type cases raise the clear need for preventive detention. Those cases involving violence, sabotage, or treason do demand some special control of the defendants. The others might be dealt with in the same manner as other criminal charges. Some procedure to cope with both these classes of subversion cases will be suggested in the concluding chapter.

Having pointed out the vexing, complicated nature of this dilemma, and having shown some illustrative examples of some of the various cases where the problem arises, one can return to the basic question: Considering all of the competing interests involved, what is the best resolution? Should we leave matters as they are and resolve particular conflicts with specific compromises in the context of our present bail system? Or is there some other way to deal with this recurring, problematical situation, a way that would avoid or better resolve the perplexing issues raised by bail and the practice of preventive detention? An answer to this, the most difficult question for one who is critical of the current bail system, will be offered in the concluding chapter. There an attempt will be made to propose a system which would improve upon and liberalize the ordinary bail case while providing a procedure to deal with these special cases where preventive detention seems appropriate.

CHAPTER V

Alternatives to the Bail System

In the past several years there has been an awakening to the inadequacies and unfairnesses of the traditional American bail system. Recently, both the Department of Justice and the United States Senate have begun to move for reform in the sphere of the federal law. In some states inquiries are being made into various possibilities for change. In certain cities innovative bail reform programs have begun, are catching on, and are spreading. The ROR and summons work of the Vera Foundation in New York City, and a number of ROR (release on recognizance) programs in the courts of several cities, the program now being tried on a test basis in Illinois, and the Tulsa Bar Association's new program are in the vanguard of this reform movement.

VERA

Any consideration of modern bail reform must begin with a look at the work of the Vera Foundation in New York City. Its story is testimony of both the basic and fundamental fallacy of the traditional American bail system and the probably narrowing but still hearteningly limitless amount of good that can be done by a few men with a good idea.

In 1960 a chemical engineer and industrialist named Louis Schweitzer was taken through a Brooklyn detention prison by Commissioner of Correction Anna Kross of New York City.

Mr. Schweitzer was shocked by and indignant at what he observed. He learned that some people were held in pretrial detention for periods up to a year because they could not afford bail. Adolescents (sixteen to twenty) were thrown into men's prison with hardened criminals. The facilities were worse than those provided for convicted prisoners who were serving their sentences in state prisons. Encounters like this happen all the time. But Louis Schweitzer was more than appalled. He was moved. Not being familiar with the workings of the criminal part of the American judicial process, Schweitzer discussed this situation with people who were. There was no reason at all, he felt, why men should be punished for their poverty, or why those who were wealthy enough to afford bail could go free while the economically disadvantaged had to suffer the indignity and privation of imprisonment without regard to their guilt or innocence, their reliability to appear for trial, or their dangerousness to society. He discovered that, in 1960, 114,653 people were detained before trial in New York City, and of these only 30,827 were subsequently convicted and given jail sentences. The others served time in prison for no other reason than their poverty.

At first, Schweitzer thought of establishing a fund to pay the bail for those people who were worthwhile risks but who could not afford to pay for the bail bonds upon which their freedom was conditioned.

This idea was eventually abandoned as misaimed. It would have treated the symptoms and not the disease. He would rather, he concluded, attempt to change the basic thinking about bail than perpetuate a bad system. He decided that, if he paid the bail costs for indigents who were good risks but could not afford bail bonds, he would be supporting what he had concluded to be the basic erroneous flaw in the bail system, that reliance upon money is a valid criterion for pretrial release. Instead, he felt that it would be both better and fairer to find a workable way to release individuals on their own personal responsibility. He felt that a way could be found to help courts decide whether men were responsible and trustworthy by setting up a system to investigate their backgrounds. However, there was no way of knowing then whether this would be a reliable alternative to the safeguards provided by bail. It seemed like a good idea, but even among those who were critical of the bail system, a number were skeptical about whether this plan would be really effective. This quandary and the motivating idea for Vera was described to the Senate Subcommittee on Constitutional Rights by Herbert Sturz, the executive director of Vera:

Months of study preceded our first day in court. Our early thought was to provide a revolving bail fund which would be available to indigent defendants. But helping the poor to buy their freedom is no solution; it merely perpetuates reliance upon money as the criterion for release. We wanted to break the pattern and stimulate a more basic change in bail thinking. The release of greater numbers on their own recognizance appeared the broadest and most potentially valuable approach. We decided to test the hypothesis that a greater number of defendants could be successfully released in this way if verified information about their stability and community roots could be presented to the court. This was the goal of Vera Foundation's first undertaking: the Manhattan Bail Project.

Eventually, Schweitzer created and endowed a charitable organization which he named "Vera" after his mother. The Vera Foundation was established in 1961 to further equal protection of the laws, inquire into law enforcement, aid the indigent accused, and develop programs to further "law, justice, and civil liberties in the United States."

Supervised Release

Vera's first undertaking was the Manhattan Bail Project, which the New York Times has called ". . . a quiet experiment in human trust." It was begun in October, 1961, by Vera with the cooperation of New York University Law School and its Institute of Judicial Administration. The project was, according to Herbert Sturz, "based on the hypothesis that the courts will be willing to grant release on recognizance—release on one's honor pending trial, called 'pretrial parole' in New York—instead of setting bail if they can be given verified information about a defendant's reliability and his roots in the community." After much careful planning and many preparatory meetings with judges, prosecuting officials, defense lawyers, educators, and city officials, the Manhattan Bail Project was launched.

This is how it works: The Vera staff is provided with an office high in the Criminal Court building in Manhattan. The detention pens for the felony part of the Magistrates Court for New York City is ten floors below. Each morning prisoners are brought into this detention area prior to their appearance in court. It is here and at this time that the Manhattan Bail Project swings into action. Under Herbert Sturz's direction, New York University law students, who are employed full time by Vera while they attend night school, interview about thirty recently arrested defendants in the detention pens just prior to their arraignment. The Department of Correction provides Vera with a small cell in which these interviews are held. The prisoners' permission is first requested, but almost all are happy to be helped. In fact, only about 1 per cent refuse to be interviewed. The interviewers ask a series of questions that are listed on a form, and record the defendant's answers. The questions are aimed at establishing the individual's community ties, whether he is a good pretrial parole risk and whether he could be reasonably trusted, if released on merely his word, to return for trial. Originally, defendants charged with homicide, narcotics, or sex offenses were not eligible for consideration, although recently some experiments with narcotics and sex crime defendants have been successful. Within a few minutes the defendant is asked a series of questions about his residence, family, job, background, prior criminal record, and associations. His answers are scored by the Vera personnel according to a set formula. Originally, Vera's basis for decision was subjective. Now it is quite refined. A point-weighting system is used. The defendant's responses to Vera's questions are scored in points, and, to be recommended for release by Vera, the individual must score a certain total of points. While at first Vera was recommending about 29 per cent of those interviewed, they are now recommending about 65 per cent.

Here is an example of how the system works, as recently described to a Senate subcommittee by Sturz:

[One suspect] is charged in 1964 with felonious assault and S. 1897 of the N.Y. Penal Code (possession of a concealed weapon). His prior criminal record consists of a felonious assault charge which was reduced to simple assault, for which he received 30 days suspended sentence in 1952. In 1957 he was convicted of driving while intoxicated and his sentence was $100 fine or 30 days. He couldn't post the fine, and went to jail. In 1961 he was convicted on a disorderly conduct charge, and got a suspended sentence.

He is 35 years old, has been living at his present residence for 6 months with his wife and child, and has a verified previous one year residence in Manhattan. He has been working as a counterman in a restaurant for the past 3 months, and his previous job has been verified as lasting 3 years. His current employer says he is a good worker. If he is released on recognizance, the employer will volunteer to help him get to court. But the employer adds, "If he isn't back to work by tomorrow I'll have to hire someone else."

Should [the suspect] be recommended for ROR? Well, this is how we calculate his score:

−1 point for three misdemeanor convictions
+2 points for a stable residence
+2 points for family ties
+2 points for good ratings on present and prior jobs
[The suspect] totals 5 points.
Although this is a minimum score, he would be recommended for parole.

Examples of Vera's forms used in the evaluation and supervision process appear at the end of this section.

The information provided by the prisoner is then checked for accuracy by one of the Vera staff. This is usually done quickly over the telephone or sometimes right at the visitor's section of the courtroom. An interview takes about ten minutes, and the verification takes less than an hour. If by Vera standards the defendant is a good risk, a summary is made of the gathered information. Copies of this summary report are provided for the arraigning judge, the district attorney, and the defense lawyer (usually a legal aid lawyer) who reads the recommendation into the record.

To test the validity of its theory and the efficacy of its work, Vera did not recommend pretrial parole for all the defendants who were eligible by these standards. A control group was segregated, and in some cases no action was taken by Vera except to keep records about the fate of those in this control group. Thus their fate could be charted alongside the fate of those for whom Vera did take action, though both groups were qualified for recommendations for release by Vera standards. The purpose was to see how accused persons who met Vera's criteria for release fared without a Vera recommendation.

The action that Vera does take is simply to recommend release on recognizance in those cases where it appears appropriate, based upon Vera criteria, and to provide the court with the summarized information which supports their recommendation. Ordinarily, the arraigning judge knows only the defendant's name and prior police record. Vera provides additional factual background information relevant to the key questions facing the court at arraignment: What assurance is there that this defendant will show up at trial if he is let free now? And upon what reliable facts can this prediction be made?

From the beginning, the results of this experimental pilot project have been clear and convincing. Of the first hundred cases disposed of where Vera recommended release and it was granted, sixty were acquitted or released, thirty received suspended sentences, and six received only a fine. Only four were ultimately given jail sentences after trial and conviction. Of the first three hundred cases where Vera recommended pretrial parole, two hundred were in fact granted parole, and of those, only two did not appear for trial. This nonappearance rate was better than analogous statistics of defendants who were released on bail. But Vera was conservative during the first days of its program. Sturz reported that "During the first month of the Manhattan Bail Project we found that 25 percent of those interviewed qualified for pretrial parole. Nine months later we were recommending parole for close to 50 percent of those interviewed." Now about 65 per cent of those interviewed are recommended for pretrial parole by Vera.

Defendants have not changed. But Vera is now more confident of its original thesis and it has the proof to bear out its high hopes. Back in the planning stages some magistrates had argued that the Vera approach was wrong, that it would do a disservice to society by turning loose defendants who were likely to commit more crimes. When the Manhattan Bail Project began, the courts were cautious, following Vera recommendations only about 50 per cent of the time. Today, the courts follow Vera's suggestions about 70 per cent of the time. The district attorneys also have displayed faith in Vera's discretion. Originally, the district attorneys concurred in Vera's recommendations about 50 per cent of the time; now they concur with Vera about 80 per cent of the time. Originally, Vera dealt only in the felony part of the Magistrate's Court; now it operates in the felony, misdemeanor, and adolescent parts of Manhattan's Criminal Court. During the first year of the project, Vera was responsible for the release of about five defendants a week; now Vera is averaging about seventy released defendants a week. During the first three years of the Manhattan Bail Project over 10,000 defendants were interviewed and approximately 3,500 defendants were released on their own recognizance due to Vera's work. Of these 98.5 per cent appeared in court for trial when they were supposed to. Almost three times as many defendants who were on bail during this period failed to appear for trial. This experience has provided good proof that a sound and sensitive investigation of a defendant's background is a more reliable criterion for pretrial release than is his ability to afford bail.

Vera also has proved that even amongst those who fail to appear in court at the appointed time, some are less delinquent than naïve or uninformed. Vera makes it its business to follow up on those defendants whom it recommends for parole. A letter (in the language of the defendant) or a phone call, or even a visit, can avoid failures to appear which are the inevitable results of mistake or ignorance. Just a little care by someone in society can easily convert what may appear to be outlawry into conformity and cooperation.

The control groups of those whom Vera would have recommended but did not recommend due to their calculated random selection for the purpose of comparison has now been dropped from Vera practice. Its point was proved. Herbert Sturz was able to report recently that "While the court granted pretrial parole in 60 per cent of the Project's recommended cases, it did so in only 14 per cent of the parallel cases in the control group. In other words, judges paroled four times as many accused persons with the aid of verified information." And 60 per cent of those recommended by Vera for pretrial parole were not convicted, while only 23 per cent of the comparative control group were not convicted. Finally, in the group recommended for parole by Vera, of the 40 per cent who were found guilty, only one out of six went to jail, while in the control group, of those 77 per cent who were convicted, 90 per cent were given jail sentences. Since the same criteria were applied and the same results were reached for both groups by Vera, "verification" to the court could be said to have made the difference between release and detention before and after trial for a significant number of defendants. These statistics, therefore, are not subject to the questions that might be raised concerning the comparison of Vera defendants with defendants who were treated in the ordinary ways. As far as Vera was concerned, all these defendants warranted pretrial release. Those they recommended for release fared much better than those they did not recommend, in terms of those released, those convicted, and those sentenced to prison. The only question that can be asked about the efficacy of Vera's intervention is whether their failure to recommend worked to prejudice these defendants.

There are presently indications which, although admittedly lacking in conclusive, empirical proof, indicate that the conclusion implicit in Vera's results is true: Dependants fare better at trial and in their sentences after trial and conviction when they have been free before trial. If accepted, this startling revelation would mean that the innate inadequacies of the current bail system so compound themselves that a defendant who is free before trial has a better chance for acquittal or, if convicted, for a suspended or nonjail sentence. This matter is under investigation now by Vera. The indications so far, although admittedly lacking in complete development and refinement, are that the court's original decision about freedom before trial follows a defendant throughout the trial process, in a prejudicial way.

It is submitted that there is a deep and far-reaching truth to be gathered from Vera's experience. Aside from Vera's accomplishments in low "jumping" statistics (its utilitarian success), and its significant savings to the city (its economic success), the humanitarian aspect of Vera's work is perhaps most noteworthy. Out of the first 2,800 cases of pretrial release based on "Vera-fication," the following were the case dispositions: In 47 per cent of the total cases, the defendants were acquitted or the charges were dismissed; 53 per cent of these defendants were convicted. Of these convicted defendants, 72 per cent received suspended sentences, and only 8 per cent were given prison sentences. The other 20 per cent of those found guilty received fines. Only 114 men, out of 2,802 who were ROR'd with the help of Vera, ended up in jail. Of the 2,802 defendants, 2,688 might have been in prison prior to their trials for, in retrospect at least, no reason.

Are these statistics deceptive? Are there other criteria which must be added to Vera's figures in order to garner the truest message from Vera's work? Is the comparison of Vera to the traditional bail system loaded, stilted, or unfairly presented? These questions and others ought to be considered now because they bear upon the validity and meaning of Vera's experience.

The Vera reports show that they apply the same criteria for deciding who should be released on personal recognizance as do most bondsmen. The latter apply these criteria related to community ties and personal background in a less formalized, institutionalized, or social-scientific way. But a recent survey of bondsmen around the country (by one attorney for the Department of Justice) disclosed that the bondsmen do use these criteria subjectively in making their personal decisions about providing bond for individuals. The idea that community ties are a key to a good release risk is generally conceded.

Most bondsmen are cynical of Vera's statistics, which indicate that those defendants on bail "jumped" three times as often as did "Vera-fied" defendants during the same time and at the same place. The skeptic will point out that after Vera takes the best of the lot for their statistics, the bondsmen take what is left. And what is left is, by Vera's own exclusive standards, a group not worth releasing on trust. It is this kind of person for whom the bondsman is the key to pretrial freedom. Those who have questioned Vera for frequently refusing to recommend for release fail to acknowledge that bondsmen often refuse, too, and for reasons having less to do with the risk of flight. The further argument is made that because the bondsman has money at stake, he is more anxious than Vera to release the right people and return the wrong ones, since Vera can write off their mistakes as experience. This is simply not borne out by the comparable results of Vera and bonded defendants.

One could also question whether Vera defendants would have appeared for trial without "Vera-fication." And, when Vera rejected a defendant, was his bail ever lowered by the court, or was his release attained in any other way? If so, in these two classes of cases, Vera might be unnecessary. Another question that could be raised is whether the failure of Vera to recommend release itself prejudices other defendants? Out of almost a thousand arrests each day, Vera aids in the release of only a relative few. What about the rest? One can also question Vera's role in the cases of wealthy or middle-class defendants. Since Vera ignores them, if they do not have sufficient personal wealth they may have only the bondsman to turn to for help.

The obvious answer to some of these inquiries is that any overall system of reform must, of course, deal equally with all defendants. Vera was modest in its initial programs for reasons of politics, economics, and other pragmatic demands. No Vera agent has ever advocated justice solely for the poor, only that reform should properly begin where it is most needed. Vera is not the absolute answer to our questionable bail system, but it does provide key evidence of a basic and important truth which should be used in formulating an overall answer. Obviously any systematic program adopted by the law ought to cover all defendants.

Another question about the interpretation of Vera's statistics can be raised. If those out on bail are less frequently indicted, convicted, and imprisoned than those in jail before trial, is not society better off with all defendants in jail? Is there some obvious relationship between poverty and crime which accounts for the statistics showing more convictions against those who cannot afford bail? If this is so, then does Vera do a disservice in securing releases? If the guilty plea is a by-product of pretrial detention (as is indicated), does this mean that pleas are being coerced, or is it more likely that this proves that pretrial detention is an effective way to resolve crimes and expeditiously dispose of cases? Is the injustice not one of wrongful incarceration as Vera argues, but rather one of wrongful release prior to trial? Are the acquittals of released defendants miscarriages of justice, more so than the conviction of incarcerated defendants?

I do not know an irrefutable answer to these wry questions. One response is that not all defendants are guilty, and our social and legal values do not condone punishing many inno-

cent people to assure the punishment of *some* guilty people.
Yet this would be the necessary concomitant of a system that
incarcerated all defendants in order to raise the odds of con-
victing the guilty. It is more likely that the truth behind Vera's
figures is that pretrial incarceration may itself have prejudicial
side effects, and hence the relative conviction statistics. There
are also metaphysical issues which can be raised concerning the
relative injustices to innocent men under the present bail
system compared to those against society at large which might
be occasioned without it, and the proper amount of injustice
which a social system simply must sustain as the price of its
less-than-perfect existence. I leave these questions with their
mere mention, as their exact answers are beyond the kind and
quality of proof needed for present purposes. The philosophy
behind the proposed overall solution in Chapter VII actually
includes value judgments about these issues.

The validity of the theory about the prejudices running from
pretrial detention was bolstered by a recent report of a study
which analyzed the basis of Vera's release program.[1] This
fascinating report was based on the Vera program during one
year, October, 1961, through September, 1962.

The report first found that defendants who were in jail
continuously between the times of arrest and final adjudication
received unfavorable dispositions much more often than did
those who were free on bail during all or part of that period.
For example, defendants in jail were 20 per cent more likely
to be convicted. And 64 per cent of 358 defendants jailed from
arraignment to adjudication were sentenced to prison while 17
per cent of 374 who made bail and were free during this time
received prison sentences. The nature and type of the crime
charged showed little relationship to detention. These figures

[1] Rankin, "The Effect of Pretrial Detention," 39 *New York University Law
Review* 641 (1964).

still leave questions about the impact of variables other than the detention itself.

The report did examine the effect of the addition of certain other ingredients to see if their presence or absence altered the final disposition of bailed and jailed defendants. It was found that the existing differences did not disappear or decrease appreciably because of the addition of any of five tested characteristics: the existence of a previous record, the amount of bail, the type of defense counsel, the defendant's family integration, and the defendant's employment stability.

The reporter concluded from the statistics gathered that those defendants who were in jail before trial were more likely to receive jail sentences than were bailed defendants, regardless of whether they had been previously arrested or convicted. The implied conclusion is that the existence of a previous criminal record itself would not vary the difference between the disposition of bailed and jailed defendants.

It was also concluded that bailed defendants received fewer prison sentences than did jailed defendants—regardless of the amount of bail. However, the amount of bail did raise a perplexing question. Could the relationship between pretrial detention and ultimate disposition have reflected the fact that there are special qualities about high-bail defendants which (prejudicial effects aside) make it likely both that they would be detained and that they would receive prison sentences? If so, the mere fact that they are in jail before trial because they cannot afford bail may not be the important factor in any equation. If the likelihood of guilt was great, and bail was unattainably high as a result, then pretrial incarceration was less a causal condition for conviction than had been indicated. The author of the report concluded otherwise. Among low-bail defendants who received prison sentences, 54 per cent had been detained and 12 per cent were free on bail, a difference of

42 per cent. Among high-bail defendants the figures were 68 per cent and 25 per cent, a difference of 43 per cent. These differences were only slightly smaller than those where the bail amount was held constant. (There it was 47 per cent.) Therefore, the reporter's conclusion was that ". . . detained persons are more likely to be sentenced to prison than bail persons, regardless of whether high or low bail amounts had been set." The report conceded that a person on high bail is less likely to make bail and therefore is more likely to receive a prison sentence because of the consequent pretrial incarceration. Assumedly this means that though pretrial detention leads to post-trial sentences regardless of the amount of bail which led to the pretrial detention, there are more of both kinds of detention in the high bail cases.

The type of counsel a defendant had, although it might appear to be a likely point of differential, was not in these instances. Bailed defendants who had private counsel received prison sentences 16 per cent of the time compared to jailed defendants who were sentenced 60 per cent of the time. The difference was 44 per cent. Bailed defendants with court-appointed attorneys received jail sentences 21 per cent of the time; jailed defendants did 64 per cent of the time, a difference of 43 per cent. These differences between the dispositions of bailed and jailed defendants were comparable to the difference (47 per cent) before the type of representation was held constant. The conclusion one can draw from these figures is that the kind of attorney may make a difference, but that the differences are the same with regard to bailed and jailed defendants. Therefore it is the pretrial status itself that remains the key differential in the ultimate disposition of these cases.

Neither family integration nor employment stability bore a marked relationship to disposition, according to this study.

The two factors were strongly related to pretrial detention (as would be likely), but were themselves less strongly related to ultimate disposition than the other three characteristics. Of course this relation to pretrial detention would have had an effect thereafter, since that status has been shown to have continuing impact throughout the trial process. These two factors also undoubtedly affected the other three, and therefore had other incalculable effects upon disposition.

In sum, these five characteristics taken into account separately did not appreciably alter the disposition of jailed or bailed defendants. The conclusion of the report was that *these* characteristics alone do not provide a notable relationship between detention before trial and unfavorable disposition after trial. Even when considered in combination, they accounted for only a small impact upon final disposition. These findings strongly support the notion that a causal relationship *does* exist between the factor of pretrial detention alone and unfavorable final disposition. This conclusion supports general, and thorough-going reform of the bail system as much as it corroborates the validity of Vera's theory.

While not scientifically conclusive, the Vera results to date do indicate at least that investigation is helpful in determining whom to release; that supervision without detention can be quite effective in assuring the presence of defendants at trials; that the availability of money for a bond premium is not necessarily related to whether a defendant will flee; that most defendants will appear for trial voluntarily if humanely assisted; and that a tremendous amount of pretrial detention is unnecessary and wasteful to the state, and terribly prejudicial to the defendant.

Fortunately the results of the Manhattan Bail Project are not limited to the approximately 3,500 individuals who became the beneficiaries of its noble experiment. The Vera Foundation proved its point. Now New York City is appropriating money to enable the city's Probation Office to take over the work which Vera was doing. In January, 1964, the New York City Board of Estimate appropriated $181,600 to the Office of Probation to take over Vera's work. Moreover, the Vera program has spread to the criminal courts of other nearby counties. In fact, cities all over the country are beginning programs modeled after the Manhattan Bail Project. New York City has incorporated Vera's procedures into the courts of the city's five boroughs. Experimental projects fashioned after Vera are underway in Chicago, Des Moines, Denver, Albuquerque, Los Angeles, San Francisco, Syracuse, St. Louis, Orlando, Charlestown, and the District of Columbia. Plans for more projects are underway in thirty-five cities in twenty states. Vera has become a nationwide counselor to other places that want to emulate this mode of bail reform. Plans are underway for Vera to serve as a coordinating center for incipient programs around the country. All of Vera's experience and information is readily available, and soon field representatives will be able to travel around the country and give personal assistance in starting new programs.

And in large part, Vera's Manhattan project awoke the country to the inequities and waste of the bail system. Much of the national reform which has begun is due to the stimulus provided by Vera. Its results were praiseworthy, and the press has given it deservedly good coverage. When the vastly influential United States Department of Justice sponsored the first National Bail Conference in May, 1964, the cosponsor was the Vera Foundation. And Vera has not stopped with this one bail-reform program.

THE SUMMONS

The summons is commonly used in minor cases to simply bring a case to disposition. The summons expeditiously charges one with an offense and as quickly as possible releases him without jail, bail, or the cranking up and invocation of the whole judicial machinery. (The parking ticket is the most obvious example of this.) The arrest and bail process is replaced by a simple matter of paper work. Through this simple, nonpenal substitute, one is notified to appear for trial. Already used in millions of minor cases, the expanded use of the summons into misdemeanor cases or the more serious felonies is a potential solution to some of the problems caused by the bail system.

A summons can be used by the court or the police to substitute for arrest and bail. In a majority of the states and in all federal courts, summonses may be issued by lower-court judges instead of arrest warrants at the time of the complaint or after indictment. Local practice determines whether it can be used as an alternative to arrests in misdemeanor cases or felony cases, or both. Its use (on the increase around the country) spares the police and the courts administrative troubles and allows the defendant to avoid the punitive aspects of pretrial detention. Police summonses also may be issued at the time of arrest where the police are not required by law to seek arrest authority from a court first. The authority exists in the majority of American jurisdictions for on-the-spot arrests in misdemeanor cases; but police summons authority along with or in lieu of arrest and bail does not exist in most places. Police summonses could be used in a variety of instances: instead of arrest, on-the-spot but after an arrest, and in the police station sometime shortly after the arrest.

Increased use of the on-the-street summons is being considered now in certain places as an alternative to arrest and the later issuance of a summons at the police station. One potential problem may exist with this projected practice. In big cities, tens and even hundreds of thousands of arrests are made each year. If the local cop on the beat is given the power to decide between jail or a summons in this large number of cases, great opportunities for graft and abuse would be created. So far, this fear has not been borne out. However, the experiments to date have been conducted under restrictive and carefully observed conditions. What might happen if the practice became more far-flung and inevitably less controlled is impossible to predict. Millions of summonses are already used each year in minor traffic-variety cases, and this experience raises some legitimate fears of potential abuse. Assuming no administrative difficulties such as this, on-the-street summonses could be the technique of the future. With criminal information computerized, a policeman could easily obtain enough facts upon which to determine whether a summons would be more appropriate than arrest.

Vera has recently begun a project aimed at evaluating the use of a station-house summons to replace arrest and bail. This technique, though something less than on-the-spot release, nevertheless avoids the problems of arrest and bail quickly (if not immediately) and significantly (if not completely). If instead of arresting a person who is charged with a crime, the police quickly issued that person a summons calling for his appearance at arraignment or trial, there would be no need for bail or any of its substitutes. The defendant would have been ordered to appear for trial without having been kept in prolonged custody. Vera is trying out this technique now with the cooperation of the New York City Police Department. Writing in the *New York Times Magazine* on July 26, 1964, Gertrude Samuels optimistically reported this new program: "Now the new Manhattan Summons Project adds a dramatic dimension to the Bail Project, testing this proposition: many defendants can be safely released *in the very first stage*—by converting an arrest into a simple 'summons to appear.' "

The Manhattan Summons Project, begun in March, 1964,

incorporates the Vera technique at the local precinct police station. The project begins in point of time when the formal arrest is about to take place. Vera personnel are stationed at the police station. Then, with the cooperation of the police, and in only certain specific kinds of cases, the Vera staff conducts its interviews of defendants to establish eligibility for disposition of the case through a summons instead of arrest. The desk officer at the police station is the final decision-maker, but he uses the Vera report much in the same way as do the judges under the Vera bail project. If the summons is used, Vera assumes the similar supervisory role to assure the defendant's presence. This procedure is all accomplished in a matter of minutes or hours, and it avoids the penal aspects of this early part of the criminal process. In Miss Samuels' words: "During these interviews the mood of the prisoners shifts from hostility and suspicion to glimmering hope. Perhaps it is the need to talk to someone—perhaps it is the lack of uniformed and official brusqueness—not one prisoner has refused to cooperate."

Between April, 1964, and January, 1965, 848 cases were considered under this program: 664 petit larcenies, 57 assaults, and 127 disorderly conduct cases. Vera-recommended summonses were issued in 246, 25, and 44 of these specific groups of cases. Vera's recommendations were made in 67 per cent of the cases they surveyed. The police rejected the recommendations in only a few of these cases. Of these test cases, only a small fraction of the ultimate dispositions included jail sentences. Most cases resulted in suspended sentences, acquittals, dismissals, or fines. Thus the avoided pretrial incarcerations resulting from Vera's supervision were particularly critical.

An especially interesting and encouraging aspect of this experiment is the attitude of the police, which has so far been not merely cooperative but enthusiastic. In a recent speech,

Deputy Commissioner Leonard Reisman of the New York City Police Department pointed out that the Vera summons experiment, even on its present modest scale, is saving the police department thousands of hours of manpower and is responsible for significant savings of hitherto useless public expenses. Costs of welfare and detention have been considerably reduced with no corresponding economic or social costs as a result of this conservative beginning. Considering that there are hundreds of thousands of arrests in New York City each year, the proportions of these savings could be vastly increased by the expansion of the use of summons to other areas of criminal charges.

Every arrested defendant must be taken to jail, booked, fingerprinted, questioned, and eventually brought to court. The police must accompany the defendant through the beginning steps of the judicial process until the arraignment when the court takes over. Thus police are detracted from their primary responsibilities of detecting and preventing crime. And facilities such as cars and cells, and custodial personnel, are diverted and used up. These administrative chores are expensive, time consuming, and wastefully unproductive. And, of course, the human savings to defendants in terms of the practical corollaries of their individual freedom are inestimable. The early machinery of the administration of justice is improved. And in the words of Deputy Commissioner Reisman, "Ultimately, we think, the dignity of the law enforcement process will be enhanced."

The project has shown no negative aspects and is being expanded. Moreover, it has kindled an interest in other cities which have begun or are planning to begin similar programs. Some federal courts are also developing plans to expand the use of summons procedures. Another Vera success seems inevitable.

Would this work in the cases of more serious crimes? According to Vera's results, and according to one report early this year to the Governor's Conference on Bail in Louisville, Kentucky, it can and in fact it already has been working well in some places.

One recent study has been made of the use of the summons throughout the nation. The author of that study recently reported her tentative results to a regional conference on bail:

The fact is that we have now had sufficient experience with summons in a wide variety of situations—in many different areas of the country—to know that most of the fears concerning summons as an alternative to arrest and bail are unfounded. Where a carefully planned summons program has been undertaken, its utility has been hailed by the law enforcement officials who were originally most skeptical. And where summons hasn't proved out, or where it has been grudgingly or inadequately used, analysis shows that the police have had poorly defined authority and inadequate standards from which to work. If the offenses for which summons may be issued are plainly understood in advance by the police and the courts; if the criteria for citing or releasing prisoners are agreed upon and properly articulated to the police administering the program, the program works.

In short, the record in those cities where summons programs have been successful should provide a strong incentive for other jurisdictions to consider expanded use of summons as an aid to more effective, fair, and humane law enforcement.[2]

If this estimation is not overly optimistic, and if experiments like Vera's around the country provide the successful experience from which to make a realistic appraisal of the use of the summons as a way of getting defendants to trials, still another technique may be added to the alternatives to bail.

Since a defendant is so carefully protected nowadays as a

[2] Address by P. M. Ward, Governor's Conference, Louisville, Kentucky, January 22, 1965.

result of recent constitutional adjudications dealing with the rights of the criminally accused, there is decreasingly little which the police have to gain from pretrial incarceration. In fact, whether or not the whole concept of detention prior to trial is in conflict with our noninquisitorial legal system and our traditions, Vera's present experiments may prove that it is not worthwhile.

Others are now joining in the bail and summons work which Vera could only begin. But Vera's work and the vision and action of Louis Schweitzer and his associates is a modern re-vindication of the American notion of equal justice.

VERA FOUNDATION, NEW YORK CITY:
PRETRIAL DETENTION FORMS

EXHIBIT A

1. Name_____ Q No. _____
          last   first   middle

R1	N
R3	N
R4	N
CT	A NA

Date_____Ct of appearance_____D. No._____

Reason for Excl or Int_____

Pvt Atty_Y N P_ Investigator_____

Co- Def_Y N_ (Names)_____Ages_____

2. Age_____Description N W S / M F__Ht_____Wt_____English_Y N__

3. Are you on drugs_Y N__ Ever_Y N__ When last_____

4. Presently living at_____
                   no.   street   boro   apt   floor

For_____On and off_Y N__ Phone_____

With (Name and Relation)_____

5. Previously lived at_____

6. NYC resident for_____

7. Relatives in NYC that keep in close contact with.

Name	Relation	Address	Phone	How Often See

8. Now married?__L CL N__ Status_T LS S__ How long?_____

   # Children_____Spouse Name_____Address_____

9. Presently employed by_____
                              company & address

   For_____ As a _____

10. If unemployed, how long_____

    How supported__UI W Sav Spouse Other_____

11. Previously employed by_____

    For_____ As a _____

12. If employed, support anyone?_____

13. What is your state of health?_____

    Ever hosp'd for physical or mental disorder?_Y N_When?_____

    How long?_____ Where?_____

174

EXHIBIT A (continued)

14. Birthplace: City_____ State or Country_____

15. Where will you go if released today_____

16. Belong to a Union __Y N__ Name _____ Local _____

17. How many times arrested before_____ Convictions_____

    What for: _____ Disp _____

    _____ Disp _____

    _____ Disp _____

    Ever on Probation __Y N__ Now __Y N__ Violate __Y N__

    Ever on Parole __Y N__ Now __Y N__ Violate __Y N__ Officer_____

    Address_____ Phone _____

18. Have you had anyone called __Y N__ Who _____

19. Any papers with you __Y N__ Info_____

20. Is there anyone we can call or speak to as a reference, someone that knows where you live, etc. (Relative, employer, friend, union, landlord, neighbor, religious leader, teacher, credit reference).

Order	In Ct	Name	Address	Phone	Occup	Relation	Yrs. Kwn

Does the complainant know you __Y N__ Is it OK to speak to him __Y N__

I AGREE TO ALLOW THE VERA FOUNDATION TO CALL THE PEOPLE LISTED IMMEDIATELY ABOVE IN QUESTION 20 IF THE FOUNDATION WISHES TO CHECK MY REFERENCES.

Signature_____

EXHIBIT B

Q number _____

Name _____

Alias _____

Previous Record: N   C   INC   No. of pages _____

Year	Charge	State	Disposition & Court

Current charge: _____

Name of Arresting Officer: _____

Name of Complainant: _____

Court of Arraignment: _____

Assault Victim in Hospital   Y   N   Name of Hospital: _____

Officer's statement of victim's condition: _____

Remarks:

EXHIBIT C

To be recommended, a defendant needs:
1. A New York area address where he can be reached, AND
2. A total of five points from the following categories.

Int	Ver	
		PRIOR RECORD
2	2	No convictions
1	1	One misdemeanor conviction
0	0	Two misdemeanor convictions or one felony conviction
−1	−1	Three or more misdemeanor convictions or two or more felony convictions
		FAMILY TIES (In New York area)
3	3	Lives with family AND has contact with other family members
2	2	Lives with family OR has contact with family
1	1	Lives with nonfamily person AND gives this person as reference
		EMPLOYMENT
3	3	Present job one year or more
2	2	Present job 4 months OR present and prior job 6 months
1	1	On and off job in either of above 2 lines
		OR Current job
		OR Unemployed 3 months or less with 9 months or more prior job
		OR Receiving unemployment compensation or welfare
		OR Supported by family
		RESIDENCE (In New York Area: NOT on and off)
3	3	Present residence one year or more
2	2	Present residence 6 months OR Present and prior 1 year
1	1	Present residence 4 months OR Present and prior 6 months
		TIME IN NEW YORK CITY
1	1	Ten years or more
		DISCRETION
+1	+1	Positive
−1	0	Negative
		TOTAL INTERVIEW POINTS

R   NR

TOTAL VERIFIED POINTS

R   NR

Reason(s) for discretionary point.

EXHIBIT D
VERA FOUNDATION, INC.
Room 1330
100 Centre Street

Recommends PAROLE in the case of _____

On the basis of the following VERIFIED INFORMATION:

RESIDENCE—FAMILY

Presently living at _____

for _____

with _____

Previously lived at _____

for _____

with _____

NYC resident for _____

EMPLOYMENT—SUPPORT—HEALTH

Presently employed by _____

for _____

as a _____

Presently _____

_____

_____

Previously employed by _____

for _____

as a _____

NOTIFICATION

Should the defendant be paroled, the Vera Foundation will notify him by mail of all future court appearances in this case.

In addition, _____
will also help to see that the defendant appears when required.

Previous record: _____

Current charge: _____

Legal Aid _____DA_____DA Rec_____Judge_____

Court Action _____

178

EXHIBIT E

CHECK-OUT

Name of defendant ———————————————————
Name of check-out ———————————————————
   Address and phone ———————————————————
   Relationship ———————————————————

RESIDENCE—FAMILY

Presently living at ———————————————————
         for ———————————————————
        with ———————————————————
Previously lived at ———————————————————
        for ———————————————————
       with ———————————————————
NYC resident for ———————————————————
How often see other relatives ———————————————————

EMPLOYMENT—SUPPORT—HEALTH

Presently employed by ———————————————————
         for ———————————————————
       as a ———————————————————
If unemployed, how does he support himself? ———————

———————————————————

Previously employed by ———————————————————
         for ———————————————————
       as a ———————————————————
Does he support anyone? ———————————————————
(For employer only) what type of worker is he? ———————
       Does he have his job to return to? ———————
Health? ———————————————————
Accept notification? ———————————————————
Remarks? ———————————————————

———————————————————

EXHIBIT F

Vera Foundation
Room 1330
100 Centre Street
New York 13, New York

Dear

This letter is to remind you that you are to appear in
                              on
                    at 9:25 A.M. This is located on
the   floor of the Criminal Courts Building at
100 Centre Street.

It is very important to be in court at the proper time. As
you know, failure to be in court is a crime.

As we helped to get you paroled, we would like to talk to you
in our office in Room 1330 on the 13th floor of the court
building. If convenient, please stop in at 9:15 A.M. or
after your case has come up in court. If you have a change
of address, if you change jobs, or if you have any problems,
please notify us. Our phone is RE 2-0990.

                                        Sincerely,

EXHIBIT G

Vera Foundation
Room 1330
100 Centre Street
New York 13, New York

Estimado Señor

Esta carta sirve para avisarle que usted tiene que
presentarse en la corte de
      el   de   a las diez. Esta
corte está en el piso número   del edificio de la
Corte Criminal en la calle Centre número 100.

Es muy preciso que usted se presente a esta hora. Como
usted sabe, falta de presentarse es un delito.

Nosotros queremos hablar con usted en nuestra oficina en el
cuarto 1330 en el piso número 13 del edificio de la corte.
Si le es conveniente, puede venir aquí antes de las diez
o después de su apariencia en corte o nos puede llamar por
teléfono al RE 2-0990.

Cordialmente,

EXHIBIT H

Follow-up Questionnaire

Name _____Date _____

How is everything going?

PA?

                           Name?

LA?

Court Notification?

Other Notification?

Family:
  (Where living?   With whom?)

Employment:
  (Are you working now?   Where?   (with address)
   If job is different or lost—probe)

Been in any trouble since parole?

EXHIBIT I
Daily Log

DATE _____

| NAME | VERA | | | | | | MAGISTRATE'S FELONY | | | | |
	VERA #	ADDRESS	CT.	FINAL VERA REC.	DOCK #	DISPOSITION	BAIL	M	LA PA	CHARGE

EXHIBIT J
Weekly Log

SUMMARY RECORDS   WEEK OF _____
Yellow Sheet Man _____

EXCLUDED WITHOUT INTERVIEW

DATE	EXT. or TRANS.	F.A. POLICE	SEX	NAR.	HOM.	TOTAL EXCLUDE WITHOUT INTERVIEW	# AFTER 1:00	FIRST INT. # LAST
WEEK TOTAL								

INTERVIEWS NOT COMPLETED   **INTERVIEWS COMPLETED**

DATE	PA	REFUSE INT	MISS INT.	SCA	S. INT.	SR1	SR2	SR3	SR4	SNR	C.INT.	CR1	CR2	CR3	CR4	CNR
WEEK TOTAL																

ROR

The most obvious and the simplest way to deal with the pretrial custody of a defendant is to release him outright. Releasing a defendant conditional only upon his own promise to appear relieves the court of the administrative waste of time and money necessary to fulfill the role of custodian. The Vera experiment has shown that, if properly supervised, outright release is feasible because basically most people are trustworthy and could be released without the danger that they would flee. Could this supervisory role be assumed by some government agency, or could it even be dropped completely? Our whole system of criminal justice is predicated upon the voluntariness of the citizenry. Without that, our affairs would be chaotic. For the few defendants who could not be trusted on their own, or for those whose freedom would present special problems, might special procedures be devised? We have not yet progressed to the point where this completely trusting approach is used in the United States. One step in that direction is the practice of release on recognizance. ROR may take any one of several forms: outright release on trust, release on the unsupported bond of the defendant alone, or release on the promise of the defendant to return backed by a fractional cash deposit.

The meaning of ROR and the difference between bail and release on recognizance has been differently defined by various courts. Essentially, a bail bond is a contract executed by the accused and requiring sureties or bail by third persons, to whose custody the accused is committed; whereas a recognizance is an obligation of record, entered into by the prisoner before some court or magistrate, to do some particular act, usually to appear and answer the charges against him. A recognizance may be a mere promise, without any financial conditions, to appear for trial. It may also include some personal token or symbolic deposit by the defendant. It may also be an unsigned bonding obligation of the defendant on the court's records (as compared to a bond, which is a more formal contract between a surety, the offender, and the government, the consideration being release of the accused from custody).[3] ROR is not quite bail, nor is it usually quite the same as outright, unconditional release. The term *release on recognizance* (ROR) has been used to mean both release on trust, or on nonfinancial conditions (as is the case with Vera), as well as the more standard personal bonds whereby in effect the defendant personally goes bond for himself without collateral or sureties, and with or without some deposit. Under this latter practice (also called ROR), a defendant may execute a personal bond to the court in the amount of the bail and thus be granted his pretrial release without having to supply additional sureties or securities. In some cases he will be required to leave a cash deposit too.

Actually, ROR on faith alone when appropriate is more realistic than is ROR on a personal bond. While in the latter case the bondsman is eliminated, this program really provides little deterrent to flight. If a defendant was going to flee, his personal promise to pay a stipulated amount to the court probably would not keep him, especially if he did not have the money to forfeit anyway. So, since in effect there is no financial deterrent, why not set the man free on his word to return, thus at least encouraging some personal responsibility and exhibiting some faith in him. Assumedly, he would have been checked out as a good risk to qualify for this type of ROR.

The Attorney General's Committee on Poverty and the Administration of Criminal Justice reported in 1963 that the

[3] Ewing v. U.S., 240 Federal 241 (1917); Reine v. U.S., 135 Federal 2d. 914 (1943); U.S. v. D'Argento, 227 Federal Supplement 596 (1964).

practices varied widely among federal district attorneys insofar as recommending release of defendants on their own recognizance. In Connecticut, for example, during one three-year period, 65 per cent of all defendants were released on their own recognizance, while in Delaware, the District of Columbia, certain districts of Georgia, and Washington there were no such releases during the same period. When it was used, this release technique worked satisfactorily. A very minor percentage (less than 3 per cent of 3,390 cases) failed to appear. Yet, there was no national policy about ROR in the federal courts. The Committee suggested that ". . . significant gains could be achieved by a more liberal use of the ROR procedure, even without other alterations in the present system." As a result of the Committee's recommendations, the Department of Justice instructed all United States attorneys on March 11, 1963, as follows:

It is the view of the Department that the use of r.o.r. should be broadened in order to preserve the traditional right to freedom before conviction and thereby to insure that a defendant is able to provide financially for his family and his defense and to take an active part in the preparation of that defense.

While recognizing that the granting of release on recognizance is the prerogative of the courts, the Department at the same time feels that, to the extent that United States Attorneys can be instrumental in effecting a more extensive use of the practice in appropriate cases, they should do so. United States Attorneys and their assistants are therefore urged to take the initiative in recommending the release of defendants on their own recognizance when they are satisfied that there is no substantial risk of the defendants' failure to appear at the specified time and place.

A determination as to whether there is a substantial risk of non-appearance will necessarily rely on the sound judgment of the United States Attorney and his assistants and their consideration of the particular circumstances of each case. Some of the circumstances to be assessed are the nature and seriousness of the offense charged, the weight of the evidence, the defendant's character, prior record, family situation, residence or ties in the district, and any other circumstances peculiar to the district or to the offense.

As a result of this memorandum, it could be reported to the National Bail Conference a little over a year later that the rate of ROR had almost tripled from 1960 to 1964. Over 6,000 defendants were released by federal district courts in the year 1963–1964, and their default rate was only 2.5 per cent. The courts usually follow the district attorney's suggestions, so the Attorney General was able to make a notable advance through his administrative control of federal prosecutors.

One committee of the United States Judicial Conference recently proposed that the federal rule covering bail should be amended to allow judges to release defendants without bail upon their agreement to appear "and upon such conditions as may be prescribed to insure his presence." And among the bail-reform bills recently proposed by Senator Sam Ervin, Jr., was one which would assure that no person will be denied bail because of his financial inability to give bond or provide collateral security. The pertinent part of this bill reads as follows: "Any indigent person in custody . . . shall, if otherwise eligible for bail, and except for good cause shown to the contrary, be admitted to bail on his personal recognizance subject to such conditions as the court . . . may reasonably prescribe to assure his appearance."

The method of administering an ROR program is important. If the matter of determining who is worthy of release on his own recognizance is left to the judge alone, he is at quite a disadvantage. Although the responsibility for decision is and ought to be his alone, a judge's competing demands are too great to allow him time to make the appropriate inquiries necessary for him to determine whether ROR would be appropriate in each of the hundreds of cases coming before him. Obviously, ROR is a tailored, personalized device. It is necessary for someone to investigate the circumstances of each case so that no individual is improperly denied release and also so that dangerous or untrustworthy individuals are not let loose without adequate controls.

Different district courts have resolved this problem in different ways. The Vera practice, wherein the investigative and supervisory role was filled by a private group aided by local law students, is the beacon. Many courts are adopting Vera's investigatory technique. However, there is only so much that can be expected from private or charitable institutional sources. It is simpler and less costly for an existing governmental agency to assume the investigatory and advisory duties which Vera performed for the New York City court. Different cities around the country are now applying the Vera approach, but are using a variety of government officials to do the Vera work. In many cities, the Vera pattern is closely followed; but in some places in California the police are being used to fill the release advisory role; in Denver, it is the sheriff; in some cities in West Virginia, the welfare department; in Chicago, the public defender; in other places, the Probation Department and the United States attorney.

Detroit

In Detroit, Michigan, the United States attorney has joined the District Court judge in attempting to assure the maximum successful use of ROR. There, the trial judges hold hearings for bail every day, including Saturdays, in order to avoid unnecessarily locking up a defendant over a weekend. The United States attorney presents the judge with a report detailing the defendant's background. Relevant information is provided for the court, such as the defendant's residence, employment, community ties, family situation, and prior record. Although there is an inclination to question whether an adversary could apply the detachment that is necessary to fairly fulfill this function, the program seems to be working well. As Judge Wade McCree of that court recently stated: "The United States Attorney knows our philosophy about bail and most conscientiously and fairly reports his findings to the court. I have never experienced a situation where a member of his staff has falsified or shaded a report. . . ." Defendants are notified by mail of the court's demands, and this seems to work at least as efficiently as bondsmen. Sometimes, periodic calls are made by the marshal or United States attorney as an extra check on ROR defendants. Weekly jail inventories are presented to the court by the United States attorneys in order to insure that no defendants are overlooked or are forced to remain in jail for lack of bail money alone.

A significant aspect of this program is that it is open to defendants charged with serious offenses such as bank robbery and narcotics traffic. And this liberality is made all the more impressive since the opportunity or temptation to jump must be especially great here. Detroit is minutes away from Canada. Judge McCree reported to the National Bail Conference in May, 1964, that ". . . in the Eastern District of Michigan we sit in a court house which is five minutes from the tunnel which leads to Canada, and 15 minutes from a bridge which connects with the same country. We have found this not to be a complicating factor."

Statistics comparing ROR cases with bail cases are telling, too. Judge McCree advised the Bail Conference that the default rate in 1962, for example, was 7.5 per cent on bail bonds and only 1.1 per cent on personal bonds. And personal bonds were allowed for serious offenses, mandatory sentence offenses, and even guilty plea cases. And bondsmen turned down many bail cases, too. Only 40 per cent of the defendants who were required to put up cash or a security bond were able to do so. This reflects both an element of financial deterrence in the ROR program (average bail was $2,500) and a reluctance on the part of bondsmen to assume risks in non-ROR cases. And still the ROR defendants jumped only one-seventh the amount of times that bailed defendants did. In Judge McCree's words again:

". . . we believe that we judges can, with adequate information, make as good an assessment of the defendant's likelihood of appearing when required as can a bondsman, and that the defendant might better employ his funds for counsel than for a bond premium. . . . This system of ours has worked for some 20 years now. It is by no means perfect, and continues to evolve as our experience indicates. We are, however, convinced that the approach is sound.

San Francisco

In the federal district court in San Francisco a trial project is underway. The function of advising the court about the releasability of a defendant is being conducted by the probation officials. Upon request of the defendant, or the commissioner or the court, the probation office will conduct a bail investigation. This had been done informally and occasionally in the past and was formalized as a pilot project resulting from the recommendation of the Attorney General's Committee on Poverty and the Administration of Justice.

The marshal notifies the probation officer when a defendant does not intend to make bail, and will sign a consent for bail investigation. Then the probation officer interviews the defendant to determine factors indicative of his stability, such as his criminal record, employment, financial resources, and residence. The offense for which he is charged is not discussed.

SAN FRANCISCO:
PRETRIAL DETENTION FORMS

EXHIBIT K

CONSENT FOR BAIL INVESTIGATION

I, _____ hereby consent to a bail in-
(Name of Defendant)
vestigation by the probation officers of the United States
District Courts. This investigation is for the purpose of ob-
taining information useful to the Court in establishing bail.

By this consent I do not admit any guilt or waive rights and
I understand that any report prepared will be shown to the
Court only for the purpose of establishing bail.

I have read, or had read to me, the foregoing consent. No
promise has been made to me as to what final disposition will
be made of my case.

Date: _____   _____
                              (Signature of Defendant)

_____
(Witness)

EXHIBIT L

TIME STUDY

BAIL FACT-FINDING INVESTIGATIONS

OFFICER _____ DATE _____ 196 ___

Time of Day	Hrs in Tenths	Name of Case	Location	Action	Purpose	Communicate to:	Remarks
			1. Office 2. Jail 3. Marshal 4. Field	1. See & Talk 2. Phone 3. Paper Work 4. Travel 5. Wait 6. Other (Expl)	1. Def. Inter. 2. Job 3. Home 4. Financial Resources 5. Record 6. Counsel 7. Other (Explain) 8. Dictate	1. Case 2. Relative 3. Employer 4. Law Agent 5. U.S. Atty 6. Def. Counsels 7. Judge or Commiss. 8. Social Agency 9. Supervisor 10. Other (Explain)	

EXHIBIT M

CASE TRAIT RECORD SHEET   Officer_____   Sheet No._____

Post appropriate number in each column – also, where entry is "Other," briefly indicate what is involved.

Name of Case	*Sex & Race	Age Last Birthday	Current Offense	Most Serious Prior Record	Usual Occupation	Longest Job In Last Two Years Free	Marital Status
	Men 1.Wh. N-Sp. 2. Sp 3. N. 4. O Women 5. Wh. N-Sp. 6.Sp. 7. N. 8. O	0.17 or less 1.18-21 2.22-25 3.26-30 4.31-35 5.36-45 6.46-60 7.61 or over	1. Auto Theft 2. Narcotics 3. Burg.-Larcen. 4. Forgery 5. Income Tax 6. Embezzl. or Fraud 7. Liquor Law 8. Obscene Lit. 9. Robbery 0. Other	1. None 2. Fine 3. Prob. w/o jail 4. Prob. with jail 5. Jail 6. Training School 7. Ref. or 1 prison 8. Two or more prison prison or reform	1. Student 2. Housewife 3. Farming 4. Labor, unskilled 5. Machine Operator 6. Skilled Trade 7. Clerical 8. Sales, Bus. Mgr. 9. Professional 0. Other	1. None 2. Less than month 3. 1-3 months 4. 4-6 months 5. 7-9 months 6. One year 7. 13-18 months 8. Over 18 months	1. Single 2. Separated 3. Divorced 4. Common-Law 5. Marriage Intact 6. Other (Widowed, etc.)

*Sex and "Race":   Men   1. White, Not Spanish Name; 2. White, Spanish Name; 3. Negro; 4. Other, Including U.S. Indian & Oriental
Women 5. White, Not Spanish Name; 6. White, Spanish Name; 7. Negro; 8. Other, Including U.S. Indian & Oriental

EXHIBIT N

BAIL FACT-FINDING INVESTIGATIONS
NORTHERN DISTRICT OF CALIFORNIA

NAME: CASE NO.:

Date of Investigation:
Original Bail Amount:
P.O. Recommendation:
Date of Recommendation:
Court Action:
Date of Court Action:
Date of Release: How Released:

FOLLOW UP

Date of Plea: Nature of Plea:
Status at Time of Plea: Custody   Bail   Personal Bond   O.R.
If Trial, Judge or Jury: Date of Trial:
Final Disposition: Date of Disposition:

Did defendant show for all Court appearances: Yes   No
If no, explain and give result.

Sources for quick information are sought to verify the facts gathered. Then a report is made and submitted to the judge or the commissioner. If release under supervision is decided upon, the probation officer will designate a schedule for reporting. This program has only recently started as an experimental project for the federal courts at the request of the Justice Department. Statistics from which its success can be evaluated are still incomplete.

St. Louis

This same system is used in St. Louis.[4] That city's probation office administers an ROR program which has been going on for several years. It was originally begun as a result of the concern of certain probation officials about the harm, from a correctional standpoint, being done to juvenile delinquents. The obvious dangers arising from indiscriminately throwing youngsters into jails with hardened, depraved criminals were drawn into awful focus by one recent episode in Farmington, Missouri. There, a seventeen-year-old boy was homosexually assaulted and beaten to death by two other prisoners, one of whom had three prior convictions.

To these probation officials, it was coincidentally evident, too, that equal justice was being denied the poor who had to suffer pretrial confinement only because they could not afford bail. There were approximately nine hundred indigent defendants a year before that court. Yet 45 per cent of all cases ended without prison sentences. It was to everyone's advantage to reduce the population of the jails as long as that was consistent with the safety of the community.

Beginning informally in 1961 and continuing until 1963, the St. Louis Circuit Court Probation Office ran investigations

[4] Shultz, "Bail for the 'Have-Nots,'" The Recognizance Program of the St. Louis Circuit Court for Criminal Causes, Probation Office, 1963.

and made recommendations to the court calling for the release of certain defendants on their own recognizance. Interviews were held as soon as possible after arrest. The probation staff based their recommendations upon indices of stability that they would gather, such as the nature of the offense, the criminal record of the defendant, age and home and job of the individual, and community references. The judge, of course, made the final decision. The program worked well and won the support of the judges of the criminal court, the district attorneys, and the public defenders.

Early in 1963 this approach was formally commenced in a full-scale recognizance program. Investigations, verification, and release under supervision, these are the facets of the program. And to date, it has been a success. The task of supervision is really insignificant, sometimes merely a periodic phone call to the probation office. But the probation officer, along with keeping track of the whereabouts of defendants, also advises them and counsels them. He will, for example, try to recover employment for the defendant who lost it due to his arrest. In fact, according to Deputy Chief Probation and Parole Office LeRoy Schultz, the probation officer was chosen to fill this role because, for a number of reasons, he was likely to be best qualified for this particular job. Probation officials are not part of the adversary system. And they have experience in the techniques of investigation and social appraisal. Plans are underway to use students of law and social work to assist in recognizance investigations. This is a valuable aid to the busy probation office (as it was to Vera) and a valuable experience for students.

At last report, about 15 per cent of all defendants in this court who were released before trial were released on their own recognizance. Only one person committed another offense. Though this is a relatively conservative start, Charles

Mann, the sensitive and optimistic chief probation officer, has hopes for greater strides in this direction. Since an estimated 70 per cent of all defendants coming before that Circuit Court cannot afford bail in the amount set by the court, and since the average pretrial jail time was forty-eight days, the savings to defendants and the public resulting from this program can be significant.

The Illinois Plan

Since January 1, 1964, Illinois has been experimenting with another way of improving the traditional bail system. The Illinois legislature initiated this new plan, to be tried for two years. It differs from other new approaches, and interestingly its conception stole the thunder from the bondsmen. The essence of the plan is this: Instead of requiring that a defendant secure a bond from a bail bondsman prior to his pretrial release, this law allows a defendant to post with the court an amount equal to the premium for a bond. In other words, if bail was set at $100, a defendant could post $10.00 with the court, instead of paying the bondsman a $10.00 premium to put up a $100 bond. If this defendant shows up for trial, instead of losing the $10.00, as he would have to the bondsman, he gets $9.00 back from the court. One per cent ($1.00) would be kept by the court for the cost of administering this plan. The cost to the defendant is minimal, only enough to pay for the added paper work for the court, and for the occasional costs of tracking down bail jumpers. In case of nonappearance, the full amount of the bail would be forfeited (for example, using the figures above, $100 would be forfeited for nonappearance). There are also penal provisions provided by statute which make bail jumping a crime.

An alternative is also provided. Instead of depositing the 10 per cent of the bond in cash with the court, a defendant may put up the full amount of bail in cash, or he may deposit with the clerk collateral of stocks and bonds in the full amount of the bail, or he may pledge as his collateral any real estate worth twice the amount of the amount of bail. If he appears as required, the *entire* amount which he deposited is returned to him. The bonding experience would then cost him nothing.

Actually, the appeal of this 10 per cent cash deposit concept is deceiving. While it does restore the administration of bail to the court, and while it saves bailed defendants most of the money needed to secure their bail (which heretofore had gone to the bondsman), it does not really solve two critical bail problems. It does not provide for the utterly poor defendant who does not have even the 10 per cent to give to a bondsman or to a court. Unless he can borrow the down payment (he would still only get 9 per cent back from the court), he would still have to go to jail. Secondly, it is questionable, as bondsmen have not failed to point out, whether the 10 per cent down payment would ever really deter anyone from fleeing. And, if it does not, why have even the 10 per cent requirement? Thus, two essential problems are left, though the bondsman and the problems that he raises are eliminated.

In the words of Professor Charles H. Bowman, one of the drafters of this legislation: "As originally submitted to the legislature, we intended the 10 per cent deposit provisions to put the bail bondsman out of business, and restore the control of pre-trial detention to the courts, where it belongs." Upon proof of the preferability of a noncommercial bail system, more thorough-going reforms could be instituted.

However, it must be admitted that in addition to eliminating the bondsman through this aspect of the Illinois plan, not only may the defendant save some money, but also more defendants are likely to be able to afford bail. The defendant who can borrow enough money to put up the 10 per cent of the bond does not have to worry about being refused by a bondsman who might insist upon further collateral security.

This provision was one of many which together comprised an entire recent recodification of the criminal laws of Illinois. Other provisions allowed notices to appear and summons to replace arrests before trial, and required the posting of notice in police stations and jails of the right to bail. The code also expressly states the public policy of Illinois to be that defendants should be released on their own recognizance where all circumstances indicate that they will appear. Criminal sanctions for the completed wrong of bail jumping replace economic punishments for what are no more than potential or prospective wrongs, as is the case with traditional bail. Another wise and fair provision adopted by Illinois provides that only one bond may be required from arrest through appeal. This dispenses with the need, the trouble, and the costs of posting different bonds at different stages of criminal proceedings. For example, it has been estimated that in the federal courts, there are an average of two bonds required in the course of each criminal proceeding. It can be more. And for each bond, the bondsman receives a separate fee.

The Illinois programs also provide that credit must be given for any detention that is necessitated in lieu of bail, and that the defendant is compensated for this detention against any fine imposed upon conviction. An attempt was made to allow credit for all time spent in pretrial confinement in reduction of any subsequent sentence after conviction. This was not passed by the legislature.

The ancient peace bond allowing detention to prevent threatened but uncommitted offenses was also eliminated. And to avoid onerously protracted pretrial confinement, a provision was passed requiring the discharge of any defendant who is not tried within 120 days of his arrest or, if he is on bail, within 120 days from the time he demands trial. All these new provisions and others form part of an overall attempt by the state of Illinois to deal fairly and rationally with the problems of pretrial control of defendants.

One criticism made about the efficacy of the 10 per cent deposit provision is that so small a sum really provides no deterrent from flight. While this fear might apply in the case of the wealthy defendant, the danger of flight certainly is no more likely in the case of an indigent defendant than it is under the present system. And although $25 or $50 might not keep most men from running away, the possibility of its return might very well make pretrial release *possible* for some men. If a defendant, in order to make bail, gives a bondsman the $50 premium for a bond, that money is gone. If he gives an equivalent amount of money to the court under this plan, he would get back almost all when he appears. Moreover, for the defendant who has some property but cannot afford the cash for bail, and who knows that he will not violate the conditions of his release, the alternative exists to post his property as security at no cost and get it back when he appears for trial.

So, although the Illinois type of plan might not assure high enough bail to assure, in and of itself, the presence of the accused at trial, it would greatly broaden the access to release for those against whom bail would work a hardship. It would also stress the personal involvement of the real parties in interest in the bail process, and exclude the arbitrary and unrelated commercial aspect present in the present bonding system.

The newspapers have reported that the bondsmen brought a taxpayers suit to declare this Illinois law unconstitutional.[5] They argued that this scheme puts the state in the position of

[5] *Chicago American*, Mar. 31, 1964.

soliciting bond business at a loss to taxpayers. By keeping only
1 per cent, they argued, the state keeps less than it costs to
administer the bonding process. Moreover, the program puts
the state in a preferred position over free enterprise. And
finally, they argued, the possibility of the state keeping only
a 10 per cent forfeiture, as compared to 100 per cent when
the bondsman is involved, creates a false sense of security.

The bases for this suit are questionable. The state need not
be satisfied with a 10 per cent forfeiture, only a 10 per cent
deposit. Assumedly, they could collect the full value of the
bond upon forfeiture if the defendant had it. The preferred
position of the state argument and the free enterprise argument fall upon recognition of the fact that justice is not
business. In fact, the state never should have put any part of
the trial system into the marketplace of business. This program
only returns to the courts the duty, not the business, that is
rightly theirs.

Actually, the 10 per cent deposit aspect of the Illinois program was not a completely original idea. New York City has
a law that allows judges to set cash bail as an alternative to
ordinary bail. As an example, bail could be set in the form
of a $100 bond or a $10 cash deposit. Thus the defendant
has the option of paying for a bondsman or leaving with the
court a deposit somewhat less in amount than the premium for
a commercial bond. The New York Assembly recently praised
this practice and noted an increase in its use. Cash-bail programs ought to eliminate bondsmen. There is no function
which bondsmen serve that would warrant defendants using
them when as much could be accomplished in another fashion
at considerably less cost.

The Attorney General's Committee on Poverty and the
Administration of Federal Criminal Justice recently recommended that the federal government adopt this practice.

On May 14, 1964, Senator Sam Ervin, Jr., along with

several other senators, introduced a bill in the United States Senate which would adopt, among other bail-reform provisions, the Illinois 10 per cent bail-deposit idea for the federal courts. The pertinent parts of the proposed bill, S. 2840 of the 88th Congress, Second Session, read as follows:

> Whenever the amount of bail has been fixed in the case of any person charged with an offense against the United States, such person shall execute a bond for his appearance, and, in lieu of providing other collateral security or securities, may deposit in the registry of the court a sum equal to 10 per centum of the amount of bail so fixed. Upon the deposit of such sum such persons shall be released from custody subject to the conditions of his bond. If there is no breach of condition of a bond . . . the court shall release such person . . . but shall retain 10 per centum of the sum deposited by such person to defray bail bond costs. The balance of such deposit shall . . . be returned to him. . . . If there is a breach of condition of a bond . . . the court shall declare a forfeiture of the full amount of the bail fixed. . . .

Hearings have been held regarding this bill, and the leading bail authorities around the country have praised it and called for its passage. Aside from the aspect of the bill which would tend to equalize the access of the poor to pretrial freedom, Senator Ervin noted in his remarks before Congress that this bill would properly take away from the commercial bondsman his presently omnipotent power to control the question of who goes free and who stays in jail.

The Tulsa Plan

When the traditional bail system in Tulsa, Oklahoma, began to operate unsatisfactorily a few years ago, that city developed a unique new program to replace it. The story of Tulsa's bail revolution is worth telling because, so far, the new plan is working admirably.

It all began in the early 1960s. The newspapers in Tulsa ran several critical articles about the local bail practices. Few people were happy with the way the system was working. A handful of lawyers were handling all the criminal trial work. Defendants frequently disappeared and forfeited their bonds even though they were supposedly under the scrutiny of paid bondsmen. To make matters worse, the bondsmen were not paying these forfeitures to the court with sufficient dependability. Local citizens with solid ties in the community, but without sufficient money to post bail, languished unhappily in jail pending their trials. No one seemed to profit from the system except the bondsmen who provided dubious service.

The Tulsa *Daily World* and the Tulsa *Tribune* in a restrained but persistent coverage of the local bonding business began to create some public pressure early in 1963. Tulsa previously had experienced a bondsman scandal in 1960. Dale "Cowboy" Bryson, a colorful local character, was one of the most prosperous bondsmen in the area. He quickly ascended to the top of the local bonding business. Then all of a sudden he was arrested and convicted of a narcotics violation and sentenced to five years in prison. He had been the United Bonding Company's local agent, and in a very short period of time was writing a major share of Tulsa's bonds. His fees were reported to have run up to $5,200 a month. When he was ousted within the year, he left almost $100,000 in outstanding bonds which he had written. In their articles covering Bryson, the newspapers listed the names of all local bondsmen and the amounts of fees they had earned. Bryson topped the list, but one of the unsympathetic newspapers reported: "There wasn't too much surprise when Bryson was arrested in connection with the crackdown and raids; he had been spending more and more time with many of the persons who were charged along with him."

For a while nothing sensational happened in Tulsa, though

bonding practices were annoying some of the local prosecutive and judicial officials. Then in 1963 the newspapers began to cover the machinations of Lewis Malone. Malone represented the Peerless Insurance Company of New Hampshire. He also rose quickly to the position of top success in the local bonding business. However, his irresponsibility with respect to guarding against and paying up for forfeitures eventually brought Malone into conflict with David Hall, the energetic and dynamic Tulsa county attorney.

It was Hall's duty to seek the collection of forfeited bail. Malone's clients had forfeited often and Malone's debts ran into the tens of thousands of dollars. When Hall brought suits in the local courts to collect these sums, Malone and the Peerless Insurance Company refused to pay up and fought him adamantly. Hall tried to have Malone's right to engage in the bonding business revoked, but the State Insurance Commissioner refused to take action because Peerless had the assets to pay their debts, and there were no civil judgments for these sums outstanding against Peerless. But in the municipal court, Malone was not covered by Peerless, and here too there were unpaid forfeitures for which he was responsible. Hall brought suits, but suits take time, and there were indications that all legal delaying tactics would be taken to stall satisfaction of these debts. Apparently, they hoped to settle some cases and get favorable rulings in some others. At one point, the county attorney had thirty-nine pending suits against Peerless for forfeitures. Meanwhile, Malone left town. Peerless has now paid off all of its debts, but the unpaid forfeitures in the municipal court for which Malone was personally responsible have not been paid off to date.

But County Attorney Hall's actions were enough to spur the press into action. The papers called for strict regulations to govern the bondsmen.

The bondsmen retaliated. One bonding company induced a state senator to submit a bill to the Oklahoma Legislature. One of the bill's provisions would have repealed the existing 25 per cent fee which county attorneys get for collecting forfeited bonds. Newsmen asked Representative Harper, the legislator who introduced the bill, whether this clause in fact made bondsmen virtually immune from suit. He replied that he had not yet studied the bill and would talk about it later.

In January, 1963, the president of the County Bar Association appointed Ollie Gresham, a bright, young Tulsa attorney to be chairman of a committee to work toward solving the local bail problem. Unlike many lawyer committees, this one acted and accomplished quick and tangible results. After meeting with his committee, Gresham talked with bar association officials, the local judges, and Tulsa's County Attorney David Hall. Hall, a friend of Gresham's and an agreeable and conscientious public official, was particularly embarrassed by the local bail situation. By Tulsa law the county attorney collects forfeited bail and personally keeps a percentage of what he collects. Forfeitures had been running so high that Hall was afraid he would be improperly accused of having some collusion with the bondsmen and this unsatisfactory condition which they had created. He was more than happy to try a promising new plan, as were the local judges and officials of the bar, if Gresham could devise one.

In Ollie Gresham's words, "After reading the articles in the paper [about] the trouble that the bondsmen were in [and] the fact that the bondsmen were not paying their forfeitures, our committee then decided to try to find some way to alleviate this matter. Keeping in mind that several of our bondsmen had criminal records or eventually were found guilty of criminal matters, we then struck upon the idea of looking into the possibility of doing away with a portion of the bonding business in Tulsa County. . . . We then decided to investigate the program that the Dallas system had." Attorneys there may sign a bond for the defendants and charge a fee for this. Oklahoma law forbade that practice, but the idea of shifting the responsibility of supervising defendants to their attorneys struck Gresham. This idea, the pressures created by local problems, and the imaginative follow-up work of Hall and Gresham led to the conception of Tulsa's unique new program.

Oklahoma State law allows judges to release defendants on their own recognizance or to an attorney. Release to an attorney is unusual, since it is a strict bar rule of ethics that lawyers should have no financial interest in the outcome of a case. Some feel that if an attorney were to make bail for a defendant, it would improperly involve the attorney with that client both in the bail proceeding and in the prospective trial. While this kind of association could degenerate into an oppressive one, there really is no reason why it should, and under proper circumstances and proper scrutiny the attorney could play both a logical, an efficient, and a useful role in the pretrial procedures for control of defendants. Gresham grasped the idea that if properly controlled, the trial bar could be the salvation of Tulsa's bail problems. And he set his plan into motion on a sixty-day trial basis in the Tulsa Municipal Court and the Common Pleas Court of Tulsa City.

A book was compiled listing the names of all practicing attorneys in good standing who were members of the Tulsa County Bar Association. Every attorney who wished to participate in the new program signed an agreement through which he could request the court to release a client to him without requiring a cash bond. By this agreement, the attorney made an undertaking to the court as shown on page 210.

A roll was kept of attorneys who were part of this plan and

in good standing. If any of the stipulated conditions were violated, the attorney's name would be stricken from the roll and he would be deprived of the privilege of securing clients' releases without cash or a bond in the future. If the client did not appear at trial time, the vouching attorney's name would be taken off the list until the case was finally disposed of or the defendant was incarcerated. In each case, the vouching attorney would sign an affidavit to the effect that he was in good standing with the Bar, that the defendant had not been convicted of a felony or a crime involving moral turpitude within the past six months, and that he, the attorney, would hold himself personally liable to the court for the defendant's appearance until final disposition of the case.

An example of that form is shown on page 211.

During the trial period of Gresham's program, the plan was used only for misdemeanor cases. Attorneys would assume this new responsibility only when they were satisfied that their client was a secure risk. However, so far the plan has worked successfully, and it has cured just those defects in the old system which were aimed at and which had originally provoked the call for change.

One month before this plan went into operation in July, 1963, four attorneys had represented 80 per cent of the defendants in the municipal court. During the first month of the operation of the new program, thirty-two attorneys represented 85 per cent of the defendants in the municipal court. This statistic could well lead one to question whether under the old system there might have been some collusion between the bondsmen and those few attorneys who were getting all the cases. Of the seven hundred members of the Tulsa County Bar Association, over three hundred attorneys are now participating in this program—an astoundingly high percentage, especially considering how few attorneys are regularly involved in criminal litigation. And more than 2,500 defendants have availed themselves of this service since the program was begun.

During the first half-year of the program alone, almost a hundred thousand dollars in bonds was avoided by releasing defendants to their attorneys. This was a loss of almost $20,000 to bondsmen with a specific corresponding savings to the many affected defendants. This is to say nothing of the general public savings that accrued as a result of the lower costs of lost work, resultant welfare, and of maintaining defendants in jail at public expense prior to their trials. After almost a year, only thirteen attorneys have been stricken from the approved list because their vouched-for clients did not appear. This is a lower fleeing percentage than that which prevailed under the traditional, commercial bail-bond system. Thus the savings in money were paralleled by no loss in effectiveness; in fact, the new system appears to be more efficient than the old one. Most of the bondsmen have left town.

The proportion of the economic and human savings under this plan cannot be fully measured by the successes so far. Only misdemeanor cases were eligible under the original plan, and in not all these cases do the attorneys request release into their custody. Still, at present, almost two hundred defendants use this plan each month. The plan could be expanded, as could its likely successes. Under consideration now, and likely to occur soon, is a plan to extend the program to include felonies. Close to three thousand defendants have been released to attorneys since this program began, and less than 1 per cent have failed to appear in court for trial. The bondsmen operating in Tulsa have diminished correspondingly. Their profits are remaining with the people of Tulsa. The bench and bar of Tulsa are happy with their program. The newspapers and assumedly the community in general are behind it. Ollie Gresham was awarded the Bar Association's "Attorney of

EXHIBIT O

COMMON PLEAS COURT OF TULSA COUNTY
MUNICIPAL COURT OF THE CITY OF TULSA

ATTORNEY'S AGREEMENT OF RESPONSIBILITY
FOR COURT APPEARANCE OF CLIENTS

I, _____, a practicing attorney, and member in good standing of the Oklahoma Bar, and a member of the Tulsa County Bar Association, respectfully request that the Court release, without cash bond, clients of mine charged with offenses in Tulsa Municipal Court, and the Common Pleas Court of Tulsa County.

If granted the privilege of having client-defendants released to me without the usual requirement of cash bond, I agree:

1. That I will not knowingly request the release of a previously convicted felon, nor the release of a person convicted of an offense involving moral turpitude within the six months preceding this request, nor the release of a person without bond who is charged with a type of offense deemed not suitable for such release by the Judge of the Municipal Court and Judges of the Courts of Common Pleas.

2. That prior to the release of a client-defendant, I will execute and deliver an ATTORNEY'S AFFIDAVIT OF RESPONSIBILITY FOR COURT APPEARANCE OF CLIENT to the Booking Desk Sergeant (Deputy Court Clerk) of the Tulsa Police Department, or the County Sheriff's Office.

3. That I will have my client execute a bond form before release.

4. That I will be personally responsible to the Courts for having my client present in court at any stage of the proceedings where his presence is required, knowing that my failure to keep this agreement will result in my name being removed from the list of attorneys granted the privilege of having clients released to them without cash bond.

5. That when I request and receive the release of a client-defendant who is intoxicated or otherwise mentally or physically impaired to any degree, that I will personally accept the transfer of custody and be responsible for his protection from injury or his injury of others.

6. That the privilege of having clients released without a surety bond is at all times subject to the approval of the Courts and can be terminated at any time at the discretion of the Courts.

7. That I have read the above subject matter and on my oath agree to comply with the same.

_____
Attorney at Law

_____
Date

EXHIBIT P

COURT OF COMMON PLEAS OF TULSA COUNTY

ATTORNEY'S AFFIDAVIT OF RESPONSIBILITY
FOR COURT APPEARANCE OF CLIENT

State of Oklahoma   )   Number _____
) ss
County of Tulsa   )   Defendant's Name _____

    I, _____, of lawful age, being first duly sworn on oath state: That I am a practicing attorney in good standing in the State of Oklahoma, and a member of the Tulsa County Bar Association. That I represent the above named defendant in the above numbered charge pending in the Court of Common Pleas of Tulsa County, State of Oklahoma. That the above named defendant has never been convicted of a felony, nor has he been convicted of an offense involving moral turpitude within the past six months, and that said defendant is a resident of Tulsa County, Oklahoma.

    That I will personally hold myself liable to the Court for the appearance of the above named defendant at all proceedings until final disposition has been made of the case to the satisfaction of the Court.

    Further affiant sayeth not.

                                      _____
                                      Affiant Attorney

Subscribed and sworn to before me this ___ day of _____, 19___

                                    _____
                                    Court Clerk by Deputy

the Year Award" and he and Prosecutor David Hall were applauded spokesmen at the recent National Bail Conference where they described their program to representatives of all the fifty states. Other cities around the country—Buffalo, New York, Tucson, Arizona, Salem, Oregon—are consulting with them and considering adoption of the Tulsa program. And Ollie Gresham, David Hall, and the people of Tulsa are justly proud of their bail reform.

All these various programs have amply illustrated that there are better ways of dealing with the problems now controlled by the traditional bail system—fairer, wiser, and more utilitarian ways. With thoughtfulness and ingenuity, the experiences under these exemplary programs can be built upon and we can move even farther along the way toward needed bail reform.

CHAPTER VI

Pretrial Detention in Other Countries

Another paradox of the American bail system is that it is less reflective of many of America's social ideals—equal justice under law, for example—than are phases of the systems used in other countries less renowned for a commitment to freedom and equality. This is not to say that the systems used by other countries are, overall, more just, but rather that certain aspects of some of these systems lead to more justice than do certain aspects of the American system. It is useful to examine these alternative ways of dealing with pretrial detention, for if a system is unjust and unworkable it is often better not to patch it up but to try an entirely different method. It is refreshing and enlightening to see the methods with which others with completely different systems and senses of values and ways of doing things cope with common problems.

ENGLAND

England, like the United States, has an accusatorial trial system and shares many traditional, Anglo-American trial procedures. Law court magistrates initiate the English bail system. The role of the police in the bail procedure, however, is nowhere as downplayed as it is in the United States. In most other countries the police have much more to say about quasi-judicial processes such as pretrial custody. In the United States it is the district attorney who ordinarily recommends bail to the court; in England it is the policeman. According to the Botein-Sturz report, "In over 95% of the cases [the magistrate] follow[s] the recommendation of the police and also consult[s] them about the solvency of the sureties."[1]

According to T. B. Smith, University of Edinburgh professor, Fellow of the British Academy, and Queen's counsel, in Scotland the public prosecutors have the most to say about pretrial confinement. Release is discretionary in all cases. The accused appears before a magistrate with little delay (within two days), and the court determines the bail question with regard both to the likelihood that the defendant will appear for trial and the expectations about his conduct upon release. If release is deemed appropriate, the defendant's lack of funds will not preclude his release.

Sixty per cent of those indicted in England are released prior to trial; the other 40 per cent are detained. However, of those convicted, only a few are released pending appeal. While those detained prior to trial are given preferential trial dates, pretrial incarceration averages about a month in urban areas and almost twice as much elsewhere (because the trial court simply does not get to more remote places as often, a distinction from our trial problems which are multiplied in the large congested areas due to the lack of enough judges and adequate facilities to handle the large amount of litigation). In 1962 these interesting figures were gathered: Over thirty-five thousand defendants were detained prior to trial without bail, of which over one thousand were found not guilty, approximately 3 per cent of those held in pretrial custody without bail.

Though England does employ a bail system akin to that in the United States in terms of exacting financial conditions for pretrial release, its system varies in one essential aspect.

[1] Report to the National Bail Conference, 1964.

Bail may be provided only by the accused or a person who will act as his surety. However, cash or a security is not posted with the court. An agreement is made to forfeit a stated sum of money if the defendant fails to appear. This is a kind of contract between that person and the Crown. However, the relationship cannot be commercialized. There are no professional bondsmen. In fact, furnishing bonds for profit is outlawed. The aim is to personally involve the surety in assuring the presence of the accused at trial. The court will explain this responsibility to the surety before releasing the defendant. The court may not accept a surety if it does not feel that he would be suitably responsible for the defendant. Bail is also only a fraction of the amount fixed for similar charges in the United States. This is probably attributable to the personal rather than the commercial nature of the surety undertaking in England. A relative needs less financial inducement to assure his agreement to produce a defendant than would a large, detached, and impersonal insurance company. This difference also accounts for the fact that fewer defendants in England are not able to arrange bail. "In only one percent of cases in which a bail amount had been set were persons detained pending trial because of inability to find sureties acceptable to the police or to the court." And forfeitures for failure to appear are so rare that statistical records are not even kept. The chief magistrate of London recently stated that "in his long experience not more than four defendants had failed to appear when required."

Nonfinancial conditions of release are sometimes used, too. Defendants are occasionally required to forfeit their passport, or to report to the police periodically, or to stay home, as conditions upon their pretrial release. Such conditions decrease the incidence of repeated crimes as well as flight. Sometimes criminal cases are instituted by the issuance of a summons instead of arrest. This eliminates the issue of release by avoid-. ing the taking of the defendant into custody in the first instance. Botein and Sturz felt after their overseas observations that the English system worked better and was fairer and wiser than the American bail system. "And," they concluded, "the halls of justice are rendered no less pure by the absence of professional bondsmen."

FRANCE

As Robert Vouin, a professor of law at the University of Bordeaux, described the French practices of provisional release in the University of Pennsylvania symposium, insofar as pretrial status is concerned, two practices prevail: they are preventive detention and provisional release. The former is supposed to be "an exceptional measure." Where the maximum sentence in a case is less than two months, there can be no preventive detention. This restriction is significant as it eliminates the problem of detention in a vast amount of relatively unimportant and minor cases where often the defendants probably could not afford any bail, and where they would provide little danger to society if released.

Preventive detention is otherwise discretionary. Where it is imposed, the time spent in pretrial custody is reduced from the sentence ultimately imposed. This is not the case in the United States. It is fair and this practice ought to be adopted. A bill providing for this is now before the United States Senate.

Provisional releases in France are of three kinds. *Mandatory release* comes either when the crime is minor or where the defendant falls into a certain category (no previous offenses, a French resident). This release must come within five days after the defendant's first appearance before the court. *Dis-*

cretionary release is a matter of judicial authority and it is ordered where there are no "very serious indications of guilt" or reasons to fear misuse of provisional release by fleeing, pressuring witnesses or destroying evidence, or committing new crimes. Necessary release is provided to cover the situation where preventive detention has lasted as long as the law authorizes (two months, with the possibility of another two-month extension by court order) or where the reasons for detention have ceased to exist. It can be seen that pretrial detention, when called for, may be extended.

Provisional releases are subject to three conditions: (1) that the defendant undertakes to appear at all stages of the proceedings and to keep the court apprised of his whereabouts; (2) at the discretion of the court some financial form of security may be required; and (3) the defendant must agree to inform the court whenever he changes his residence.

ITALY

In Italy, according to the Botein-Sturz report, criminal cases originate in one of three courts, the designation of court depending upon the gravity of the possible sentence. All three of these courts have the power to order pretrial arrest and detention. This power depends "on the term of punishment that can be meted out for the crime charged." Italy's inquisitorial system of justice allows the police and the prosecutor a period of time (from periods of nine days up to six months for certain crimes and two years for others) during which the suspect may be detained for investigatory purposes. In the courts where crimes of lesser magnitude are tried (Pretura) defendants are not frequently detained. In those courts where the moderately serious (Tribunal) and most grave (Assizes) crimes are tried, pretrial detention is often ordered. The main consideration relevant to release is whether the defendant will misbehave if he is free, more so than whether he will show up for trial. Government officials involved in the pretrial situation also give consideration to the cooperation or usefulness of the individual to the prosecution in determining whether to grant release or to detain.

Botein and Sturz noted that there has been recent native criticism about the illiberality of the criminal law in Italy and that a new criminal code is being prepared which is intended to be more reflective of the country's democratic principles. One aspect of this reform is supposed to be more lenient procedures governing pretrial treatment of accused defendants. The allowable nature and duration of pretrial detention is extremely onerous. A defense counsel has limited access to the defendant he represents, who can be detained for forty days before he is even indicted. This power is inquisitorial in the bleaker sense of that term.

On the other hand, when a defendant is released, he is ordinarily totally free. Sometimes release is made provisional upon such conditions as the surrender of the defendant's passport, living in a certain town, or periodic reporting to the police. But conditioning liberty upon financial conditions is considered undemocratic and is not done. However, long detentions are common, and pretrial release in the case of serious crimes is rare. Still, only about 10 per cent of all those arrested for criminal charges are imprisoned at all.

Norway, Sweden, and Denmark

That the overall philosophical attitudes of a nation are often reflected in its laws becomes obvious from an examination of the bail practices of the Scandinavian countries. This is especially so in the case of laws like those governing pretrial release, which are so central to the ideology of a system of government and its attitudes about individual freedom.

Norwegian laws of arrest and detention are required by the constitution to be specified by statute.[1] The Criminal Procedure Act of 1887 now governs the law of arrest and detention. Under this Act, an accused can be taken into custody "when there are reasonable grounds to suspect that he has committed an offense for which the statutory penalty is a term of imprisonment longer than six months." By American standards this would include all misdemeanors and felonies (federal law defines a petty offense as one with a maximum allowable sentence of six months; misdemeanors allow sentences to one year; every crime for which the sentence could exceed one year is a felony).

As a matter of practice, imprisonment before trial seems to depend more upon the gravity of the offense charged and the extent of the allowable sentence for that offense than upon the reasonable predictability of flight. The accused may also be imprisoned when there is reason to believe that evidence would be destroyed, or witnesses suborned, or where there is a likelihood that another similar crime would be committed (general danger of criminal activity, interestingly, is not enough). The court will determine whether detention is appropriate in each case. Its key considerations are supposed to be whether a "less drastic means than physical restraint" would suffice, and whether "the deprivation of liberty . . . is out of proportion to what [is intended to be achieved]."

The periods of detention before conviction are significant in Norway. Professor Bratholm presented some statistics compiled during 1952 indicating that the greatest percentage (about 70 per cent) of those persons who received jail sen-

---

[1] The *University of Pennsylvania Law Review* symposium contains an essay by Anders Bratholm, professor of law at the University of Oslo. This discussion was part of a larger study of arrest and detention by the author which was published by the Oslo University Press. It describes Norway's pretrial incarceration practices.

tences in their trials were also detained prior to trial. This correlation between pretrial and post-trial imprisonment has also been noted in the United States. The correlation may indicate the efficiency of investigatory processes that include the power of detention; it may represent more sinister circumstances such as the unreliable coercive aspect of inquisitorial powers like pretrial arrest. The average periods of the duration of detention varied from 72 days for stealing, to 101 days for acts of violence, to 175 days for sex offenses. Especially in jurisdictions like our own where pretrial detention does not delete subsequent sentences of imprisonment, figures like these compose a significant consideration. Interestingly, Norway's system is stricter than are the systems in Sweden and Denmark.

The Botein-Sturz report described how the inquisitorial system which exists in Sweden and Denmark allows the prosecutor the discretion to determine whether an accused should be "released or detained pending charge and trial." There, as elsewhere, the authors supposed that "the courts strive consciously or unconsciously to detain pending trial persons charged with the most serious types of crime or those which the community regards as particularly outrageous or horrendous." Of course in countries like ours, where bail is allowed, the dangerousness of a defendant becomes less significant than his ability to raise the money for bail. Often the most dangerous defendant is the most financially able.

The Danes abhor bail because it is "an instrument oppressive to the poor but convenient for the rich and well-connected," according to Botein and Sturz. Denmark is a strongly democratic country, as is Sweden. Both countries care a great deal about the fair treatment of criminally accused and the equality of treatment of the rich and the poor defendant. While Sweden has no bail system "either by law or in practice," Denmark has one by statute, although it is not applied.

In Sweden the police may detain a suspect up to twelve hours. After this time, they must release him or obtain authorization for his arrest from the prosecutor. The prosecutor must petition the court within five days in order to prolong detention, and thereafter the court must hold a detention hearing within four days or try the case within one week. So, actually an accused may be detained from nine to twelve days before trial. However, Botein and Sturz report that in practice prolonged detention is rare.

By statute, a defendant must be detained before trial if there is reason to believe that he will flee, destroy evidence, commit other crimes, or if the crime is of a certain kind for which imprisonment at hard labor could be adjudged. It is no wonder then that less than 1 per cent of those individuals who are released pending trial fail to appear in court at the appointed time. All the bad risks may not be given the chance to flee.

The police have great influence in the determination about pretrial release. The courts order detention in 95 per cent of the cases when the police recommended it and, in one study, in 80 per cent of the cases when the prosecutor recommended it. However, trials ensue quickly, and at least pretrial detention is not prolonged. One study in Stockholm showed that 57 per cent of all persons detained for criminal investigation in 1962 were released within twenty-four hours; the remaining 43 per cent were detained from four to five days until formal detention hearings could be arranged. The average length of pretrial incarceration after these court proceedings was fourteen days, and altogether nineteen days.

Ordinarily, those freed before trial are released on their word to return for trial. The judge or prosecutor may require additional nonfinancial conditions such as geographical limitations on travel or the duty to report to the police periodically.

These practices are consistent with the existing overall Swedish legal policies which go far to safeguard the rights of the accused.

In Denmark, although the practices of pretrial control of defendants generally follows that in Sweden, one major difference exists. It has been estimated that "two-thirds of all [Danish] prosecutions originate with a summons" rather than an arrest. The defendant, in this case, is free until after trial. This practice is now being experimented with in New York City by the police department along with the Vera Foundation. This approach is very humanitarian and one which could be a key technique of the future. As Botein and Sturz point out: "Danish authorities feel that seizure is very upsetting to persons accused of crime for the first time. The Danes are concerned with keeping the accused person's record free from the stigma of arrest, as well as giving him an opportunity to keep his job and life intact."

Otherwise, the Danish practices with regard to pretrial freedom are similar to the Swedish system. The nature of the crime and the background of the defendant determine whether the defendant wil be confined or set free pending trial. The alternative is more extreme than in the United States: outright freedom or absolute detention. The law allows bail, but it is not used, nor are the other authorized forms of provisional release. As a general rule, defendants are released on their promise to return to court. Youths in both countries (from fifteen to twenty-one) are given special treatment with regard to imprisonment generally.

RUSSIA

According to Dr. Armins Rusis, Department of European Law, of the Library of Congress, pretrial release practices in Russia vary widely from our own. In the case of serious crimes, the investigating magistrate has wide discretion about whether to release the accused defendant. If the local prosecutor sanctions it, the defendant could be arrested and detained for a period of up to two months. The Republic attorney (who is one step up the jurisdictional ladder) can detain for another six months, and the attorney general can add another three months of detention. This potential eleven-month pretrial detention can be extended for unusual circumstances, at the discretion of the state. Pretrial arrest like this is usually applied in the cases of serious crimes. For lesser crimes, the defendant may be released by signing an agreement not to leave the place of his residence. Between these two extremes—long arrest and detention, and outright unconditional release on trust—are other security measures. For example, another person or some organization may vouch for the appearance of the accused at trial. It is common for public organizations such as an employer to do this. Such practices are part of the recent Russian policy toward increasing the participation of the general public in the administration of criminal procedures. There are no public statistics to tell how often either of the described practices are used or whether fleeing is common. Escape is considered a separate crime.

Bail, the pretrial release on financial conditions which is the general practice in the United States, has an interesting history in Russian law. In the past, bail was not to be tolerated in the Communist society for two reasons: Under the bail system the wealthy are better off than the poor and that would not be fair; and also the policy was to arrest and take the defendant into custody or not to, and it was felt that one should not be able to pay to avoid these alternatives. However, recently one Soviet professor wrote that since Russian society has changed and there are now no capitalistic elements in existence, bail might provide a proper alternative in certain circumstances. He felt that it could now be envisioned that the situation might exist where it would not be necessary to arrest and detain a defendant, and yet more ought to be required of the defendant than his mere promise to show up. Here, bail (release conditioned upon the private deposit of money) might be appropriate. This idea is controversial in Russia and the practice is used seldom and only in rare cases, though it is provided for by statute in the Criminal Codes of Procedure. However, even when bail is allowed, there is no practice like that engaged in by our bail bondsmen. Commercial bonding would be equal to profiteering and speculation and would constitute a crime. Bail may be provided only by the defendant or a friend or relative, and never for profit.

The Soviet bail system is typical of its philosophical attitudes about law, government, and man in general. While the profit system in the judicial process is condemned and commercialization of pretrial release would be treated as a crime, there is provision for long imprisonment in many cases. And no one can ever really know what is going on as long as the state controls all media and other avenues of inquiry, and the facts are not public. While the economic policies behind the Soviet pretrial release system seem fair, the neglect, even abuse, of human values which this system allows could never be tolerated in a country like ours, which is so particularly concerned with the dignity and value of man.

JAPAN

In the *Pennsylvania Law Review* symposium,[2] Professors Shigemitsu Dando of Tokyo University and Hiroshi Taniya of Hokkaido University described the Japanese practice in the

[2] "A Symposium: Conditional Release Pending Trial," 108 *University of Pennsylvania Law Review*, 290–365 (1960).

conditional release of an accused: "Since the physical restraint of an accused prior to and during trial affects so fundamental a human right as personal freedom, such restraint should be permissible only in those limited cases where it is absolutely necessary for the investigation of a crime or for the conduct of trial." The possible jurisprudential inconsistency that is implicit in this attitude is at the crux of the disputes about when and why pretrial detention should be allowed. On one hand is the attitude that human freedom is an ideal to be fostered by the legal system; on the other hand is the vague qualification that this ideal can be sacrificed only when "necessary for the investigation of a crime or for the conduct of trial." This may mean, depending upon how the law is administered, that freedom will be protected except where it is not expedient to the prosecution. If this is the way the rule is applied, then the latter part of the law renders the earlier part of it voidable and meaningless. Freedom is more than an abstract notion. It is meaningful only when its vigor is retained in times of dispute, or passion, or even emergency.

Under modern criminal procedures in Japan, release is often allowed as a matter of right (depending on the kind of case) and may also be granted as a matter of judicial discretion when it is not demanded. As a matter of practical policy, statutory exceptions to the release rule are being progressively ameliorated and liberalized by the legislature.

Detention is allowed, however, to prevent escape and to avoid the suppression of evidence. Conditional release as a matter of right is limited to the period after investigation and before sentence. This qualification is critical. Often it is the period up to the completion of the investigation when the defendant is least protected. After this, his protections may be illusory, since the case against him could be perfected. This is the zone of time that is so much disputed nowadays in the courts and the press of this country with regard to the protections which society ought to guarantee individuals. Though this issue of prearraignment protections is not solely one of bail, it is inextricably entwined with the bail issue. In Japan, the courts may never release an accused during investigation (in the United States, the accused is generally entitled by law to release with or without bail during this time) or after a sentence that includes imprisonment. The Japanese courts apply the European qualifications, too, and often add to financial bail qualifications such as restricted travel, confinement to residence, or periodic reporting to designated officials.

Another interesting procedure which exists along with those release procedures just described is the oriental practice called *Oazuki* and *Sekifu*. This is a form of conditional liberation which suspends the execution of detention, a practice peculiar to Asian law and with roots in eighth-century Chinese law. Under this practice, the court, whether or not financial bail is imposed, may entrust "the accused under detention to the charge of his relative, a protective institution and the like . . . or restrict[ing] his dwelling." Thus the law provides for suspension of the execution of detention on financial and nonfinancial conditions. Nonfinancial release is especially important, Dando and Taniya recognized, when the accused is too poor to afford bail, where financial conditions alone are not considered sufficient deterrent to flight (where the defendant is too rich for bail to be effective), or where other special circumstances warrant suspension of early detention. The beauties of this practice are that it minimizes "the likelihood of repetition of criminal offenses" and "enhances the opportunities of an accused to secure conditional release." Unfortunately, Dando and Taniya admit that, owing to the complexity of modern life in Japan, the practice of suspension of detention is rarely used now.

The courts have the power to rescind all conditional releases for any one of several, reasonable statutory grounds (flight, suppression of evidence, violation of imposed conditions). The Lord giveth and the Lord taketh away. This attitude is consistent with liberal release policies, and is far more appropriate than is detention on the suspicion that certain conditions *could* come about.

It is telling to observe that the one chief, distinguishing characteristic of American release practices is the primary reliance upon financial conditions and the commercial sureties who administer them. An examination of the practical implications which flow from this phenomenon makes it quite clear that the American system could better be noteworthy for other, more enlightened reasons. In attempting to improve the pretrial release system, America can learn some lessons from other countries.

No other country besides the United States and the Philippines has a commercial bail-bond system. The uniform rejection around the world of our crass commercialization of even a part of the judicial system is, as we shall see, quite proper. Ironically, other countries reject this practice for philosophical reasons that are more appropriate to America's form of government. Unequal justice, as prevails under the financially oriented bail system, is especially unfortunate and inappropriate to our way of life, generally so conscious of the dignity of all men without regard to their station, and ordinarily so wisely protective of maintaining the proper balance between the needs of government and the rights of individuals.

Release based on money need not operate in a way prejudicial to poor people. In Korea, for instance, bail must be what one can afford. Money is not used in a discriminatory way, only as an inducement. Whereas money may be a valid conditioning device, it should not be the sole one. And its role should remain with the people involved and the court.

Personalizing the surety relationship by using relatives, employers, or private organizations spreads the responsibility of government throughout society. Furthermore, it bases judicial discretion on personal responsibility, a more mature criterion than money.

One valid result of the foreign systems is that they accomplish what they intend and the American does not. The overriding intent of the foreign systems is to release or detain defendants based on definite criteria. This is done. The American money system does not accomplish this result. American courts often set low bail intending to release a defendant, who for one of several reasons is not released; or they set high bail intending to detain a defendant who simply attains his release and feels no deterrence by virtue of the money bail. Perhaps this is because the prime concern regarding pretrial detention in foreign jurisdictions is with the potential danger to the public should the defendant be released, while the stated main purpose in the United States is with deterring flight.

Another characteristic of foreign systems is the use of non-financial conditions of release such as house arrest, deposit of passports, periodic reporting to authorities, and other like controls. These techniques are fair and effective, and our country would do well to consider adopting similar practices.

Avoiding arrest in the first place by using a summons to appear at trial instead of arrest and incarceration is another promising technique. Trial programs underway now ought to provide the pragmatic proof that will help evaluate this method. It seems like a good one.

Long detentions before trial are nonetheless possible abroad and in the United States. This result is reached for different *stated* reasons, and through different procedural avenues. American procedures seem less candid, and possibly less efficient. But even if the results are similar, questions must be raised if America is to continue its proud boast of being the most freedom-loving country.

On the positive side of this ledger, Americans can take pride in the fact that, more than in most other countries, people suspected of criminal activity are protected early in the investigatory process and have numerous legal means (aside from bail) to avoid long pretrial detention. Imprisonment for strictly investigatory purposes is rare and is shrouded with constitutional safeguards aimed at reducing the opportunities for abuse.

CHAPTER VII

An Evaluation and Proposal

Almost a half-century ago, Arthur Lawton Beeley, now Dean and Professor Emeritus of the University of Utah School of Social Work, wrote his doctoral dissertation about the Cook County (Chicago) bail system. His work was published as a book in 1927.[1] In it, he pointed out that many people imprisoned before trial were later acquitted of the charges. Many were not transients; quite the contrary, they were people with solid ties to the community. Many were youngsters. Many had favorable references; only about a quarter had ever been imprisoned before. One-sixth had pathological problems which warranted hospitalization more than imprisonment.

Dean Beeley urged then that a summons be used as an alternative to arrest before trial; he argued that pretrial detention lasted too long; that the amounts of bail which were being set were determined arbitrarily and insensitively; that the bondsman's role was inflated and his value exaggerated. These conclusions and suggestions may have been called radical in their time. Sadly, for the most part, his observations would hold true in Chicago and in most places in the United States today. A very recent survey[2] of bail practices in the Municipal Court of Chicago showed that in one year, out of

[1] Arthur Lawton Beeley, *The Bail System in Chicago*, University of Chicago Press, 1927.
[2] T. F. O'Rourke and S. Wizner, "Bail in Chicago," unpublished Master's thesis, University of Chicago (1962).

approximately fifty thousand cases in which bail was furnishable, only 1 per cent of the defendants were released on their own recognizance—only 1 per cent!

This is not to say that there has been no progress at all since the time of Dean Beeley's pioneer disclosures. There have been some significant steps forward recently. These have been chronicled earlier in this book: The work of the Vera Foundation and its proselytization around the country, the Tulsa and Illinois programs, the experiments with ROR and summons, the National Bail Conference in 1964, and the stimulation of thought and change by the Justice Department under the leadership first of Robert F. Kennedy and now of Nicholas deB. Katzenbach, the scholarly and provoking works of people such as Arthur Beeley, Caleb Foote, Herbert Sturz, and Judge Bernard Botein, the legislative leadership of men such as Senator Sam Ervin, Jr. and Charles Bowman, the landmark opinions of Justices Robert Jackson and William Douglas and Judge Skelly Wright. Contributions such as these have combined to bring us to the brink of what is now needed—complete reform of the American bail system. All these people and projects have offered parts to the puzzling picture of possible bail reform.

EVALUATION

Serious questions can be asked about the operation of the American bail system. Does it work and accomplish the ends for which it was conceived? And even if it does, are there abuses of such a degree as to raise the question whether the system is worth the cost? It is hoped that at this point the reader has serious reservations about the workings and value of the bail system and that the basic questions raised in the introductory chapter of this book have been answered on the way to this conclusion.

Does bail serve a legitimate purpose? Utilitarianism as the reason for bail can be successfully contested. We have seen that the requirement for money-bail works to cause imprisonment, but does not serve to protect society from those who arguably may be considered the most dangerous criminals. The latter can buy their freedom, or extract it from bondsmen whom they control. The poor cannot afford bail. For the middle class defendant, bail is simply a waste of money which does not even serve a useful public purpose. And it is only the rarest cases where the added ingredient of pledged money would either be necessary or would serve as a real inducement to a defendant to appear for trial.

Even as a practical matter, one can also question the utility of bail as a way of getting defendants to court on time. Experiments like Vera's in New York City indicate, admittedly inconclusively but nonetheless persuasively, that more people failed to appear for trial from the bail status than did those who were treated more leniently and permissively. At least these experiences show that there need be no relationship between the availability of money to afford bail and one's reliability to appear for trial. And bondsmen are an ignoble and ineffective substitute either for personal responsibility on the part of the individual involved or for social responsibility on the part of the court that is in control of the matter.

Some say that while assuring the appearance of defendants at trial may be a primary purpose of bail, other rationales exist. Protecting society from likely harms is the alternate purpose most frequently suggested. And yet this rationale for bail offends the important notion that to imprison one because he is dangerous is in effect to conclude that he is guilty. Theoretically our law does not condone the denial of bail because of a defendant's evil reputation or because of community resentment of a defendant. Otherwise, the criminal status of a defendant (based on this earliest contact with the criminal law process) would affect the further disposition of that same criminal process regarding that same defendant. This is a compounding kind of injustice which, though theoretically wrong, is in practice commonplace. Though the attitude which presumes a man's dangerousness is repugnant to our way of thinking, the very real problem which gives rise to the attitude must be dealt with carefully and thoughtfully. But is bail the way to deal with the very difficult problems of preventive detention? Is it fair, wise, or effective to manipulate the power to set bail in order to accomplish the tangential end of preventive detention? I suggest that it is not, and that a more appropriate way to treat this issue can be found.

Caleb Foote has been outspoken about the lack of wisdom in the present polarized alternatives currently available to the defendant during the time prior to his trial. Absolute freedom or imprisonment need not adequately serve either of the legitimate ends (protecting defendants and protecting society) involved in this perplexing problem. Pretrial supervision is necessary, but that need not be synonymous with imprisonment. Nor should the responsibility for supervision during pretrial release be ignored or delegated to the bondsman as it now is in most cases. Procedures that encourage (or at least leave room for) individualization of the treatment of defendants would be more proper. The present bail system is no example of the libertarian, humane, and democratic form of government action of which America so proudly boasts. Even in 1832 this paradox was noted when the astute political critic Alexis Clérel De Tocqueville wrote that the ". . . criminal procedure of the Americans has only two means of action —committal and bail. . . . It is evident that a legislation of this kind is hostile to the poor man, and favorable only to the rich. The poor man has not always a security to produce, . . .

and if he is obliged to wait for justice in prison, he is speedily reduced to distress. . . . Nothing can be more aristocratic than this system of legislation."

We have also seen that the bail-setting power is easily manipulated for improper ends and has been abused—against unpopular defendants, against poor people, against those out of favor with the authorities in a given time and place. It has been abused by judges who have used it to accomplish private and personal goals.

The legal propriety of the bail system is also open to serious questions. Certainly the theoretical argument could be made that preventive detention and perhaps any incarceration before release or any restrictions upon freedom before trial and conviction violate the guiding thought behind our legal system's presumption of innocence. Most American jurisdictions deny bail at least in capital cases, thus doing away with the presumption of innocence in the cases where the charges are most grave. This is a questionable inconsistency which has always been a part of the law of bail. Although the presumption of innocence is only a rule of evidence which comes into play at the time of trial, the philosophy of the rule that guilt should not be prejudged or assumed should guide the whole process of criminal justice if it is to have real meaning.

More significant than the violation of this rule of evidence is the serious and vital question whether the workings of our bail system violate the guarantees of our Constitution. The Bill of Rights mentions bail only indirectly in the Eighth Amendment, which directs that bail must not be excessive. This admonition includes two implicit judgments: that there is a bail system; and that one is necessarily entitled to protection only from the excesses of bail but not necessarily from its outright denial. Yet, arguably, the denial of bail is perforce excessive. However, when the Eighth Amendment is read in the context of our jurisprudential history, and the recently invigorated due process and equal protection clauses of the Fifth and Fourteenth Amendments, the spirit of the rules governing bail seems to demand a more expansive view of the right to pretrial release and a more restrictive view of the meaning of the Eighth Amendment. It seems more reasonable to conclude that the bail system is not mandatory but only one restricted way of treating pretrial custody. As such, the only inhibition of the Eighth Amendment is that if bail is resorted to, it must not be excessively applied. But where bail does not afford an opportunity for release, the philosophy behind the legal system would demand some alternative to gain freedom unless strong countervailing considerations exist. If the bail system works systematically to prejudice clearly identifiable groups because of their lack of money or property, and this is clearly the case, the system may be an unconstitutional one, at least with regard to those persons in the prejudiced class. In this instance, the class is so large as to bespeak a breakdown of the whole system. The Supreme Court has already said that ". . . in criminal trials a State can no more discriminate on account of poverty than on account of religion, race, or color."[8] Yet, the operation of our bail system does discriminate on account of poverty. We have clearly seen that pretrial detention is quite extensive. To take just a few examples that have occurred in recent years, 75 per cent of all defendants in Baltimore, 50 per cent in Philadelphia, 78 per cent in St. Louis, 65 per cent in the District of Columbia, and 62 per cent in Chicago were forced to go to jail before trial because they could not afford bail. And these detention rates rise in ratio to the amount of bail demanded. In New York City in one year, 28 per cent of all defendants could not afford $500 bail; 45 per cent could not afford $2,000 bail. Thus it is

[8] Griffin v. Illinois, 351 U.S. 12 (1956).

clear that the poor are especially prejudiced by the bail system and that the national number of those who fall into this particular class of prejudiced defendants is very significant. The Supreme Court has not yet been faced with the case where this question was raised against the operation of the bail system. Justice Douglas has intimated a disposition to apply the rule against discrimination on account of poverty should the opportunity arise in a bail case. The role of wealth in our administration of justice has been receiving considerable attention in recent years, and it may well be that this question in relation to the bail system will soon be treated by the Supreme Court.

Another constitutional issue was suggested in the conclusion of Chapter II. When the bail-setting power is abused as it has been in so many cases, constitutional questions should be raised. Were not those civil rights defendants being deprived of due process of law or the equal protection of the laws? No doubt this question will be raised soon by someone connected with the civil rights movement. Litigation questioning the constitutionality of clear and concerted bail manipulation could cause far-reaching changes in present practices.

One judicial decision of the right magnitude and scope could go far toward accelerating and indicating the direction of change. But the judicial process, while inexorable, is often tediously, sometimes defeatingly, slow. Short of judicial reform, executive or legislative action will have to suffice as the mainspring to bail reform. This has been the case in the federal government and with many state and local governments in recent years.

The new programs described earlier in this book have been palliatives. But alone they will not cure the deep and important questions raised by the workings of the American bail system. They will not do so because they have been created to work within that system. Therefore it is permissible and profitable to depart from all the individual reform programs already described, without displaying any disagreement with their essential principles, in order to question whether these programs have gone far enough. For the most part, these programs, presupposed the existence of and deal with the bail system as it is and as it has been. They have tried to make the system fairer, more workable, more just. But they dealt within the context of our traditional bail system. In proposing reform, one need not make this essential concession.

It must be frankly admitted that these new programs reflected the wise and realistic attempts of good men to bring about reforms in a dynamic society that was unlikely to accept utopian, radical, even extreme changes. Transitions such as that which would be involved in completely reforming our bail system come slowly, after trials and chances for proof. The wisdom of this kind of conservatism is only weakened by the fact that this very gradual process is sometimes overdone and the efforts for law revision are often inordinately time consuming. The bail-reform programs that have been discussed were both necessary and useful in bringing about change. They dealt within a world of competing pragmatics and ideas. And in making an improvement at the same time they made it possible to go further. Congress now seems ready for bail reform.

It is submitted that we should now go further. I am convinced that the whole American bail system should be scrapped —completely—and that a new system should be substituted for it. The evidence is clear and commanding that the American bail system fails for three reasons: (1) It has lent itself to excessive and inexcusable abuses; (2) it has caused the proliferation of evils which are part and products of the bail-bond business; and (3) it is not utilitarian, which is to say it does not even work as well as other less troublesome systems. This conclusion is based both on the evidence presented in the examination of the present system in earlier chapters and on the conviction that a better procedure ought to be and can be devised. In the belief that one ought not to dismiss an ongoing system in a cavalier fashion without attempting to find a better alternative, a proposal is suggested.

PROPOSAL

To describe my proposal it is necessary to assume hypothetically that there is a void to be filled between the time when an arrest would ordinarily have been made and the subsequent time when a criminal trial would be commenced pursuant to that arrest. During that period the individual charged with committing a crime has, ideally, one interest— to be free to live his life and, additionally, to prepare for his trial. Society has an interest in this same ideal, since the rights of one man are inextricably entwined with the rights of all. Society also has a competing interest. Ideally, society also wants its cases against charged individuals properly prepared. And it wants to be protected from wrongs to its citizens during this interim time between arrest and trial. Finally, it wants the accused to be present for his trial.

This latter interest is the crux of the voluntary system of our law: It is the beautifully interesting and crucial phenomenon of the democratic form of government and of the accusatorial system. In order for people to run their government, they must also submit to government. Under the American criminal law process, people indict and try each other. Defendants dispute charges against them in an ordered procedure before their fellowmen. The balance between the individual and the law would not be the same without this aspect of voluntarism. The idea that one will voluntarily succumb to trial by his fellowmen is at the foundation of our form of government. But it is at war with the notions upon which bail is rationalized. Justice Frankfurter once stated that bail (in that case, bail on appeal) presupposes the confidence that defendants will respond to the demands of our system of justice. Thus, he said, the amount of bail should be whatever is necessary to insure the defendant's presence. And, according to Justice Frankfurter, it also follows that, "Impliedly, the likelihood that bail within tolerable limits will not insure this justifies denial of bail."[4] Against this viewpoint it could be argued that bail presupposes just the opposite of what Justice Frankfurter suggested. Bail presupposes (I think, on the whole, wrongly) both that men cannot be trusted to appear for trial and that only money or prison can rectify that weakness. This is a very pessimistic viewpoint which conflicts with our main experiences and our aspirations.

To digress no further it is now timely to consider how better to cope with this situation, with this time period in the process of criminal law enforcement, and with these competing interests. If the present bail system is eradicated, what would be the better substitute?

I propose a two-step pretrial procedure to deal with all situations now covered by bail. Step 1 would include the greatest majority of cases, those when release is deemed appropriate. Step 2 would involve special procedures to deal with the special cases when it is thought that for exceptional reasons pretrial detention should be ordered. Step 1 would include two classes of situations: one, for the majority of cases when the judicial process is called into play and some Vera-like supervised release is ordered; the other, when a summons would suffice, and the judicial pretrial process could be avoided or significantly limited. There would never be an incarceration prior to trial under a step 1 proceeding; there could be pretrial im-

[4] Ward v. U.S., 76 S. Ct. 1063 (1956).

prisonment only after a step 2 proceeding, which would deal only with this issue and which could be instituted only in prescribed situations and carried on in a prescribed manner. Let me explain.

When the state determines formally to begin its criminal process against a man who it believes or suspects of having committed a crime, it should proceed under step 1 in one of two ways.

If the crime is not a serious one (a petty offense, possibly some misdemeanors), a lesson can be taken from the experiences with the summons. Either instead of arrest or at the time of arrest (and often instead of taking a person physically into custody), or a very few hours thereafter (here there would have been an arrest, booking, perhaps some brief incarceration demanded by the particular exigencies of the case), the defendant should be summoned by a delegated police official to appear in court for trial. If refused the summons, he could demand to be brought before a court which would, except for some extraordinary reason, then order him to appear for arraignment or trial. This phase of step 1 would include both the true police summons (instead of an arrest) or police ROR (that is, a summons soon after arrest, along with some limited investigation). The defendant would have to agree to appear in court as a condition of his release.

If the crime were a serious one (aggravated misdemeanors or felonies), the accused should immediately be brought under the control of the courts for initial action. This should be done as soon as possible, under similar time requirements as now exist in federal practice regarding mandatory appearance before a commissioner. Depending on the nature of the crime, the background of the defendant, and any other meaningful circumstances of the case, the court could then proceed, either by merely ordering the defendant to appear for later arraign-

ment or trial, or by placing him under the control of a designated official for investigation and then ordering his future appearance and releasing him under the supervision of that court
officer.

Under either phase of step 1, both prolonged imprisonment
and release based upon money bail would be eliminated, and
with it would disappear the role of the bondsman in the administration of justice.

Where a summons was issued, there would be no significant
imprisonment. In other cases, at the first meeting with a defendant the judge would be called upon to decide which techniques would be appropriate to assure the defendant's presence
at trial. This might be a simple order by the court to be there;
or it might be an order when to appear with an assignment to
and the assumption by the defense attorney of the responsibility to insure his client's presence. If appropriate (and it would
be in most cases) the court would make an assignment to the
district attorney, or preferably to a court official such as a parole
officer, to investigate the defendant and administer the order
to appear. This function could be assigned to any court
official, even one who dealt solely with this task. The repon-
sible court official could fulfill this duty by any program short
of imprisonment.

The supervisory officer for the court could draw on the
techniques of any of the existing programs to suitably administer the defendant's release. He might require a defendant to
report periodically; or to submit a driver's license or a passport;
or to deposit a bank book, even a sum of money if it were an
appropriate control and as long as release was not dependent
solely on the ability to make a financial deposit. Perhaps only a
letter or a phone call would be all that was necessary. Third
party parole could be used. Under this concept, the assistance
of an employer, a relative, or a member of the clergy is en-

listed to supervise the defendant prior to trial. This is done now in Albuquerque. It has long been a practice in juvenile courts. The point here is that the court official, with the opportunity to satisfy himself that the defendant is no danger and can be released, as would be the case most of the time, should not be limited in the variety of methods by which he could administer this step 1 proceeding and assure the defendant's presence at trial.

I suggest that this supervisory task should be a public one, not one for private agents, as is the case where the Vera program is in operation. All the techniques of the existing ROR and Vera-type programs could be used as models for administering this quasi-control prior to trial without incarceration or bail charges. No more action would be necessary in the greatest majority of cases. Experience and experiments have proved that.

This aspect of the judicial process, calling for some supervision by the court or its agents to insure against failures to appear, should not be relegated to the bondsman. Rather the function should remain with the court. The means of administering this essentially clerical and administrative function could be developed with an eye toward present experiences with programs like Vera's. The essential truth to be derived from Vera's work, and from programs like it, is that pretrial investigation and supervision of defendants is wiser and fairer than reliance upon the enterprise of commerce insofar as providing the assistance for release and avoiding flight before trial.

Certainly programs like those in St. Louis and Detroit, for example, have demonstrated that the courts can do this job of administration better in every sense than can the bondsman. And the programs of Vera, Tulsa, and Illinois have sufficiently shown that defendants free on bail are no better risks than those released on their own recognizance. In fact the suggestion is that the latter group are better risks. As Justice Douglas pointed out in *U.S. v. Bandy*, quoted in Chapter I, ". . . there may be other deterrents to jumping bail: long residence in a locality, the ties of friends and family, the efficiency of the modern police. All these in a given case may offer a deterrent at least equal to that of the threat of forfeiture." Since the premium for a bond is usually about 10 per cent of the amount of the bail, it is unrealistic to believe that the fear of forfeiting the premium will deter flight if the defendant is so disposed. And the collateral supporting a bail bond is unattainable for the poor and is often ineffective for the rich. Thus its addition does not add to the utility of bail. Enough should have been said in Chapter III about the faults of the bondsman to warrant dispensing with the restatement of that indictment here.

If there is flight, this should be a problem for the court and police, not the businessman. The responsibility and cost of bringing a defendant to justice should rest with society. And although the deterrence of flight is the prime reason for our bail system, flight is no longer a serious problem. James V. Bennett has pointed out that fugitives from justice are so rare that bonds are really unnecessary. In his experience, of 750,000 prisoners, fewer than 12 escaped and were not captured. And of those, there is no reason to believe that the bail-bond system would have prevented or terminated their escape. To this low figure of fugitives must be added the impressively efficient record of the FBI in hunting down and capturing even this small percentage of people. The police investigative agencies are quite adept at this function and have proved the fact that of the few defendants who become fugitives, even fewer get away. Natural deterrents like lack of money to hide indefinitely, or ties to home, people, and community also all combine to minimize the problem of flight.

Courts also have the contempt power, the power to swiftly punish any violation of their orders. This would include an order to appear for trial. And there are adequate devices other than contempt with which courts can deal with fugitives. Fleeing from a trial could be made a crime in those places where it is not already. And in some places, proof of flight may be offered in a trial as evidence of a defendant's consciousness of guilt. So, as a practical matter, courts can deal adequately with the few cases of flight.

Thus the courts have both punitive as well as administrative powers to deal with the inevitable but unusual cases when a defendant does not appear for trial. Charging fees for bonds or imprisoning other nonrisk defendants, as is now done, is not a worthy cost for dealing with these few cases. The present system charges or imprisons the mass of defendants to protect against the potential few who might flee or do harm. The proposed system frees the mass of defendants who deserve freedom and provides a special machinery to deal differently with the exceptions.

To return to my proposal, under the proposed step 1 situation all defendants would be released prior to trial:

a. In petty offenses and minor misdemeanor cases after only a summons to appear, or a brief arrest and then release with a summons by a police official who would administer the bookkeeping needed to record and administer the event, or

b. in more serious cases after being brought swiftly before a court and either

(1) simply ordered by the court to appear, or

(2) ordered to appear and in the meantime placed under the control of his attorney, or a court officer, who would interview the defendant and assume the administration of the Vera role of investigation and supervision.

Step 1 would no doubt cover 90 per cent or more of all criminal cases and the release of most defendants.

In addition, some further procedure must be provided to cope with the small, special, but very important class of cases mentioned in Chapter IV when the court or prosecution feels that compellingly strong reasons exist to warrant special treatment of a particular defendant until his trial. As a second step a special procedure is necessary to deal with the problems of preventive detention. This procedure should attempt to balance the safety of society reasonably with the rights of accused individuals, to secure the proper relationship between control and freedom. Any such proposal must take into account two vital values: (1) the need to prevent unnecessary crimes, especially crimes of violence or crimes truly involving the nation's security, whenever possible; (2) the importance of maintaining and encouraging the working philosophy about crime that no man should lose his liberty without due process of law, that accusation is not conviction, that until conviction a man is presumed innocent, and that the burden is on the government to prove otherwise.

To do this I would propose the establishment of a special step 2 proceeding in the nature of a civil commitment proceeding at the time of arraignment, to deal only with the special cases where preventive detention is sought by the government. In appropriate cases, if the prosecutor should feel that there are strong reasons why a defendant should be imprisoned prior to trial, he could resort to this special step 2 proceeding to seek the court's sanction for a special commitment. The court could initiate this proceeding, too, as could the court officer who is in charge of the administration of defendants prior to trial, when the step 1 circumstances made it appropriate. For example, if in the step 1 proceeding a defendant should refuse to cooperate with the court official, so that the court could not determine whether release would be appropriate, no other recourse would exist except automatically moving into this step 2 proceeding. This instance might arise in cases where defendants are unknown or uncooperative. If the official in charge of release procedures under step 1 could not gain sufficient facts to administer pretrial supervision, he would have no recourse but to seek pretrial imprisonment. Here, the defendant himself would have frustrated the machinery set up to prevent his pretrial imprisonment. He could not complain about incarceration, since it would have been in his power to avoid it and he would have chosen not to exercise it.

Appropriately careful and sensitive procedures would have to be developed to avoid the touchy constitutional questions of self-incrimination and the right to counsel, which could arise during these early proceedings.

A statute should list the cases where the step 2 proceeding would be permitted. This law should include crimes of extreme violence, obviously pathological crimes, subversion cases where violence, sabotage, or treason were involved, and cases where recidivism or obstruction of justice is reasonably anticipated. Situations where a defendant would not cooperate with the court official in charge of release could also be a category permitted under this procedure.

The government should be required in this class of case to make a very strong showing of the existence of these special conditions, to warrant the invocation of commitment. In the step 2 proceeding, of course, the defendant would have the fullest and fastest opportunity, with counsel, to oppose the government by presenting full arguments in his defense. All doubts would have to be resolved in favor of the defendant.

It should be noted that the government would not be without certain recourse should its request be denied. For one thing, the court could carefully instruct the defendant about his responsibilities regarding the matter that raised the issue of detention. Any later misconduct could be quickly handled by the court in a contempt proceeding. All government witnesses and evidence could be subpoenaed immediately so that any subsequent interference with them could be prosecuted under existing obstruction of justice statutes. Police surveillance could be instituted to protect anyone endangered and to frustrate further criminal acts by the defendant.

Only if the court should decide after a speedy, full, and fair hearing to order special commitment would the defendant be incarcerated. Even in this case, every step should be taken to make this a special kind of arrest. I do not suggest this in any hypocritical or euphemistic sense. No imprisonment is pleasant, I realize, and calling it something else does not make it any better. Even Blackstone, who argued that preventive detention was not only necessary but eminently fair, recognized the prejudicial penal aspect of preventive detention:

> But this imprisonment, as has been said, is only for safe custody, and not for punishment; therefore, in this dubious interval between the commitment and trial, a prisoner ought to be used with the utmost humanity, and neither be loaded with needless fetters nor subjected to other hardships than such as are absolutely requisite for the purpose of confinement only; though what are so requisite must too often be left to the discretion of the gaolers, who are frequently a merciless race of men, and, by being conversant in scenes of misery, steeled against any tender sensation."[5]

A great deal can be done to make this incarceration less personally destructive than is present pretrial detention. For example, a special facility for pretrial incarceration (separate at least from convicted prisoners and possibly even from the prison for convicted criminals) should be considered. All

[5] Blackstone (Jones), Vol. 2, p. 2523, S. 337.

facilities should be made as physically pleasant as possible. A prisoner's family should be allowed to visit at any reasonable time. The defendant should be able to work at controlled employment to earn some reasonable income during this time before trial. He should be assisted to find re-employment if he is acquitted. All social and medical services that would be helpful to him or his family ought to be provided. Where the crime charged or the background of the defendant indicates a mental problem, treatment could begin immediately. Particularly in the cases of the uncontrollable recidivist criminal, or the pathological or insane criminal, this proceeding could convert into a more permanent medical incarceration if that were found to be appropriate. This pretrial incarceration should not be counted as an arrest record if the defendant should be acquitted. Trial dates should be expedited by giving calendar preferences to these cases. The time of pretrial detention should be reduced from any subsequent sentence after the trial. The defendant should be released at the time of trial, and the fact of his incarceration should not be brought to the jury's attention.

I fully realize that this suggested proceeding raises serious constitutional problems which cannot be dismissed lightly. To deprive any accused defendant of his liberty without a trial by jury, for committing no consummated wrong or no proscribed action, is fundamentally in conflict with the basic American way of doing things. This is so no matter how the incarceration is specialized.

I realize that there is a chance that step 2 would be declared unconstitutional because, no matter how circumscribed and how restrained, it does sanction imprisonment without the traditional trial and all its valuable concomitant protections. There is some precedent for this kind of a proceeding in existing civil commitment practices where individuals may be incarcerated without the ordinary trial process because it is deemed necessary to society and to the individual himself to do this. This is so, for example, in certain places in narcotics cases and in mental incompetency proceedings. Could the rationale be extended? How different are these proceedings from the one recommended? Is the title "civil" in a matter the critical factor? Would not the courts be doing the same thing in cases under the proposed step 2 as they have done in civil commitment proceedings?

Could not the pragmatic argument be made in defense of step 2 that since (a) we frequently practice preventive detention under the bail system and (b) it has never been considered unconstitutional, then (c) doing it under step 2 in a much more clear and direct fashion, surrounded with careful safeguards, should not be considered unconstitutional either? This is really the converse argument to the proposition that since imprisonment without trial is unconstitutional, dressing it up in a special case cannot change a weed into a rose. To this the response may be that no matter what principles we espouse, we do practice preventive detention within the workings of the bail system—so why not here?

How carefully step 2 was implemented would be an important factor in assaying whether it would be a reasonable and fair procedure. The courts would have to build a body of law around such general guiding propositions as: How much proof would be necessary to invoke step 2 successfully? Precisely what crimes would fall within the general categories of eligibility that were suggested? How could the time factors be controlled to allow defendants realistic and fair opportunities to oppose or appeal from these proceedings?

The trenchant question has been asked me: Once condoning preventive detention under these restrictive circumstances, how can one stop there? Would this lead to arrests for investigation? Once accepting the idea behind preventive detention, why wait for a formal indictment or criminal charge to detain? Why not detain all the evil people and prevent their future crimes? Why not have preventive detention even after acquittals or dropped charges, to protect society? The answer must be that lines must be drawn and that the suggested contours in this situation seem fair and right. Concepts need not be taken to their logical extremes so as to test their validity in limited cases. But the question does raise the visceral reaction to, and the theoretical caveat about, preventive detention. If used, it must be done carefully. Notwithstanding its questionable constitutional character, it is suggested that the proposed step 2 proceeding would result in less improper official conduct and less incarceration than goes on under the present bail system, and it would better protect both society and defendants.

On balance step 2 should cause less of a loss of personal liberties or of public security than results from the present system. First of all, the bail power would not have to be perverted to deal circuitously with these problem cases. For judges to misuse their judicial powers as they do now in denying bail for preventive purposes is wrong and degrades the judicial process, no matter how noble may be the motivation. Secondly, a distressing situation would be faced, and dealt with clearly, and I should hope sensitively. In those cases where preventive detention was proper, there would be some specified mechanism to deal with the particular exigencies of that particular case. The individual against whom this procedure is invoked could insist that the charges against him be specified, and proved. And he would have an opportunity to refute them. There would be less chance for judges to abuse their powers—their reasons and the basis for them would appear on an appealable record. Moreover, any incarceration would be less punitive than it is under existing penal procedures. Every possible consideration would be afforded the defendant. His trial would be expedited. His period of incarceration would be made as tolerable as possible. He could receive medical and other special services if they were warranted.

I grant this is not equal to freedom, but it would intend to be as close to it as possible, or at least as far from traditional imprisonment as possible. These cases would undoubtedly be few in number, but they are often the most important and socially demanding cases. A proper procedure for such cases, and one which would not be applied to any others, must be provided. Whatever extra costs would be occasioned by the administration of this program would be worthwhile. The expenses and the personnel could, for the most part, be drawn from existing sources.

Some means for preventive detention exists in all other systems of law. Currently there is no such procedure in the United States, though the problems that create the need for one are recognized as serious. Presently, in an ad hoc unofficial way we treat these situations either by reacting after the damage is done or by misusing the bail procedures (which are not meant to take care of this situation) as a makeshift substitute. The proposed procedure is an attempt to accommodate many competing interests clearly, directly, and with fairness.

A POSTSCRIPT PROPOSAL

It is recognized, nonetheless, that such a procedure as I have suggested for step 2 of my proposal is subject to two serious and possibly fatal objections. Should it be determined that (1) the idea may be good but is unconstitutional, or (2) that the idea is not good and therefore not worth adopting even if it were declared constitutional, then we must ask if there are still other, better alternatives for dealing with these special step 2 cases, aside from the present bail system. There are.

To deal with these other methods, it is necessary to break down this class of step 2 cases into specific problem areas. Each specific area could be dealt with in a special way. The cases that fall into step 2, or which do not fall into step 1 of my proposal, are these: certain subversion cases, certain organized crime cases, patently pathological crimes, egregious recidivist cases, and possibly some minor vagrancy-type cases.

Without going into great detail, ways of treating these categories of cases can be generally suggested. All would be better both to society (in terms of self-defense and the deterrence of flight) and to the defendants (in terms of helping them and protecting their rights) than is the bail system in these cases.

In the class of subversion case where there is not a real danger to society if the defendants are released (a danger in terms of flight or the commission of further serious criminal acts), release and surveillance ought to suffice. Where there is a strong showing that one of these conditions does exist, the defendant could probably be detained under present procedures. Either the imminence of flight or of the commission of serious (possibly capital) offenses would warrant pretrial detention. Detention could be required by statute in these cases just as it is now for capital offenses. In the other cases, conditional release under the careful supervision of the court (step 1, with any reasonable conditions) and of the FBI ought to keep the defendant under suitable control.

In organized crime cases where the fear is that evidence or witnesses are in jeopardy, several steps could be taken. The evidence or the witnesses could be taken under protective custody (not imprisonment). Or a reverse material witness bond could be demanded, this time operating against the cause of the fear instead of the object of it, as is now the case. Again, surveillance of the victim and the threatener by investigative bodies could afford some deterrence. Quick subpoenaing of all evidence would also afford some protection. Speedy trials would also reduce some of the pressures.

In the case of the pathological criminal, civil commitment proceedings for mental observation could be extended and perfected. This would rid society of the danger and provide the individual with the most appropriate incarceration and treatment.

The professional criminal, the repeater by choice, presents a special problem. One way he could be curtailed would be to require by law that anyone indicted for a second crime during pretrial release before his trial for a first crime should be detained. This is a nuance of the negligence law which allows a dog just one bite before the master is held responsible for his misconduct. The idea that the benefit of the doubt can be extended only so far and then the beneficiary becomes responsible could apply to these criminal cases as well. This would at at least curtail certain recidivism.

The case of the man with no identity or no place in the community, the poor vagrant, presents an even more difficult problem. In number, if not in import, these cases might well be significant. Flight may be a real danger. And the court might have no basis to undertake supervision under step 1.

Perhaps the solution to some of these cases lies in the daytime release concepts now being used with convicted prisoners in some places.[6] Under these programs, prisoners are released to work during the day and return to prison at night, and this is after conviction and during the serving of sentence. It allows

[6] For examples, see Maryland Dept. of Correction, "Report on Work Release Program"; North Carolina Law 148–33.1; Wisconsin, Huber Law; Minnesota Work Release Program. Many states are now considering the adoption of plans of this variety. Also see Judge Allen Gwyn, Work, Earn, and Save (1963).

some freedom but at the same time keeps prisoners under control. The prisoner earns some money while rehabilitating himself, and he contributes some of his salary to the state to cover the costs of his incarceration. Where this is too risky, and where no device under step 1 seems reliable, incarceration would be proper. These trials should be as speedy as possible.

The primary purpose of the bail system or any other system which takes its place must be to serve the administration of justice. Delicate, rational, intelligent compromise is necessary to balance the competing interests of the government and the individual. Where the American bail system has failed, reform must transform the system and do away finally with the ransoming of people and the ransoming of justice.

Index

Ronald Goldfarb was born in Jersey City, New Jersey, in 1933. He received his A.B. and L.L.B degrees from Syracuse University and LL.M. and J.S.D. degrees from the Yale Law School. After serving as a trial attorney for three years in the Air Force JAG, he was an Arthur Garfield Hays Fellow at the New York University Law School in 1960–1961, when he also served as a Staff Counsel for the Commission on Law and Social Action.

From 1961 to 1964, Mr. Goldfarb practiced law as a special prosecutor for the Organized Crime and Racketeering section of the Department of Justice, conducting grand jury investigations and trials of nationwide criminal activities. He served also as a member of the President's Task Force for the War Against Poverty. Later in 1964, he was a speech writer on Robert F. Kennedy's staff for the New York Senatorial campaign.

He is the author of *The Contempt Power* and of numerous articles in the *New Republic*, *Commonweal*, and in many legal journals. He is a member of the District of Columbia, New York, and California Bars, and has been admitted to practice before the United States Supreme Court. Mr. Goldfarb lives in Alexandria, Virginia, with his wife, Joanne, who is an architect, and their infant daughter, Jody Anne.